Gift *of* Time

DISCOVERIES FROM THE DAILY RITUAL
OF READING WITH MY FATHER

*In honour of my parents
and with love for my children*

Gift of Time

DISCOVERIES FROM THE DAILY RITUAL
OF READING WITH MY FATHER

FRANCES PRINCE

PRINCES PHARMACY

DAVID PRINCE, Ph.C., M.P.S., M.C.P.P.
JAMES PRINCE, J.P., Ph.C., M.P.S., M.C.P.P., M.A.
Member Society Hospital Pharmacists of Australia

350 BRIDGE ROAD, RICHMOND, VIC. 3121
TELEPHONE   9428 1953
FAX   9427 0160

We rolled up our sleeves and prepared ours
Verification Commission to gain admission t
Maximillian 'Universitat or Technische Hochschul

Our attempts to succeed at all cost were
by willpower and determination which offered
the goal Jewish post-war students strove fo
Feldafing, Landsberg and few other camps were of

With few exceptions we lived in rooms rent
families. Life was not easy, but with youth
had the capacity to cope.

We also had fun. Dances, excursions,
romantic encounters even marriages. As for me,
the Isator Pl. Jewish students cafeteria. We
on 23 December 1947 and hope to celebrate our
Anniversary this year. We have two child
grandchilren.

Most of us left Germany (apart from a handf
However only Israel recognized our qualificatio
dentistry and pharmacy. Consequently all tho
in other countries had great difficulties ti
to have the hard earned de
it was a matter of perseverance
of the kind we strove for in Ge

Deutsche Bundesrepublik
Internationaler Kraftfahrzeugverkel

Internationaler Führerschein

Internationales Abkommen
vom 24. April 1926

Ausstellung des Scheines

Ort .... **München**

Tag .... **11. Jan. 1954**

Landeshauptstadt München
für öffentliche Ordnung
(Name der Verwaltungsbehörde)

(Unterschrift)

München, Kreuzstr. 2

Form approved.
Budget Bureau No. 43-R321.2.

Rosa W. Nelson

The validity of this permit expires

MONTH	DAY	YEAR
SEPTEMBER	14	1960

ISSUED AT
NEW YORK, NY

MONTH	DAY	YEAR
SEPTEMBER	14	1959

APPLICATION FOR EXTENSION SHOULD BE
SUBMITTED TO DISTRICT OFFICE AT:
NEW YORK, NY

Approved:

Arrived by   Arrived by   Arrived by   Arrived by
DIST. IMF. N.Y.

NONE

SEX		MARITAL STATUS	
☐ M	☑ Married	☐ Divorced	
☑ F	☐ Widowed	☐ Single	

COUNTRY OF WHICH A CITIZEN,   COUNTRY OF BIRTH   COU
SUBJECT, OR NATIONAL

STATELESS   POLAND   AUS

NOTE.—Any erasure or alteration shall render this permit null a

E
X
T
E
N   Joseph F. Leahy
S   American Vice Consul   September 14, 1961
I   (Date)
O
N   Extended to and
S   invalid after

                                            (Date)
Extended to and
invalid after

SCHWANTHALER

Ecke Senefelderstraße
1 Minute vom Hauptbahnh

(Fortzecung)

Studienbuch
für
Vor- und Zuname:
David Prinz

ASSE 30-32

er Hotel Germania
ng Bundesbahnhotel

An episod fun trojerikn		
omre	. . .	Prinz Daniel
Eltere/s npcecha	. . .	Kubliner Leib
Toru mlejna	. . .	Uus der hebreische prese
Dunkij hammee	. . .	Getzler Israel
O teorii względnei	. . .	J. Felberbaum
Riznuj techniki fol elek-		
tennonpartejncgneh	. . .	Tudeusz Mieczc

Published by Real Film & Publishing
www.realfp.com.au

Text © Frances Prince 2021
Images © Prince family, with the exception of:
Cover images, p.14 & p.102 © Picos Media
Image p.55 © Ohrenstein family
Image p.63 © Piekarczyk family
Image p.101 courtesy of Jeremy Varon
Image p.120 © Simon Schochet, courtesy of United States Holocaust Memorial Museum
Image p.127 courtesy of Polaris Media Pty Ltd, publisher of The Australian Jewish News
Image p.163 courtesy of the Jewish Holocaust Centre
Image p.261 courtesy of Lane Shmerling

ISBN: 9780645213119

Edited by Georgie Raik-Allen
Editorial assistance by Romy Moshinsky
Designed by Marianna Berek-Lewis

Contents

In *Gift of Time*, inconsistencies in the spelling of names arise due to a number of factors including culture, nationality, war, migration, translation and bureaucracy.

Jewish children born in prewar Poland were commonly given both Polish and Yiddish names. The names of those living under the German occupation during the war, or living in Germany after the war, such as my parents, often morphed into Germanic variations. Upon immigration to countries such as Australia, these names were further modified into an Anglicised version. Some immigrants changed their names officially, and in some instances bureaucratic errors and spelling mistakes led to further discrepancies.

My father's name in Polish documents appears as David Princ, Dawid Princ, David Prync or Dawid Prync. His name in Germany was recorded as either David Prinz or Dawid Prinz. In Australia, Dad's name was David Prinz until 1957 when he changed it by deed poll to David Prince.

In this book, I have used the names as appropriate for the period I am writing about. For example, I refer to my dad as David Princ during his Polish prewar childhood, David Prinz during his years in Germany and David Prince in Australia.

Prologue

It was never my intention to write a story about my father's experiences as a Jewish student at a prestigious German university in the aftermath of the Holocaust. However, the concurrence of two significant events provided the momentum that set me on this unintended path. One event had universal significance and the other was significant for our family history: the 2020 global pandemic and my discovery of a remarkable book about the experiences of young Jewish survivors as they navigated university studies in the American Zone of Occupied Germany after World War II.

I have always known that my mother, Ella, and father, David, both born in Poland in the mid-1920s, suffered tremendously during the Holocaust. After the war, they studied at university in Munich, Germany, where they met as members of the all-important Jewish Students' Union. Dad studied pharmacy and graduated. Mum completed part of her dentistry degree but did not graduate. They married and later immigrated to Melbourne, Australia, arriving in 1950. This is the founding framework of our small family: my parents, my brother Issy, born in 1951, and me, born in 1958.

I felt familiar with the broad brushstrokes of my parents' student days. I had heard the oft-repeated anecdotes, met some of their friends from that time, seen documents and photos, and had even visited Munich with Dad in 2009. I knew that through a variety of convoluted pathways, some young Jews, including my parents, had found their way to German universities in the late 1940s. Most studied medicine, dentistry, pharmacy or engineering.

Just a couple of short years before enrolling in university, most of these young people had been starving in German concentration camps, hidden in attics and cellars, or living with false identities fearing imminent discovery. Deep-seated terror had been at the centre of their lives. Precious few had a full complement of parents and siblings still alive and next to none had grandparents.

My parents had always emphasised the importance of those Munich university years in terms of the unfolding of the rest of their lives. I sensed an emotional undercurrent at play whenever Mum and Dad talked about that time. Perhaps those years were among the happiest of their lives. They were energetic, dynamic and purposeful. They were imbued with the optimism and vigour of fledgling independent young adults. And they shared this inimitable experience in the company of others like them.

Despite my awareness of Mum and Dad's stories, there were always unaddressed questions about this little-known episode in the postwar Jewish experience. Questions that stretched beyond the family narrative.

In early 2020, during one of my sporadic searches on the internet for material on these Jewish students, I stumbled across a book, *The New Life: Jewish Students in Postwar Germany* by Jeremy Varon. A well-researched, academic and erudite masterpiece. This was the book I had long been waiting for. It had been published back in 2014—how had I missed it? No idea. Never mind. I was beyond excited. I ordered it and rang Dad all at the same time. I gushed out my enthusiasm at a million miles a minute and lost him from the start. "Slow down! What are you talking about? I can't understand what you are saying to me," he interrupted. I gathered myself—and my patience—and started again. Slowly. This time, Dad took it all in. My discovery and its gravitas. He was as excited as I was.

At last, I would find out all-important details underpinning this project that enabled Holocaust survivors to enter German universities. Initially, I think of these youngsters, including my parents, as 'Student Survivors'. However, they, like all those who endured the Holocaust, are actually 'professional' survivors. There was nothing amateurish about surviving the Holocaust. In addition, they had to have survived first, in order to become students. I decided it was more appropriate to switch my terms of reference and describe them as 'Survivor Students'. They merit their own unique category.

Growing up in Melbourne's Jewish community in the 1960s and '70s, I was surrounded by Polish Holocaust survivors. My parents' friends. The parents of my friends. It felt normal to me. What was not normal was that my parents had studied at university. It was a trajectory my family shared with nearly no-one. It was so out-of-left-field among Holocaust survivors that whenever I mentioned it, there would be stunned incredulity. It didn't make sense. Here were two Polish Jews whose worlds had been decimated when they were children. One hadn't completed primary school and the other completed just one year of secondary school. This paucity of education, together with their endurance of ghettos and concentration camps, formed their curriculum vitae. And yet they both became students at the venerated and grandiose-sounding Ludwig Maximilian University of Munich.

It is hard to find references, even amongst Holocaust academics, to this niche post-liberation experience. The late Dr Zeev W. Mankowitz of Hebrew University, a much-loved scholar and highly respected specialist in the field of postwar Germany, barely acknowledged it. His seminal work, *Life Between Memory and Hope: The Survivors of the Holocaust in Occupied Germany*, disappointingly devotes merely one stand-alone sentence to the Survivor Students. It states that at the end of 1946, "581 students were studying at German universities, mainly in Munich and with a fair number in Frankfurt". That's it. One measly sentence in a thorough and highly detailed scholarly work.

Dr Mankowitz does mention Bavaria's very important state commissioner for the victims of Nazi persecution, Dr Philipp Auerbach, but not in relation to his crucial role in supporting and advocating for the Survivor Students. The book does reference Simon Schochet, my parents' friend, and fellow Munich student (aka Szymek Schochet). However, Dr Mankowitz mentions Szymek in relation to matters that have nothing to do with his university days or his active role in the Jewish Students' Union.

I had the privilege of being taught by Dr Mankowitz on a number of occasions over many years. I learned much and have the fondest memories of him. However, I can't help feeling a touch let down.

While I was making the exciting discovery of Jeremy Varon's *The New Life* in the early months of 2020, the world was grappling with the growing threat of a new virus, Covid-19, which was spreading across the planet at an alarming rate. After much debate, the World Health Organisation declared Covid-19 a global pandemic and, in Australia, talk of restrictions on social gatherings and movement gained momentum. The virus was thought to be particularly devastating for the elderly and my brother and I began discussing how we would take care of Dad.

My 95-year-old father lives around the corner from me. When Mum and Dad moved into that street about fifteen years ago, my sons, Gali and Noey, counted the steps from their place to ours. Seventy-one. Mum is no longer alive. She passed away at the end of 2013. Dad has lived at home on his own ever since. My children no longer live in Australia. Gali is in London. Noey is in Jerusalem. In fact, even I don't totally live here. My husband, Steven, and I have a home in Jerusalem and during the last four years we have been spending substantial time in Israel. Living another life.

As coronavirus numbers continued to climb, it became apparent that our next Jerusalem sojourn would be delayed. The government began closing borders and a lockdown was announced. We were going nowhere. And then the book arrived and suddenly I knew how I would take care of Dad during this time.

And so began our daily afternoon reading ritual. At my place, on the couch in the lounge room. We would need to get comfortable. We were in it for the long haul.

Dad liked to sit up straight with a cushion behind his lower back and a footstool on which to stretch out his legs. Covered by a blanket. I liked to sprawl along one length of the couch with my pillow behind me. Covered by two blankets.

When I began reading aloud, I asked Dad to stop and interrupt me whenever he wanted me to repeat something. Or to add details from his own experience. Or comment in any way. After all, it was his imprint and overlay that I sought.

I had no plan to write about our reading endeavour. About Dad's reactions to the book, our resultant conversations or my ruminations. My sole objective was to keep Dad company and engaged in what was becoming a narrowing world. No more and no less. However, when I told a couple of close friends how Dad and I were spending our afternoons, some suggested that I write about the experience. They felt it would be worthwhile to record Dad's thoughts, reactions, opinions and the conversations that our reading project inspired. For my sake. For the sake of my kids. It would provide an important family legacy for Gali and Noey, my niece Ilana, my nephew Jeremy and the following generations. Perhaps not a linear memoir, but an insight into Dad's life and experiences. Not a bad idea. I decided to go for it. I started to jot down Dad's remarks during our reading and conversations. Then, each day after he left my place, I would sit with my laptop and the words just poured out. I found myself thoroughly enjoying the process. I envisaged photocopying twenty booklets and presenting them to family members and a few close friends. I felt focused and emboldened with this particular audience in mind.

After a couple of weeks of writing, my husband, Steven, asked to read some of my "manuscript". I laughed at his terminology. As if. I read him some sections and he listened carefully. Then he said, "You have more than a family story here."

"What do you mean?" I asked.

"I think that maybe you should be writing for a broader audience. Other people, even those who don't know us, might be interested. You don't realise it yet, but you are writing a book."

And so, here is that book.

Reading
Project
Part One

Dad as a student in Munich, late 1940s

Monday 16 March 2020

The New Life: Jewish Students of Postwar Germany
Jeremy Varon
Published by Wayne State University Press, 2014

Jeremy Varon begins his book with an acknowledgements prelude. His personal research backstory echoes the astonishment that most people feel when first hearing about the Survivor Students. A combination of wonder and disbelief. He names some of those who were instrumental in his research project including Sabina Zimering, Frederick Reiter, Andrew Kerr, Simon Schochet, Roman Ohrenstein. They had all been members of the Jewish Students' Union in Munich.

Sabina and Simon were friends of my parents. I met them both in the USA. The other names are new to me, but most are familiar to Dad. He notes, "Fred Reiter was the one who corresponded with us about the reunions. He was one of the organisers."

A number of Jewish Students' Union reunions have been held over the decades. Mum and Dad attended a few of the larger international gatherings. In October 1995 they travelled to Israel for one such reunion. They planned to stay on afterwards, to catch up with some of their friends and visit family. Then, 4 November. Prime minister Yitzhak Rabin was assassinated. The people of Israel were in shock and shattered. No-one felt like entertaining guests, not even those who had come from faraway Australia. Dad says, "Everyone was crying. No-one was in the mood for chats, coffees and dinners." Mum and Dad curtailed their trip and left the country.

Only a few years later, in June 1998, another international reunion was organised at the Concord Hotel in Upstate New York. In the heart of what was once the 'borscht belt' of Jewish east coast America. Way past its heyday, the Concord Hotel was still open. Just. In fact, it closed down for good later that year. Dad wanted to go. Mum did not. After a family discussion we decided that I would accompany Dad. We flew to New York together and Dad caught the bus directly to the hotel. He wanted to squeeze in as much time as possible with his old friends. I did too. With *my* old friends. Not in Upstate New York, but in Manhattan. We parted company for a few days. I stayed with my friends and ran around New York like a lunatic, as I always do. Having lived there for three years in the mid-1980s, I had a sense of returning home.

After arriving at the Concord Hotel, I reflected on the joy of catching up with old, close friends. It had been an exhilarating time. How much more so must it be for Dad to be reunited with his friends. For me, it had been just over a decade since we had lived in each other's pockets. For Dad, it had been five decades.

In his book, Jeremy Varon profusely thanked Professor Bella Brodzki, who connected him to many of the Survivor Students. She travelled far and wide with him to interview them. I met Bella at the 1998 reunion in New York. She is the daughter of survivors and the niece of Sabina Zimering, one of the main instigators of Varon's research project that resulted in his book. Bella is a professor of comparative literature and her areas of scholarship include autobiography and global writing. Bella was well-placed and well-qualified to play a major role in jumpstarting Varon's book. By the time I met Bella she had written an article about the Survivor Student group, which was likely the prelude and impetus for Varon's research. I remember the animated discussion about the need to have their story professionally researched and written down for posterity. There was an urgency to record the importance and uniqueness of their lives. They were right. They found in Jeremy Varon the ideal person for the job. In my opinion, he has done them proud. He has honoured their achievements for all time. He has afforded them a lasting legacy in the annals of Jewish history.

Tuesday 17 March 2020

In his introduction, Varon broadly sketches the context of postwar Germany. After Germany's surrender, the Allies divided the country into four military occupation zones: American, British, French and Soviet. His story then narrows in on the American Zone. It is a chaotic and anarchic picture. A growing number of Jews arrived there from many countries east of Germany. These people eventually became known as 'Holocaust survivors'. At that time, they were referred to, in Hebrew, as 'שארית הפליטה' 'sh'erit ha-pletah', the surviving remnant. A miniscule percentage became, what I have coined, the Survivor Students, including my parents.

We read about the inconceivable misfortune and unimaginable suffering that these people endured. Their losses, grief and anguish are gut-wrenching. When we read Varon's words, "Likely, the majority now had no parents", Dad adds, "Mum and I were exceptions. I had my father and Mum had her mother. It was very rare. I knew how privileged I was." This resonates with me, a generation later. Growing up, I had these two grandparents. This was two more than most of my friends. In Holocaust survivor families, grandparents were extremely rare.

The heartbeat of the Survivor Students' lives in Munich was the Jewish Students' Union. I grew up hearing about this group but remained somewhat confused. What was it exactly? To me, it sounded mostly like a social club. My parents talked about their outings, hikes and cultural events. I knew about the Jewish student cafeteria. This was where the Survivor Students ate, socialised and discussed the topics of the day. This was where my parents met.

Now, reading Varon's introduction, I learn about the origins and myriad of purposes of the Jewish Students' Union. Formed in December 1945, its function was multilayered, complex and far-reaching. Basically, the Union (as the Survivor Students called it) organised every necessity and requirement for the potential students. It negotiated with various authorities for their entrance into university, located accommodation for them, and took care of all their conceivable needs. Dad pipes up, "The Union made it all possible. They gave me this life. It's like they took me by the hand and guided me through everything. Really everything. They created the pathway for me. I didn't have the experience or worldliness to figure out the whole system on my own. No way. My accommodation, the huge paperwork, food, travel vouchers. So many other things too. They did everything for me."

In Germany, during the late 1940s, hundreds of young Jews were imbibing the elixir of life within the rarefied environment of a European university. Despite recent experiences of inhumane horrors, Survivor Students described to Varon a time of great vibrancy and joie de vivre. Others might be surprised reading this. I am not. I have always had a sense that during this stage in their lives, both Mum and Dad were deliciously happy. Perhaps it was the wistful nostalgia with which they talked about that time? Perhaps it was the faraway dreamy look in their eyes? Perhaps it was the venerated pedestal upon which they placed their friends from their student days? Most probably, a combination of these factors.

An academic, Varon set himself an ambitious project on many levels. His multipronged study investigates many aspects of the lives of the Survivor Students in Munich during the immediate postwar years. We read about his research methodology, including wide-ranging surveys and in-depth oral histories. The research represents seven or eight years of work.

Varon travelled extensively to meet Survivor Students. He found them in different parts of the USA. He traversed Israel to visit others. He does note "…a small number of the alumni settled in Australia, with whom I had no meaningful contact". This annoys us both. "Why not?" we say at the same time. In the age of the internet, how hard could it have been? Especially given that a number of the Survivor Student instigators of this book were friends of my parents. In addition, my parents attended reunions in the USA and Israel. They were definitely on the radar. Dad and I decide to forgive Varon. After all, he is providing us with the details of the most significant years in my parents' lives.

I am excited to read the macro story of this time. Background, context, the big picture. I am already familiar with the narratives of Mum and Dad's lives. But perhaps new gems will emerge. I have seen their report books, Jewish Students' Union membership books, a myriad of other related documents and photos from that time. But how did the whole project come about? Who were the Survivor Students?

Dad with Henry Weisfelner, Hanka Prywes, Arek Lukrec &
Shulamit Lukrec at the Jewish Students' Union reunion, New York, 1998

Wednesday 18 March 2020

Chapter One
I Knew One Thing—I Have to Study:
Early Education and Dreams of the Future

Through collating and analysing information drawn from interviews with Survivor Students, Varon determines that most came from families where education was central in their lives. Their parents tended to have university qualifications and were members of the professional or business classes. Before the war interrupted (to say the least!) their lives, they hoped to grow up and attend university. It was the future they aspired to. Varon writes that going to university after the war, "was a bridge to both their pasts and their futures".

I re-read this section to Dad. Slower than the first time. This profile fits my mother to a tee. Her family occupied the upper echelons of Jewish society in Warsaw. Her mother, Rosa Gringlas, was a dentist and her father, Izak Salcberg, a civil engineer. However, it is certainly not my father's story. Dad says, "There is no way I would've gone to university if my life had continued with no war. I probably would have learned a trade. I grew up in Lodz, after all. An industrial, textile city. No way was university education part of my world." He had no idea that his prewar background was so at odds with most Survivor Students. He tells me that they didn't talk about the past. They didn't talk about their childhoods before the war. They didn't talk about their war experiences. Varon corroborates this lack of discussion regarding the past.

Varon's research is astounding in its detail and thoroughness. I love his number crunching. Within those statistics are my parents' lives. They literally count for something! For example, Varon reports that of the 402 students in Munich in July 1947, 307 were originally from Poland. I say to Dad, "If it wasn't for you and Mum there would only be 400 students and 305 of them would've come from Poland." He laughs.

I ask Dad whether he was friendly with any of the non-Polish Jews studying in Munich. He answers, "I don't think so." It makes sense. After all, they were by far the largest cohort in the group. Why stray out of your comfort zone?

The study divides Survivor Students into age brackets. The aim seems to be two-fold. Firstly, Varon is investigating what level of schooling they had attained before the war in order to ascertain how prepared for university they may have been. For Dad, his one solitary year in secondary school holds a precious place in his memories. I have often heard him lament that his secondary education was so curtailed.

The second aim of this age-bracketing is to uncover the true ages of the would-be university entrants. Evidently, a minimum age was needed for admission to some universities. We read that some students declared themselves to be older than they really were. Dad chimes in, "That's what Mum did." I have not heard this before. He continues, "Mum was born in 1927. On her application form she wrote 1925. That would place her clearly over the line in terms of any age requirement. Also, she bolstered her age so she could claim to have had more schooling than she really did." The boldness, determination and sheer audacity of Mum and her cohort astounds me.

It seems that many of the Survivor Students interviewed had been exemplary students before the war. Varon writes that they "…had to have been high achievers with great aptitude and motivation". Dad comes in, right on cue, "More motivation than aptitude for me. I had been an average student as a child in school. I was never an excellent student." In addition, their parents had nurtured them, to differing degrees, with intellectual pursuits and they had been curious or voracious readers as children. "Not me," says Dad. "That was not me and that was not my home." He shrugs. This is becoming an increasingly involuntary physical response to much that we read. He adds, "My parents weren't big readers, and neither was I." On the one hand, I am saddened by the fact that Dad did not grow up in a more highbrow environment. On the other hand, this fact makes me even prouder of Dad's achievements. Entrance to Ludwig Maximilian University, studying and graduating in pharmacy, in German, a second language. Then, in the mid-1950s, doing it all again at the Victorian College of Pharmacy in Melbourne. In English, a third language. Perhaps this is the most apt example of a self-made man.

However, Dad's parental background does concur with the majority on one parameter. It seems that virtually none of the Survivor Students came from low-income families. My grandfather, Israel Princ, was a building draughtsman employed by the city of Lodz for about four years before the war began. Dad says, "That job meant a larger salary. We—Mum, Dad and my twin brother Heniek—moved out of 17 Zawadska Street (now called Prochnika) and into Aleja (Avenue) 1-go Maja 7, once my father secured this new position." Since I have visited the exteriors of both apartment buildings, I can attest to the more salubrious accommodation of their latter home. My grandmother, Frymet Chaya Princ (after whom I am named) was a stay-at-home wife and mother, typical of the times and her social class.

We continue reading about specific Survivor Students. I want Dad to tell me about them all. He remembers some very clearly. This is especially so for people he has remained in sporadic contact with over the decades. Even more so for people he has met up with at the group's reunions in America and Israel in the 1980s and 1990s. Some names draw a complete blank. Others ring a bell of vague familiarity. Of course, I want him to remember, in detail, everything about all these people. I am acutely aware of how unreasonable this is.

Dad interrupts, "Say that name again?"

"Lidia Eichenholz," I re-read, very slowly.

"Hmm….I think she is the person who introduced me to your mother."

"What?" I bellow.

He says, "I can't be sure, but I think so."

I retort with, "Tell me more! Tell me more!" like the song *Summer Nights* in the musical *Grease*.

"Well, we were in the Jewish student cafeteria. That was the place where we all met up between classes. It's where we ate, socialised and flirted. Mum was sitting with another girl. Lidia, I think. I am not sure how I knew her. Anyway, Lidia introduced me to Mum, briefly. At a later time, Mum told me that Lidia said to her that I was a really nice boy, and that she, Lidia herself, might be interested in going out with me." I am gobsmacked and a little overwhelmed. I find myself cheering on my mum in this Mum/Lidia competition. As if my life depends on it. Which it actually does.

In Varon's exploration of the types of families the Survivor Students grew up in, one area of focus is the Polish-Jewish divide of their identities. Dad says, "There were so many Jews in Poland, of all varieties. There were so many ways of being Jewish." But I ask him how Polish he felt. I want to probe his sense of 'Polishness'. He begins, "Polish is my first language. It's my mother tongue. We spoke Polish at home. But my grandparents spoke Yiddish to us. At school I learnt Polish history, Polish literature, Polish geography. The books I read as a child were all in Polish. It was a normal part of my life. Polish and Jewish; Jewish and Polish. That's just how it was." So there seems to have been no contradiction between Dad's Polishness and his Jewishness. It seems that for Dad, the two identities sat comfortably with each other. He continues, "I never set foot in a church. We had little to do with non-Jewish Poles. We lived in the heart of Jewish Lodz." I ask him whether he related to Polish history as *his* history. He is incredulous, "Of course I did. The old kings of the Polish kingdom, the Kosciuszko Uprising in 1794, the emergence of the new Polish state after World War I. I learnt it and loved it." To this day, Dad can rattle off the names of the Polish kings with ease.

We discuss the way Dad enthusiastically embraces Polish history, literature and culture. However, this enthusiasm does not extend easily to non-Jewish Poles. He is attached to Polishness. Not so much to Poles. Dad's attitude is not rare amongst Polish Jews. Far from it. Nevertheless, it is fascinating. Isn't there something deeply contradictory and problematic about feeling warmth towards, and ownership of, a nation's corpus of creation, but antipathy towards its creators? Is it possible to identify with a nationhood but not the nation? Obviously it is. Dad can—and does. As do many others.

There are a number of layers to unpack. The easiest layer to understand is Polish-Jewish or Jewish-Polish identity. I am an avowed believer in the ability to juggle multiple identities. In fact, I am a professional celebrator of multiple identities. This is what I do on a daily basis. For the last six years I have held the multicultural and interfaith portfolio on the Jewish Community Council of Victoria (JCCV) executive. The JCCV is the umbrella representative organisation of the Victorian Jewish community. I represent the JCCV in the broader community. I sit on interfaith boards and delight in working with Australians of diverse religious and ethnic backgrounds. My life is enriched and blessed by these experiences. Nevertheless, I am acutely aware of the context of my positivity. Melbourne. The 21st century. Democracy. Multiculturalism. I don't want to sound naïve—believe me, I am not. There are numerous challenges in our society. Racism and prejudice remain significant concerns. No system is perfect. However, this is not a bad milieu in which to discuss multiple identities. There are worse. Far worse.

Life for Jews within Polish society, from the time of its modern reincarnation after World War I, and way before, was exceedingly complex, multifaceted and often fraught. Some Jews lived totally separately from Christians. Some lived partially integrated and others were completely assimilated. It is important to emphasise the diversity of Polish Jewish life. This diversity goes a long way in explaining the different attitudes of Polish Jews to their individual identities.

The next layer is much more sensitive. The attitude of Polish society— including the government, the church, academia and individuals—towards Polish Jews. I have no doubt this topic will arise again in our readings.

Dad (centre) on a Jewish Students' Union excursion. Uncle Heniek is on his left and Heniek's future wife Fela is behind Dad

Thursday 19 March 2020

We return to our Survivor Students. We read about the role that Zionism played in their lives before the war. Like all other factors, the continuum is wide. Dad tells me that his parents were not particularly Zionistic. They didn't have passionate family discussions—let alone the delicate parsing of the differing Zionist ideologies—or engage in political activities. However, he did go to a few meetings of the Zionist youth movement called Gordonia. He went because friends took him. This social imperative remains the main incentive for children to join youth movements today. Gordonia was founded in Poland in the 1920s. Its goals included the practical pioneering of the Jewish homeland for the Jewish masses. As an afterthought, Dad says, "I also went to a few Betar meetings." Betar is another Zionist youth movement. Its ideology and orientation are more right-wing than Gordonia's.

"How come?" I ask.

I get the same response: other kids took him. "I think it was in Parzeczew (a town about 30 kilometres northwest of Lodz). We went there to visit relatives from my mother's side of the family."

I ask, "Did your cousins take you?"

"Probably. But I was never a member of either organisation," he responds. I ask Dad whether he liked going to these youth movement meetings. He answers in a droll manner, "Before I could even start liking them, it was over." After a thoughtful silence, he continues, "I am sure that if I'd had even one more year of high school, of growing up, I would've become more active in a youth movement. I didn't have enough time to get involved in anything."

We read a description of the political situation in Poland in the late 1930s, especially regarding the Jews. We have often talked about this unnerving and uncertain period. I have read about it. Dad lived through it. The impact of the death of Marshall Jozef Pilsudski in 1935 was tragic, for Jews in particular. The leader of Poland had been a strong suppressive bulwark against blatantly virulent antisemitism. The late 1930s was a time of increasing antisemitic agitation, both from official quarters as well as on the street. This is part of the more sensitive and potentially sinister aspects of being a Jew in Poland that I alluded to earlier.

I remember Mum telling me that she went to Pilsudski's funeral with her governess, Panna (Miss) Liza. She was eight years old. I never figured out whether she went to the actual funeral or an accompanying procession of thousands upon thousands. Dad is also unsure. He went with his father from Lodz to Warsaw to join the mourning. "There were cheap train tickets for the event. I can't remember whether they were half price or completely free. It was just me and my Dad." His brother Heniek was not with them. Dad can't remember why. He continues, "We stayed in a private apartment for three days. Lots of people were renting out rooms for the funeral." Airbnb circa 1935.

Whenever we come across a name of one of the Survivor Students, I pause. I repeat the name, hoping Dad will recognise it, even if only vaguely. Sophie Schorr? "Yes, I remember. She was doing medicine. Her father had been a doctor before the war. But she lost both parents." This may not be much, but it's something. Isaac Minzberg? "Hmm. I don't remember him, but I do remember that there was a Minzberg who was a senator in the Sejm, the Polish parliament." Perhaps they were from the same family.

As we read a broad outline of Jewish educational options in Poland between the wars, Dad places people he knew within the various school systems. This one went to that stream of Hebrew-speaking schools, the other went to a Yiddish-speaking school and someone else to an Orthodox school. If the war hadn't happened, there is only a marginal chance that these people ever would have met. They were ensconced and entrenched in different worlds. Religiously, linguistically, ideologically and socio-economically, they were poles (pun intended) apart. In this bizarre way, the war democratised the remnant of the European Jewish world. Postwar acquaintanceships, friendships, romances and marriages crossed previous demarcations. As one of my parents' friends told me long ago, "Hitler was our matchmaker."

Dad and I discuss this statement. It irritates him. It implies that he and Mum perhaps married for inappropriate reasons. And he won't hear of that. However, he does acquiesce that some couples in their friendship circle seemed strangely matched. The search for companionship, warmth and love amongst the losses may not exactly be an aphrodisiac, but it may have been a powerful driving force. "It wasn't like that for us. Firstly, we were the right age for serious relationships. We were surrounded by only young people, like us. We socialised together in the Jewish Students' Union. We ate together. Studied together. In all our leisure activities, we were together. What do you think will happen in that environment?"

Nevertheless, I do make the point that my parents would never have met had it not been for the war. Dad was in Lodz and Mum was in Warsaw, for starters. Dad's family was lower middle-class. Mum's parents were professionals. In addition, my maternal grandmother came from an exceedingly wealthy family. Without diving into nuances, it is obvious that my parents never, ever would have met, had their worlds not been destroyed and the remnants reshuffled.

Dad & Mum, Munich, c. 1947

Friday 20 March 2020

"How about I bring over my photos from the Munich days?" Dad suggests.

"Brilliant idea!" I respond.

Dad goes home to retrieve this treasure trove. What used to be a two-minute walk is now closer to ten minutes. Dad is well organised. Everything is in its place. I am the same. He returns with the envelopes of old photos. We spread them out on my dining room table. He gets twitchy as I take charge of this spreading. Is it possessiveness? Is it fear that I will accidentally tear a photo with my dispersion tactics? I have seen these images many times but this is the first time I have really looked at them. There are about 60 photos of various sizes, shapes and shades of black and white, and sepia. Some are miniature, passport-photo size. Some are enlargements of these. Others look original. Some look like copies. Some look like copies of copies. There are multiples of the same photo.

Where do we start? Dad wants to begin where the photos have landed. He seems eager to work our way from one end of the table to the other. I find this maddening. It isn't methodical enough for me. And perhaps a few years earlier, it wouldn't have worked for him either. I want to sort them first. This annoys him. Firstly, I group photos that are identical. Sepia, black and white, large, small. If it's the same picture, it's a group. Secondly, I look for photos that seem to have been taken at the same place and time. They consist of the same people or a combination of those people. These are placed next to their corresponding first group. Even this cursory sorting compels me to closely examine each photo. Faces are becoming more and more familiar. I am beginning to identify people. Not yet by name, but by their features. Smiles, hair, postures, poses. Thirdly, I categorise photos into activities or venues. There are the obvious excursion photos. Outdoor scenery and hiking. Indoor socialising scenes. Indoor meetings. University scenes with students replete in their long, white lab coats. And of course, some photos defy easy categorisation. But I feel satisfied that this is a good start. Meanwhile, Dad is upending my system by turning photos over to see what is written on the back and not placing them back to my satisfaction. I am getting annoyed that my ordered classification system is not being sufficiently respected and adhered to. He is getting annoyed that I am nabbing the photos out of his hands. We are annoying each other.

Nevertheless, we undertake to identify names and faces, and even specific places. Slowly. We are helped by the notes Dad has written on the back of some photos, detailing names, dates and places. But only some. I have my post-it notes ready to write down any other information that Dad can recall. There is no system to this. I write down whatever Dad can remember and attach the post-it note on the appropriate photo. Every now and then we move from our reading room (the lounge room) to the photo display room (the dining room). All flashes of memory are welcome. None are wasted.

Dad (centre, front row) on a Jewish Students' Union excursion, late 1940s. My parents' lifelong friends Adolek Kohn & his future wife Marysia are standing behind Dad

Top: Dad (not wearing a lab coat) with fellow students, late 1940s

Bottom: Dad (far right) & his fellow students in a chemistry lab, late 1940s

Munich photographs spread on my dining room table, 2020

Sunday 22 March 2020

Chapter Two
You Survive Because You Survive:
Occupation, Exile, and the Holocaust

In this chapter, Varon focuses on the childhoods and wartime experiences of the Survivor Students. We read, we discuss, we unpack. The luck of being a young person during the war is a significant factor in the survival of our students. Their cohort stood the greatest chance of making it through the Holocaust. Dad and I mull over this. He shakes his head, saying, "You just had to be lucky. All the time."

I counter with, "But if you managed to evade a roundup or a mass shooting or a random beating, as a young person, you would be better placed to make it through, let's say, hard labour. Especially as you got a little older and presumably stronger." I realise, as I am saying this, the assumption that people grow stronger during their teenage years, was not necessarily true during times of deprivation and disease.

Today, we read about what Varon calls 'an experiential divide'. He refers to a split between two groups of Jews residing in postwar Germany. Or perhaps even three groups. There is a sensitive division between those who experienced the war under the brutal Nazi genocidal regime and those under the rule of the Soviet Union. The latter certainly endured incredible challenges, but, as a Jew, there was a greater chance of staying alive under the Soviets than the Germans. John Goldlust, an Australian academic, refers to those Jews who spent virtually the whole war under Soviet authority, as having experienced the 'lesser-known pathway'. He claims that of the 300,000 to 350,000 Polish Jews who survived the war, "probably at least three quarters of them spent most of the time under Soviet authority".[1]

I share Goldlust's research with Dad. But not immediately. Firstly, I ask Dad, "How many Polish Jews survived the war?" I am not really testing

---

1. Goldlust, John. A Different Silence: The Survival of More than 200,000 Polish Jews in the Soviet Union During World War II as a Case Study in Cultural Amnesia, *Australian Jewish Historical Society Journal*, Vol XXI, part 1, (November 2012), pp. 13-60

his knowledge. I know he knows the answer. My intention is to heighten his amazement at the "at least three quarters spent most of the time under Soviet authority". My set-up is successful. Dad is indeed amazed. To make Goldlust's point even starker, only two small calculations result in the conclusion that only 75,000 to 87,500 Polish Jews who endured the war under Nazi occupation, survived. These new figures shock Dad. We sit together in silence.

A third group is a type of hybrid classification, a combination of the two already delineated. Those who lived in the eastern part of Poland which, under the Molotov-Ribbentrop agreement[2], was secretly designated to be taken over by the Soviet Union. Jews living in that area largely avoided the Nazis until June 1941, when the Germans double-crossed the Soviets and attacked them and their territories. In other words, the Jews living in this region had about 21 months of reprieve before bearing the full force of the Nazis' brutality.

We have family friends from all three groups. Dad rattles off a list of names that belong in each category. I had long been aware of an unspoken pecking order to these categories of war experiences. The origin of this hierarchy of suffering began in the immediate aftermath of the war and lasted for many years. Perhaps for some, it never dissipated. This issue was linked to the question of who was considered a 'survivor', not that the term was being used at that time to describe those who had endured the Holocaust. It was, for want of a more delicate term, a competition in the suffering stakes. First-class survivors were those who had been in ghettos and concentration camps. They had endured the German genocidal assault from beginning to end. Second-class survivors were not far behind. The difference was the 21-month reprieve. But after Germany invaded, these survivors were subjected to the intense ferocity of its assault on the Jewish people. This reprieve, for Dad, meant that the Jewish people in this category managed to squeeze in another 21 months of schooling. These two categories of Jews were probably the original possessors of the title of 'Holocaust survivor'.

---

2. Molotov-Ribbentrop Pact: a non-aggression pact between Nazi Germany and the Soviet Union that was signed in August 1939. Molotov was the Soviet foreign minister and Ribbentrop was the German foreign minister.

However, it is much more complex than this. There were those Jews who survived by hiding from Germans and avoiding imprisonment in ghettos and concentration camps. Some hid in underground bunkers, others in attics, cellars, barns or bombed-out buildings. This usually, but not always, required assistance from non-Jews. Others hid 'in plain sight' after procuring, usually with great difficulty, false identification documents. They took on new names and biographies but lived in constant fear of being recognised and denounced. Some Jews, such as Jewish children living in monasteries or convents, sheltered behind both closed doors and false identities. Another group of Jews hid amongst the partisans, the guerrilla resistance fighters, in the forests. They faced danger from extreme weather as well as German reprisal attacks and antisemitic partisan groups.

In the years after the war, many of those who had avoided the concentration camps didn't consider themselves, nor were they considered by others, to be 'Holocaust survivors'. This broader and more-encompassing definition was decades away. Jews who survived in the Soviet Union, no matter how grim their lives had been, had to wait even longer for entry into this macabre club. Dad shares with me stories of friends and acquaintances who felt a little ashamed, embarrassed or sort of sheepish, that they hadn't suffered the full German onslaught.

Then there were German Jews who had been exposed to their country's brutal treatment from 1933. Many managed to escape before the war started in 1939 but, during that prewar period, they did suffer in terrible ways. These people got very belated admission to the club.

We read, in excruciating detail, the multiplicity of experiences of a number of the Survivor Students. It is mentally and emotionally exhausting, for me at least. Less so for Dad, it seems. I find even the least-horrific scenarios to be unimaginable in their deprivations, terrible suffering and cruel violence.

We are nearing the end of this chapter. I am tired and so is Dad. We are winding down for today. And then, in the last paragraph, we read about the Jewish Students' Union newspaper, *The New Life*. Dad says, "I think I have a copy at home."

"What?" I screech, with renewed vigour.

"Yes, I think I may have written something in it. I'll have to look for it tonight."

I am excited for tomorrow.

Meanwhile, I want to learn more about the newspaper's origin. It seems that the first issue was published in the autumn of 1946. Maybe this means that the edition containing Dad's article in early 1947 is only the second edition? Interestingly, the newspaper's inaugural title is *The Jewish Student*. Dad's edition is called *The New Life*. Nothing was random with these reflective and creative young people. I imagine a discussion, a forum, a robust argument about a proposed new name and, finally, a decision.

Monday 23 March 2020

Today Dad arrives with an oversized A3 plastic pocket containing the January/February 1947 edition of the Jewish Students' Union newspaper. At the top of the broadsheet it says in florid font "*D.P. Express*". Underneath, in large Yiddish block print, appears "ווידערגעבורט". This transliterates as *Wiedergeburt*, meaning *The New Life*. Below that, in English, is written "The New Life Wiedergeburt". Next to this, in Hebrew letters only, is the word "התחיה". I will transliterate this as *Hatchiya*. I assume this is the editor's translation of *The New Life*. But I feel that in Hebrew, this word packs a much more powerful punch. The 'Ha' part means 'the', so it is 'tchiya' we need to focus on. In Hebrew, this word means revival or rebirth or rejuvenation, even resurrection. According to traditional Jewish teachings the dead will be resurrected as part of the Messianic vision. Our Survivor Students have risen from the dead.

And that is just the masthead. Below that, on the right, is a logo that looks like a flame embossed on top of an open book. Perhaps this represents the students' burning desire for learning. Around the book-and-flame logo are words in Hebrew, partially concealed. What can be seen translates as: 'The Hebrew Student' and 'The Surviving Remnant'. To the left of the logo, in Yiddish script, is printed: 'The Periodic Script of the United Jewish Students in Munich.'

The front page also includes a large partial sketch of Israel and a symbolic drawing of Jerusalem. (The borders, of course, are drawn from the imagination of the illustrator. The State of Israel would not exist for another sixteen months.) This front page would surely have dissuaded those who doubted the Zionist zeal of the Survivor Students. On the bottom of the imagined map, is written the classical religious and Zionist phrase, "...From Zion will come Torah..." The implication is that Jewish life is centred in Zion, in *Eretz Yisrael*, the Land of Israel. On the left side of the front page is the table of contents listing the articles and their authors.

The newspaper consists of sixteen pages. Articles were written in a variety of languages: Polish, German, Yiddish (some in Latin letters) and Hebrew. Article number six is written by Dawid Prinz. Dad. It is written in Yiddish, in Latin letters. Dad never learnt Yiddish formally. It was the language in which his grandparents spoke to him. I wonder why he didn't write it in Polish, his first language. Dad also wonders—it would've been the easier and more natural choice.

He doesn't remember what the article is about. But he is certain that it's neither serious nor hefty in content. That much he does remember. Since it's not written in Yiddish/Hebrew letters I can't just slot it into Google Translate. I need to find a translator. I do. Danielle Charak is a highly respected Yiddish specialist. She teaches, she edits, she writes. I am friendly with her children. One of her grandsons and my younger son are close friends. This is what can happen in Melbourne.

D.P. Express

Authorized by I. C. D. under Licence
for the "D. P. EXPRESS," dated
November 14 th, 1946.

ווידערגעבורט

| Januar/Februar 1947 1-2 | | הּתחיה | The new life
Wiedergeburt |

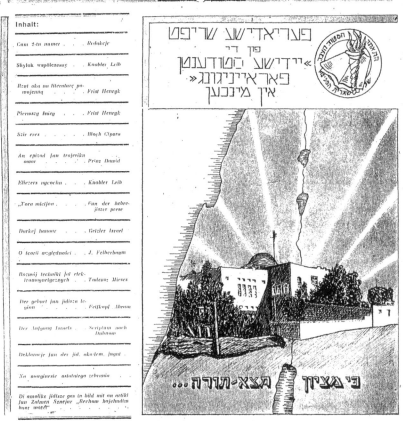

פעריאדישע שריפט
פון די
«יידישע סטודענטן
פאראייניגונג»
אין מינכען

פי ציון תצא־תורה ...

Front page of *The New Life*, a newspaper written by Jewish students in Munich. Dad's article is the sixth one listed, published early 1947

Tuesday 24 March 2020

Danielle texts me when the translation is nearly ready. She just needs to ask Dad "a couple of little things". Fine. We've waited 73 years, what's a few more days? Later, I receive this text from her:

> *It's a very moving, real, unaffected and unassuming piece, even with a touch of lightness and humour, whilst at the same time underscoring once again the cruelty, inhumanity of guards and supervisors, encouraged and let loose under a brutal and power-hungry regime…*

Dad's claim that the article is neither serious nor hefty is beginning to sound hollow.

Wednesday 25 March 2020

I am reading to Dad as usual when Danielle's email arrives. I yell out, "Here it is! Are you ready for me to read it to you?" I can see he is nervous. I think he has been modestly, but purposefully, downplaying his literary efforts. Perhaps he is fearful of being unmasked as not much of a writer.

I open the attachment. Dad is looking straight at me. I haven't seen his eyes this wide open for a long time. We both take a deep breath. I set the scene in my mind. I have no clue as to what we are about to read. All I know is that Dad wrote this for the Jewish Students' Union newspaper. The January/February 1947 issue. He was 21 years old. The war had ended twenty months earlier.

An Episode from our Sad Past[3]
By David Prinz

Translated from the Yiddish by Danielle Charak, 2020

Four o'clock in the afternoon. The gong sounds nervously and with haste: get up, get up…

I hear the call in my sleep, it reaches me like a clap of thunder from the bright and beautiful sky. A cruel fear penetrates my bones… I just lay down for a sleep and it's time to get up already? To go to work again? No! I cannot, I don't want to!

I promptly pull my head down between my shoulders and disappear under the dirty covers. And maybe I'm mistaken? But a minute later I hear the voice of my barrack-elder: "Piotrus, up!" (They used to call me Piotrus.) I see it's no dream. My head is buzzing, my bones ache, I'm tired and hungry. Then I hear my mates hurriedly pulling on their clothes. Each one of them wants to run as quickly as possible to the kitchen to bring the pot of food. Each one hopes to get an extra ladle of hot water.

I sit up slowly and, in a stupor, look at the flowers which adorn the windows of our barrack… A drop of icy cold water drops from above onto my shaven head. A shiver goes through me… At the same time I lower my legs from the upper bunk, straighten my bag of bones, wrap the damp rags around my feet and run into the washroom. I wash myself with snow because the water system is frozen and I dry my hands and face with a rag which serves me also as a scarf.

Hurriedly we still get our soup which we've been dreaming about. Nearly everyone drinks it straight from the bowl. Not everyone has a spoon and not everyone considers it worthwhile to dirty his spoon. I quickly make up my bunk, wash out the bowl and complete my dressing toilette. This consists of a Soviet summer coat with the large letters S.U. and crosses on the back and sleeves. I wrap myself in it, do it up with a wire—to keep warmer.

---

3.   See Appendix A for Yiddish original

I pull down the prisoner's cap over my ears and I'm ready in time still for the strike of the gong which calls us to the 'apel' and to the march to work.

We leave the barrack. The frost is biting, the cold winter night is falling. We hear the calls of the kommando: "Attention! Hats off! March!" And now we're stepping through the camp gates. "Left, left, one, two three, four!" We march with even steps. For the first few metres each still tries to keep up his step, but later, even with the best of good will, it doesn't work. The freshly fallen snow sticks to our wooden clogs. We haven't any strength left, our hearts are beating strongly, we walk and fall. Our SS escorts are waiting for this with a very special glee. They beat us with the butts of their rifles, they yell and curse, unloading the vilest curses in the German lexicon. Notwithstanding, we're still alive and enter the factory.

We don't speak, we all understand each other: now are we to endure twelve hours in this cold hall? It's hard to believe but we know from experience, this is not our first night shift and unfortunately, not the last. We hope to last through this one too without mishap. "Each to his job!" the shift leader calls out. We disperse in the extremely unheated hall of the V.D.M. Works. For a minute I still contemplate my five-metre-long 'rotating bench', check the Norton box and let the power into my machine.

I'm feeling exceptionally weak today. I'm shivering with cold and with fever. The noise of the saws and polishing machines resounds in my burning head. I've been working like this already a few hours, but more and more slowly… My eyes are closing, my legs don't carry me.

All of a sudden, I notice that I'm being watched. Yes, my dog of a foreman (Kurt Herdeker from Hamburg), is calmly eating his ham sandwich and doesn't take his eyes off me. I try to remember how long he has been standing near me. I exert my last bit of strength trying to work very fast and with confidence. Meanwhile he is coming closer to me. His piercing eyes are drilling through me. Now I completely lose my balance. My hand trembles and the micrometre falls into the water. So the measurements are no measurements, the 'cap' comes out too thin. "Ha! You dog! You don't feel like work today, cursed one!"

I want to speak, I want to tell him that... But before I can even open my mouth, I already feel his broad hand and the "backpfeife" as he called his blows. I almost fall over. The blood is raging inside my head. He calls over the guard and orders him to mark down my number 56497 for "verpfle-gungs-sperre" (solitary confinement). I'm no longer capable of thinking. Who can think now about what is yet to come—when I feel that today something more must happen, something out of the ordinary and may it be something good? May it be whatever, but let it come! Once and for all!

I'm quite broken, both physically and mentally. I feel ... the last moments of my consciousness are drawing near. I disconnect the completed propeller; I try to stand it up and I fall. The eighty-pound propeller falls on my foot.

The sound of the falling metal draws the attention of the foreman and of the SS officer. He runs to the propeller and picks it up quickly. "You dog, you've damaged the whole thing! I'll show you!"... and only my ears tell me about the blows which the foreman delivers to my entire body. My body has stopped feeling. I'm struggling in pain, until my kapo heaves me onto his back and takes me to the German medical hub.

A welcome warmth invades me. My foot is already swollen. The nurse believes the foot is broken. After some provisional bandaging I'm taken into the eating room where we used to sit during our break. The foreman wants me to go back to work. I tell him that's impossible. He threatens that he will send me back to Gross-Rosen or ... he will shoot me. Do what you like, I tell him. He leaves me sitting. I remain alone.

And maybe this is even for the good? I think to myself. I'll rest up in the sick room and sleep to my heart's content. Sleep, but really sleep till I feel I've slept enough. I can already imagine how I sleep for three days and three nights. The bread ration of these days I shall eat up in one go afterwards.... I spread myself comfortably on the bench and fall asleep instantly.

"Get up, we're going home," my mates wake me. "Already?" I ask. It seems to me that it's only five minutes since I lay down. They interrupted such a sweet dream...Father...Mother... A warm home... The table is set... A white, bright... Shall I live to experience all that ever again?

This is definitely something serious and hefty. A treasure unearthed. A family heirloom discovered after 73 years. I feel that I have just met my father for the first time. I don't recognise the author. Neither does he. We are both overwhelmed. Tears overbrim our eyes. Speechless.

I don't know what to do next. There is nothing more to read today. I'm not sure there is anything more to read full-stop.

I get into action mode and print a few copies for Dad. I am beside my-self with excitement. Dad is wondering about the fuss I am making. I'm not sure if he is being falsely modest or really doesn't grasp the riches we have discovered. I send an email to all immediate family members, with our newly found treasure as an attachment. In the body of the email I give background and context. I also add my bossy instruction: "Please read it slowly and carefully." I don't want anyone rushing through it or skim-reading. The article deserves dedicated time, full attention and reflection.

Thursday 26 March 2020

Everyone is gobsmacked. But by what exactly? There are doubts about the authenticity of Dad's eloquence. He doubts himself. I think I am the only one who does not. Our family is wondering about the accuracy of this translation. Did Danielle Charak take Dad's words and reconstitute them into a literary treasure? I speak to Danielle. It seems not. I feel vindicated. For me. And for Dad.

I feel the need to share our treasure beyond the family. First, I send the article to a couple of close friends. Then I decide to share it far and wide. Always mindful of doing the right thing (after all, I am my father's daughter) I ask for Dad's permission to disseminate his gem. He laughs, "Don't be silly. Do what you want. You don't need to ask for my permission." I guess I knew that would be his response but I'm glad I asked. I call Jayne Josem, director of the Jewish Holocaust Centre (JHC) in Melbourne. I tell her about our find and send it to her. She, too, is blown away. She passes it onto Ruth Mushin, editor of *The Centre*, the JHC journal. She and I communicate. She is removing something from the next edition so that she can squeeze in Dad's article. I also send it to a friend who is an academic at Yad Vashem in Israel. I want the world to read it.

***

I have the Munich photos. I have *The New Life* newspaper. And so continues the unofficial bequeathing of familial documentary and photographic heirlooms. Dad has a mini filing cabinet, with old-fashioned green cardboard dividing folders, labelled, and full of papers. At first, he brings individual documents. Some are directly related to the stories we have been reading. Some tangentially so. Again, I have seen most of them before, but not read them closely. Not with sufficient attention to detail. As we go through each one, and as Dad tells me its providence, a legacy is being handed down. I am aware of this, but I am not sure if Dad is. He asks whether I want these documents. Copies. I tell Dad that I don't want copies; I want the originals. Now, I am not so sure that he is ready to hand them over. He is not sure either. This conversation is really about mortality. That is the subtext. But he does hand them over. Not ceremoniously. A little reluctantly in fact. But hand them over he does.

To prove that I am worthy of this bequest, I make a foray to Officeworks. The truth is, I don't really need to prove my bona fides to Dad. But any excuse to go to Officeworks is welcome. After my reconnaissance, I decide on a light blue concertina-style filing case. I show it to Dad. As he bequeaths me more and more documents, I place them in my trusty plastic pockets which go into the correctly labelled section of the concertina file. I have constructed my own genre-based filing system. At sporadic times over the weeks to come, he will ask me for *our* filing case. He will rummage through it, upsetting my system. An unforeseen benefit of this interference is that I will need to re-sort the documents, affording opportunities to study yet again these all-important parental papers.

I have started to tell more close friends about this writing project. Hesitatingly.

Friday 27 March 2020

Chapter Three
We Create: The Origins and Evolution of the Jewish Students' Union

We read about the founders and leaders, the *machers* (Yiddish for movers-and-shakers) in the Jewish Students' Union. Most names are familiar to Dad. First we read about Yehuda Knobler and Josef Silberman. Later, David Fund and also, Alexander Piekarczyk who worked for the Jewish Joint Distribution Committee (JDC) with the main remit to support the Union. As such, he was considered an 'honourary' member.

Dad claims that he was not involved in political affairs, such as defending the rights of students or keeping abreast of Zionist activities but it seems that most of those interviewed in Varon's book were. Dad has no recollection of attending meetings of any sort. However, as we sort through his Munich photos, there are a few of Dad sitting at a main table, two and sometimes three people across from someone who is addressing the meeting or forum. He recognises most people in these 'activist' photos. My pencil is poised ready to write down each name as he identifies them. Dad rattles off: "Silberman, Piekarczyk, Knobler, Fund, Fund's girlfriend." I can't square Dad's words about his lack of political participation with the photos and the ease with which he names the protagonists. I think Jeremy Varon's book has triggered Dad's ability to identify the people in his photos. I am fascinated by the 'reawakening' of Dad's memories that this gem of a book has elicited.

The history of the founding of the Jewish Students' Union is unknown to Dad. How was it formed? By whom? How was entrance to the universities of Germany arranged? Who was involved? Which organisations? Who supplied textbooks, organised accommodation, food, living allowances? I am not sure if Dad does not remember or if he never knew. He isn't sure either.

But we now read about it, together. And the details are almost all here. Thanks to those Survivor Students with an acute sense of history, the founding of their Jewish Students' Union has been exceedingly well chronicled. It is not my intention to repeat Varon's painstaking research, but to highlight some of the narrative as it relates to Dad directly.

Dad presents me with a three-page, typed document that he wrote entitled 'Reminiscences'.[4] From its contents, I date it to sometime after October 1995. Not long after the Jewish Students' Union reunion in Israel. I guess he wrote it for the short-lived Union newsletter some of the American Survivor Students published during the 1990s. I hope they printed his article. He doesn't remember and can't find any back issues. I read his piece aloud to him. Dad is impressed with himself. It is beautifully written, heartfelt and moving. I tell him so. He is impressed that I am impressed. He values my judgement. Dad says, "I used to write well. Even when I was in grade five and six, I wrote nicely."

In this article, he pays tribute to 'Engineer Alexander Piekarczyk', one of the *machers* we have been reading about. Dad identifies him rather quickly in the pile of Munich photos that now dwell on my dining room table. Dad wrote in his 1995 article that Engineer Piekarczyk was "… instrumental in the logistics pertaining to the entry to tertiary institutions". He wrote that Piekarczyk, "represents one of the most practical sources of encouragement to study…" Dad listens to himself, so to speak. Now, 25 years after he wrote that article and nearly 75 years after these events, he adds, "I owe him the good life that I have had." We will keep coming back to Engineer Alexander Piekarczyk.

These underqualified students would not have been able to attend university without the efforts of the United Nations Relief and Rehabilitation Administration (UNRRA). The short version of a complex and incredible story is that UNNRA played a crucially mammoth role in providing for, and overseeing, the return to life of the displaced persons of Europe. Amidst the chaos and confusion of the time, UNRRA personnel began conducting classes for aspiring students. This quickly evolved into the UNRRA University. Both the students and the faculty members came from amongst the displaced persons of Europe.

I have never heard of this university. I know about Ludwig Maximilian University, where Mum and Dad studied. I know about the Technische

---

4.   See Appendix B

Hochschule, where those studying engineering were based. But UNRRA University? Never. I ask Dad about it. "Oh yes, quite a number of our students had gone there before attending a 'real' university." I ask him to expand. "It wasn't considered a serious place. The standard was not of a real university. It was seen as lightweight, a sort of steppingstone for many people to ease them into studying." I ask whether he thinks he would have gone there if he had arrived in Munich earlier than he had. "I'm not sure, but probably."

Dad, his father, Israel, and brother, Heniek, had been liberated from the Friedland concentration camp on 8 May 1945. The very last day of the war.[5] Dad always emphasises this. They spent three to four months in the town of Friedland, near the camp. Then they moved to the city of Regensburg. About six months later Dad found his way to Munich.

"But how did you decide to go to Munich in the first place? How did you find out about the Union? How did you even know about the possibility of going to university?" I ask.

Dad takes a while to answer. He is straining to remember. "Arek Lucrec was my friend from Regensburg. There was some incident he was involved in, in Regensburg. He decided to leave and go to Munich. He was upset about the whole matter. As his friend, I decided to go with him."

I query, "Just like that?"

Dad confirms, "Just like that." Dad can't remember the specifics of the incident or he doesn't want to tell me. Both are legitimate. I wonder what my grandfather had to say about the matter. The response I get is a shrug of the shoulders, followed by, "I was independent." Perhaps, at the age of 21, after being with his father every single day of his life, including the horrendous six war years, it was time for Dad to make his own way in the world. And so he did. "It was in Munich that Arek and I heard about the Union, the students, university. I thought it sounded interesting. Maybe I could do it? It developed from there."

***

5. World War II officially ended in Europe on Tuesday 8 May 1945 when the Allies formally accepted Germany's surrender to its armed forces.

In Varon's book there is a photo taken in 1946 of two Survivor Students who feature heavily in his research, Roman Ohrenstein and Yehuda Knobler. It was taken in the summer of 1946 and the students are standing in front of a lake with their arms around each other. Varon points out Yehuda's emaciated physique. This was more than a year after liberation.

Dad thinks he met up with them at one of the reunions. "Let's go find those photos!" I exclaim. As far as I am aware my parents travelled to three reunions: Tel Aviv, 1995; New York, 1998; and Florida, 2000. Since I attended the New York event, a good starting point is my photo albums. Of course, my albums are clearly labelled and shelved in an orderly manner. (Even if the spines on some have been chewed by our late, much-loved dog, Coco.) I have only devoted two pages to this reunion. And one is taken up by the breakfast menu! Five photos are squeezed onto the next page. Only two are photos of Survivor Students but they are worth gold. I recognise most of Dad's old friends but there are no photos of Roman Ohrenstein or Yehuda Knobler.

Now we must return to Dad's place to scour his photo albums. He doesn't share my enthusiasm. I think this is due to his dread of my speedy pace and concern that I will upset the order. His fears are totally founded. Maybe he is fantasising about a leisurely and nostalgic perusal of the 'good old days'. However, I am on a mission. I am focusing only on unearthing the Jewish Students' Union reunion photos. That's it. All other photos, no matter how sentimental, are mere distractions. And so, I find the stepladder in Dad's garage, drag it to his cupboard, and proceed to bring down album after album. I am driving Dad nuts. My doggedness and single-mindedness irritate him to no end. I find the relevant albums and take them home. There is no way that Dad is now calm enough to cast his mind back into the distant past, to recognise faces and remember names. My exasperating behaviour has seen to that. I'll wait patiently for another day.

Of course, I begin to peruse the photo albums on my own. At the 1995 reunion in Israel, Mum is 68, Dad is 70. Everyone in the photos is around the same age. Given that Dad is now 95, very few would still be alive. On the inside front cover of this album, Dad has stuck, with sticky tape now yellowed and semi-detached, a typed list of participants.[6] There are 144 attendees: 56 are from USA and 77 are from Israel. Three are from Germany, three from Sweden and one from Norway. The four from Australia are Mum and Dad, and their friends Susie and Marion Lieder. I estimate that some are spouses and adult children of Survivor Students. Nevertheless, it's an impressive number. Many of the names from Varon's research are on the list. There is at least one person I recognise from the photos whose name is not on the list. Perhaps it is not totally comprehensive.

It takes a dose of self-discipline not to focus on photos of Mum. My attention is drawn straight to these. I want to penetrate beyond her photogenic smiles. However, I force myself to put these thoughts aside and concentrate on other faces. It doesn't take long to hit the jackpot. Here is the photo I was hoping to unearth: Roman Ohrenstein and Yehuda Knobler, side-by-side again. In Israel, nearly 50 years after the 1946 Munich lake photo. Roman is on the left and Yehuda is on the right. In both photos. I place the photos next to each other and I leave them like this for days. I look from one to the other and back again. Fifty years. An adult lifetime.

I now allow myself to stare at Mum at a leisurely pace. She looks happy in the company of old friends. To be among her compatriots from nearly 50 years earlier. But was she really? I know that she carried a sense of lost opportunity throughout her life. Regret at not completing her dentistry degree in Munich and never fulfilling her destiny to be a professional woman. Like her mother had been. She carried this regret even though she was complicit in that long-ago decision to leave Germany straight after Dad had graduated, when she had merely completed her 'half-diploma'. Even though it made sense to her that Dad would be the one to try and requalify as a pharmacist in Australia. He would be the breadwinner. But regret and reason can live uncomfortably together. Lament and logic can cohabit.

I try to delve beyond my mother's posed smiles. The vast majority of her compatriots did become professionals in their post-Munich countries.

---

6. See Appendix E

Including the women. Those who immigrated to Israel did not need to requalify. The new Jewish state did not just need farmers. It needed doctors, dentists and pharmacists too. I know that those who studied medicine and then immigrated to America faced hurdles before they were legally allowed to practise. But most were working as doctors within a relatively short period of time. It required tenacity and a dose or two of luck. But most did it. Dentists faced much greater obstacles. I can't imagine any of them, upon immigration to any country, had easy lives. But they had goals and aspirations that might, eventually, lead to professional self-actualisation. To the life they were destined for.

But not Mum. How confronting was it for her to meet up with all these friends from long ago, on the cusp of retiring from their decades-old, fulfilling professional careers? I do know that she decided not to attend the next reunion, held three years later in New York. I went with Dad in her stead.

David, Israel & Heniek Prinz, Regensburg, c. late 1945-early 1946

Heniek, Israel & David Prinz, Regensburg, c. late 1945–early 1946

Top: Roman Ohrenstein & Yehuda Knobler at a lake near Munich, 1946

Bottom: Roman Ohrenstein & Yehuda Knobler, Jewish Students' Union reunion, Tel Aviv, 1995

Top: Dad at Jewish Students' Union reunion, Tel Aviv, 1995

Bottom: Jewish Students' Union reunion, Tel Aviv, 1995.
Mum & Dad are in the first row of people standing.
Mum is the sixth person from the right, Dad is standing behind her

Sunday 29 March 2020

In a more relaxed state, I go through the album photos with Dad. Together, we try to identify people. Rather than enjoying the process, Dad is getting frustrated with his difficulty in recognising faces and remembering names. The experience is less than satisfactory. For both of us.

Continuing to work our way through Varon's book, we read about the Deutsches Museum building. The offices of the organisations that supported the aspiring students and other displaced people were housed there. At least in the very early days of Jews arriving in Munich. Dad says, "I know where that was. It was on the street by the river. But I never went there. I went to offices on Sieberstrasse." Sure enough, we read that all the major Jewish institutions were to be found on this street. And there were many. The Central Committee of Liberated Jews had moved from the Deutsches Museum building to offices on Sieberstrasse by the time Dad got there. As always, I am delighted and relieved when Dad's memories and the 'facts' corroborate.

We continue learning about the founding constitution and declarations of the Jewish Students' Union. Its statutes and goals were ambitious and grandiose-sounding. The hierarchy and range of positions were worthy of a major corporation. I am amazed by the boldness of its vision and the constructed self-importance of its officialdom. The Union would need all of this, and more, in its negotiations with UNRRA, the JDC, the Central Committee of Liberated Jews, the Jewish Agency, the American military authorities, the Bavarian government and the German university administrations. Its advocacy on behalf of the students and would-be students, was nothing short of astounding. It worked tirelessly to access support for every aspect of the lives of its members. Dad repeats his mantra, "They did everything for me. Everything. They made my life."

Monday 30 March 2020

Chapter Four
The New Life: Education and Renewal in Occupied Germany

We read more about the UNRRA University. Its initial growth, its role as a conduit to well-established German universities, and its ultimate demise. It is a complex and fascinating story. Dad repeats, "I had no idea. No idea whatsoever." A number of Survivor Students describe their views on tertiary education. Some had always dreamed of going to university, some had begun their degrees before the war, some were advised to consider further education in the aftermath of the war, and others just 'fell' into it. Dad places himself firmly in this last category.

But how did they go about applying to a 'real' university? To the Ludwig Maximilian University of Munich? The many students who did not have their maturas (the Polish word for matriculation) and diplomas had to pass exams run by the intriguingly named, Verifikations-Kommision—Verification Commission. If they didn't pass, their aspirations for university were over before they began.[7] We now read that the Jewish Students' Union established the all-important Verification Commission to confirm that applicants were qualified to embark on university education. However, it seems that a clear separation between the Verification Commission and the Jewish Students' Union needed to be established. It was obviously in the interests of the Union to enable as many aspiring students as possible to enter university. This sounds suspicious to me. Wouldn't their commission be as lenient as could be? Dad and I will follow up on this point later.

In the meantime, we are informed that Engineer Alexander Piekarczyk was the chair of the Verification Commission. Again, Engineer Alexander Piekarczyk. He was central to the lives of the Survivor Students. It seems that he was always referred to by his mouthful of a full name. Engineer

---

7. A few Survivor Students were admitted into university before the commision was established and some enrolled by other means.

Alexander Piekarczyk. It's never Alexander (or God forbid, Alex) or even Mr Piekarczyk. I am intrigued by him. He was old compared to the students. They were still in, or barely out of, their teens. He was in his late thirties. He was a mature and worldly man. I look closely at Dad's photo of him. He had been immersed in this effort to support Survivor Students from the start. He was everywhere with them and for them. He held many positions—official and unofficial—all geared towards getting these young Jews an education. He was a constant presence—until he announced, in October 1948, that he would soon depart for the new State of Israel.

I wonder about Engineer Alexander Piekarczyk. About his leadership, his determination, his boldness and his vision. In Dad's three-page article, written after the 1995 Union reunion, he mentions a (then) recent photo of Engineer Alexander Piekarczyk. This photo appears in a book entitled *Konin: A Quest* written by Theo Richmond.[8] It's in my study-library. And I know exactly on which shelf. It is one of my favourite books of all time. In fact, I remember reading it, or rather devouring it, on a weekend away when our two sons were young. I may as well have stayed home. I spent the entire weekend immobile and immersed in Theo Richmond's captivating pursuit and painstaking research to uncover the rich Jewish life that once thrived in his ancestral hometown of Konin, about 130 kilometres north-west of Lodz. His thoroughness in trying to trace people from Konin was admirably dogged. Engineer Alexander Piekarczyk was one of those born in Konin. To think that I just flicked past his photo way back in my 1995 reading! How did I read nearly ten pages about him without having a clue of the indispensable role he had played in the lives of my parents, 50 years earlier? We don't know what we don't know.

I place the two photos side-by-side: Engineer Alexander Piekarczyk circa 1945 and Engineer Alexander Piekarczyk circa 1995. Old age is unforgiving. However, even a diminished Engineer Alexander Piekarczyk looks like a tour de force. He is unsmiling in both photos. His eyes are penetrating. His jawline, determined. Theo Richmond describes him as, "tall, gaunt and stern". He is not an easy interviewee for Richmond. I laugh

---

8.   Published by Penguin Random House, UK, 1995

out loud while reading to myself. He sounds like a downright battleaxe. Why would I expect anything else? How could a softer, gentler man ever have persuaded the American military government, the Bavarian state government and the German university authorities to accept hundreds of unqualified youngsters into university courses of the highest calibre and standards? How could a less authoritative personality have convinced these institutions, along with a myriad of aid organisations, to materially support these unconventional (to say the least) university students?

My parents always described their preparatory study regimen for entering the university as gruelling. They hadn't yet met; they endured this ordeal separately. "How much did you study in the lead-up to the exams?" I ask. Dad can't exactly remember. I try to stimulate his memory but my incessant questions probably make it worse. We establish that he arrived in Munich from Regensburg not long before the exams were scheduled. With some back and forth, we figure out that maybe he had three months.

"We studied like dogs!" Dad exclaims, "I don't know how I ever thought that I could catch up on five years of schooling in three months. I still don't understand how I could have even aspired for such a thing." My parents were ensconced in their respective homes. Dad studied with Arek Lukrec, who had become his roommate. Mum studied with her friend, Rosa Eichenbaum, at the apartment where Mum lived with her mother, Buba Rosa. Mum and Dad each knew that this was their one and only chance for university study. It was imperative to pass the Verification Commission exams.

***

Mum's friend and study partner in Munich, Rosa Eichenbaum, had survived the war with her parents and younger brother in the Soviet Union. They were one of the few intact families. A few years after the war ended, the family asked Dad for a favour. They wanted him to be a witness to their false claim that Rosa's brother had been in the Friedland concentration camp (a subcamp of Gross-Rosen) with him. Why would anyone want to claim to have endured such a horrifying experience?

Because the only legitimate recipients of welfare rations were those who had been in concentration camps. Other wartime experiences weren't deemed 'worthy' of assistance. Evidently, this type of request was not uncommon. Dad readily agreed. Mum and Buba Rosa were also party to this decision. End of story? Not quite.

A number of years later, in the mid-1950s, in Melbourne, Dad received a letter from the German authorities. Evidence had emerged that the Eichenbaum boy had been in Russia during the war and that Dad's testimony had therefore been false. They demanded that Dad repay the German government the full total of Eichenbaum's reparations.[9] Plus, they advised they would no longer dispatch reparations to Dad. Dad tells me that he was beside himself. These funds made a material difference to their lives. Mum and Dad were in a seriously sticky situation. What to do? Dad said he wrote to the authorities in his finest German explaining his precarious situation. He was married and had a child. He was studying, again, to be a pharmacist. Losing the reparations would mean he could no longer afford to study. His dreams would be shattered. He also wrote that the Eichenbaum boy had described the camp and the work that had been done there. He *sounded* as if he had been there. He looked like someone Dad had known from the camp. The way people looked while in a concentration camp changed a lot even a short time after their liberation. He had *thought* it was him. So, what happened? Dad looks at me and says, "They forgave me."

---

9. Reparations are payments by the German government to Jews as a type of 'compensation' for their losses and suffering. The German word is *Wiedergutmachung* (to make good again). Initially, the acceptance of reparation payments by survivors was controversial and met by mixed responses. Nevertheless, these payments enabled many survivors to financially begin their new lives.

Dad leaning in and listening intently to Engineer Alexander Piekarczyk (standing), Munich, late 1940s

Engineer Alexander Piekarczyk, Israel, early 1990s

Tuesday 31 March 2020

Dad wants me to retrieve his Verification Commission document[10] from amongst the treasure trove of files he has entrusted me with. This document of Dad's results has been translated into English. We examine it together. It attests that Dad undertook these exams in June 1946. In the last pile of papers Dad has handed over, I find his Studienbuch, student book. Here, it says: Verification 12.6.46. A little finetuning.

With the average grade of "Successfully Passed" (David Prinz) had met the scientific requirements for taking up studies at a university.

The second page lists each subject and Dad's results.

WRITTEN EXAMINATION
Literature – Good
History –
Mathematics – Sufficient
Physics – Sufficient

ORAL EXAMINATION
Literature – Good
History – Good
Latin – Satisfactory
Mathematics – Good
Physics – Sufficient
Chemistry – Very Good
Biology – Good
Geography – Sufficient

I wonder what history and literature were being tested. We read that literature was "both world literature and one's national literature". We don't learn anything about the history syllabus—it seems that Dad did not do a written exam in that subject anyway. I am relieved for him. We read that

---

10. See Appendix C

a competent level of the German language was required. But that doesn't appear on Dad's transcript. I wonder about the Latin. Varon explains that originally it was a requirement "partly due to the theological tradition of the heavily Catholic LMU". However, it was later removed as a general requisite, and only remained compulsory for students of medicine and pharmacy. Dad was applying to the faculty of pharmacy.

We return to the issue of the potential conflict of interest between the Verification Commission and the Jewish Students' Union. Or, more accurately, the potential collusion of interests that I am wondering about. It seems that the commissioners were determined not to be accused of exactly what I am insinuating. It was important for the Verification Commission to be considered a legitimate certification authority. The exams were rigorous. However, it is acknowledged that irregularities existed and "the admissions process remained somewhat arbitrary".

Dad was a case study in irregularities. On his Verification Commission document it is written: "Mr Prinz, David, born in Lodz on July 21, 1925 who no longer possesses the Maturity Certificate that was awarded to him by the Jewish Humanistic Gymnasium in 1945…"

I don't know where to start in thinking about this formal manuscript. To add to my bewilderment, in pen, the numeral '5' in the year 1945, has been altered to a '3', as in 1943. Dad explains, "I told them it was 1943. The English translation is inaccurate. I remember that I focused on needing to be 18 years old to claim that I had finished school."

There is much to unpack. There is the assertion that Dad once had a 'Maturity Certificate'. 'Maturity' means matriculation. In Polish, the word is *matura*. There are two assumptions here. Firstly, that Dad had completed his *matura*. He had completed twelve years of school education and was awarded the associated certificate. Secondly, that the certificate (which was purported to have existed) he "no longer possesses". It was lost. Due to the war. This is perfectly plausible. This explanation is the only plausible part of this claim. This document exaggerates Dad's formal education by five years. Dad is very grateful for his secondary school education. He values it highly. But it lasted only one year.

We sit in silence. Lodz, 1943. The image of a carefree high school teenage life could not be more at odds with reality. It is beyond ludicrous. As a clarifying aside, I ask Dad if there was ever such a school as the Jewish Humanistic Gymnasium ('Gymnasium' is a common term for high school in some parts of Europe.) Dad explains that this was not one specific school, but a stream of schools. The term 'humanistic' refers to schools where students specialised in the study of humanities. (I do wonder about the veracity of this translation.) In 1943, the year of his alleged *matura*, Dad and his family were indeed in Lodz. In the ghetto. At this stage, there were no Jewish humanistic gymnasiums. There were no schools at all. Dad, his brother and their parents were cramped, starving, overworked, mourning deported (and departed) relatives and friends, dispirited and enslaved.

I ask, "Surely, the Verification Commission and the German university authorities knew the sheer impossibility that you attained your *matura* in 1943 or in 1945?"

Dad butts in, "Don't think it was just me. Everyone did whatever they could to increase their chances of acceptance." He doesn't want me to think he did the 'wrong' thing. "The Verification Commission of course knew. They were comprised of our people. And I am certain the German authorities knew too and just turned a blind eye. Their guilt was probably their motivation," he adds.

Once again, I return to Dad's Reminiscences article from 1995. The part where he writes about Engineer Alexander Piekarczyk being "one of the most practical sources of encouragement to study". After that phrase, Dad had added, "to those eligible, as well as the ones who missed out on formal education through the war and depended on individual adaptation". I think that the key words here are "depended on individual adaptation". Dad found an elegant turn of phrase to ambiguously cloud the inexactitude of the qualifications of aspiring students. Dad belonged to this second group. As did Mum. As did most of the Survivor Students.

The Verification Commission document was a statement of worthiness, but it was not a statement of admission. I am baffled by the difference. What was happening here? It seems that this was a two-pronged problem. Acceptance into university entailed an additional, none-too-transparent process. Plus, students needed to pay tuition fees. Dr Philip Auerbach was the saviour for these students. As I read out his name, Dad reacts with a sort of a "huhu" sound, while he puffs out his chest. "He was a real somebody. He was older. He was a big organiser. He took care of so many things for us. We didn't even know exactly what he did, but because of him we got admitted to university. But…." Dad is straining his memory, "I do remember some scandal, and he committed suicide." As we read on, this is all confirmed.[11]

It is through Dr Philip Auerbach's determined interventions and actions that many Jews could enrol in the university. In addition, tuition fees were scrapped or reduced and a modest stipend was paid. He enabled their admission and the necessary accoutrements. We read about the Jewish Students' Union registration cards. "Stop," says Dad, "let me get mine and Mum's." He returns home to collect them.

Virtually all of Mum and Dad's friends studied medicine, dentistry, pharmacy or engineering. Now we read that, indeed, Survivor Students were significantly drawn to these disciplines. Various motivations influenced individual choices. For example, Mum chose dentistry because her mother was a dentist. There was also a collective mindset that drove these students towards a practical vocation.

Why did Dad choose pharmacy? He shrugs his shoulders. Yet again. "I think it was a mixture of wanting something that wasn't too long. I didn't want something too hard. I had so little schooling behind me. Also, I think that maybe Arek was interested in this, and since we had come together to Munich from Regensburg, we decided to do the course together."

Growing up, I often heard Dad say that if he had stuck around at university in Munich a few more years, he could have studied medicine. Evidently, first-year students of medicine, dentistry and pharmacy took the same program. It was only after that foundation year that students branched into their chosen faculty. He put this decision—not to remain in Munich and study medicine—down to his lack of maturity and impatience to finish his degree. Perhaps this is where Dad's excessive (in my opinion) reverence for physicians emanates.

---

11. Philip Auerbach, born in 1906, was appointed Bavarian State Commissioner for Jewish Affairs, to deal with reparations. He was responsible for returning stolen Jewish property and monetary restitution to Jews. In his dealings he made many enemies, until finally, on 16 August 1952, during a trial against him for embezzlement, he committed suicide.

During our reading, Dad says, "Actually, I don't think I could've studied medicine. I wasn't smart enough." I am rather taken aback. He continues, "I knew that I just couldn't do it. I might've gotten into the course—they were very lenient—but I probably would've been kicked out after the first year. My memory just wasn't good enough." Dad never pretended that he was a scholar. He always said that he had to work like a dog at his studies. Nevertheless, I am surprised. I wonder what has caused this late-in-life 'confession'. Perhaps Dad's loss of confidence in his old age is transferring to a loss of confidence in his younger self. Or, as we are now reading about his colleagues, he is reminded of just how smart some of them were, and is recalling feeling that he never measured up. Or maybe it's a combination of both factors. It is a humbling conversation. For both of us.

Throughout our reading, Dad talks about how industrious he was in his studies. It comes up again and again. This was the focus of his life. "You have no idea how little I knew about anything. Some people had gaps. I had huge amounts of knowledge just missing. I studied almost all the time. It was one big catch-up for me." It seems like it was the same for many of the others. *Almost* nothing but study. I think that the '*almost*' is extremely important. There were many activities organised by the Union. Social, political, cultural and tourist activities. These days, Dad downplays his participation in many of these events, except for the tourist outings. They are easy to recollect because he has concrete evidence of these excursions. The majority of Dad's Munich photos seem to have been taken in the countryside against the backdrop of dramatic and scenic vistas. I assume that these were mostly short day trips. Dad corrects me, "No. Sometimes we went away for a week or two weeks. The German countryside is beautiful." I ask him who paid for the excursions. He shrugs his shoulders to indicate that he does not remember. We do read about how various organisations assisted in defraying the costs. However, it was always the Jewish Students' Union who made the arrangements.

Dad and I are immersed, together, in a wonderful time-machine journey into my parents' youthful lives. Taking a break from reading about their trips and hikes, we return to my dining room table to view the many photos taken during such excursions. Dad, through his glasses, squints closely at the faces. I, through my glasses, do the same. I feel as if I know these young people. Truth be told, I'm not sure how I expect myself to identify any of them. Most I have never met. Those I have met were then aged in their seventies. Here they are in their early twenties. Never mind, I keep trying.

The recreational and social lives of the Survivor Students seem to have been joyful and invigorating, providing a welcome break from near-constant studying. These carefree activities also enabled them to experience a childhood or youth each had been deprived of during the war years. A number of romances blossomed, including between my parents. Their meeting at the Jewish Students' Union cafeteria, the Café am Isartorplatz, forms the foundation of our family. It keeps emerging in Dad's commentary. The cafeteria has assumed mythic proportions.

Dad often articulates a gratified sense of accomplishment in his studies. During our present-day reading sessions and throughout my growing-up. His pride is not empty boasting; it is always expressed with wonder. "I did it. I actually did it." As if he can still barely believe it himself. He knows his successful graduation emanated from pure hard work and unmitigated motivation. But still…. Dad is not the only one who feels this way. Other Survivor Students also seem to be in awe of themselves. They also can hardly believe what they have made of themselves.

Membership-Certification

Mitglieds-Ausweis

Nr. 185

Signature of holder   Eigenhändige Unterschrift

NAME Name	*Prinz*
Christian name Vorname	*David*
Date of birth Geburtstag	*21. VII. 1925*
Born at Geburtsort	*Lodz (Polen)*
faculty Fakultät	*Pharmazie*

term Semester	1	2	3	4	5
	6	7	8	9	10

address: domicile Wohnort	*München 8*
street Nr. Straße Nr.	*Brahms 8/0*

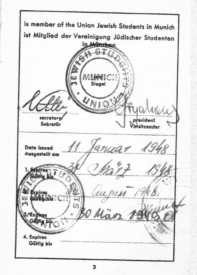

is member of the Union Jewish Students in Munich
ist Mitglied der Vereinigung Jüdischer Studenten
in München

secretary   president
Sekretär   Vorsitzender

Date issued Ausgestellt am	*11 Januar 1948*
1. Expires Gültig bis	*31 März 1948*
2. Expires Gültig bis	*August 1948.*
3. Expires Gültig bis	*30 März 1949*
4. Expires Gültig bis	

3

Dad's Jewish Students' Union membership

Membership-Certification

Mitglieds-Ausweis

Nr. 404

Signature of holder   Eigenhändige Unterschrift

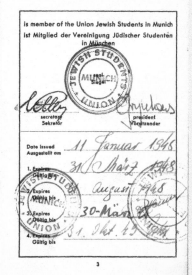

NAME / Name	Salzberg - Prinz				
Christian name / Vorname	Rachela				
Date of birth / Geburtstag	15. II. 1925				
Born at / Geburtsort	Warschau				
faculty / Fakultät	Zahn-medizin				

	1	2	3	4	5
term					
Semester	6	7	8	9	10

address: / domicile / Wohnort	München 8
street Nr. / Straße Nr.	Brahms 8/o

is member of the Union Jewish Students in Munich
ist Mitglied der Vereinigung Jüdischer Studenten
in München

secretary / Sekretär   president / Vorsitzender

Date issued / Ausgestellt am	11 Januar 1948
1. Expires / Gültig bis	31 März 1948
2. Expires / Gültig bis	August 1948
3. Expires / Gültig bis	30 März
4. Expires / Gültig bis	31. Okt. 49

3

Mum's Jewish Students' Union membership

Wednesday 1 April 2020

I have received an email from Jayne Josem, director of the Jewish Holocaust Centre (JHC). She informs me about a project that JHC is launching, in response to the museum having to halt its in-person programs during this coronavirus pandemic. JHC wants to support its Holocaust survivor volunteers who can no longer come to 'work' at the centre. The project is called Survivor Connect. The idea is for students and others who would have visited the museum to instead write to Holocaust survivors. The intention is to maintain the connection of survivors to the community during this period of prolonged isolation. The centre will send the letters for Dad to my email address. I tell Dad about the project, and he says, "Ok, sounds nice."

***

We have been reading Jeremy Varon's book for more than two weeks now. I'm suddenly overcome by the desire to contact him. I feel immensely grateful to him. He has provided a vehicle through which Dad and I can spend time together. Not just to pass the time, but to meaningfully explore a defining experience in the life of my parents. It has given Dad a much-needed boost during these early days of isolation and shaky uncertainty. As he keeps saying, "This is my life. This is what made me." It has been a while since Dad has been excited by anything.

I decide to send Jeremy an email—but I don't tell Dad so that he is not disappointed if I do not get a response.

Dear Jeremy

My name is Frances Prince and I live in Melbourne, Australia.

At present I am reading your amazing book The New Life. *I am not sure why it has taken me so long to come across it...Both my survivor parents were students at LMU during the era that you researched— my late mother studying dentistry and my father (who is 94) studying pharmacy.*

In fact, during these crazy times, I am reading your book aloud to my dad, every single afternoon. We sit together and discuss the people he knew, those he didn't know, the context and background of his experiences, what he remembers, what he doesn't remember, what he never knew, how he and Mum did or didn't conform to some of the profiles you write about and so on.

I knew quite a lot about my parents' youthful lives, and, in fact, went to Munich with Dad in 2009. Among other places, we did go to LMU. Now I am learning, and so is he, so much more.

My parents attended a number of student reunions over the years, both in USA and Israel. In fact, I travelled to one with Dad in the Catskills, maybe in 1997. So I have met a number of the people you have interviewed. I remember meeting Bella and her sister (I can't remember her name, but we hung out together at that reunion). At that time we discussed, together with some of the students, the need to have their story properly written up and recorded for all time. I remember that Bella had written an article already.

I guess that you were the person tasked with this massive undertaking. I, for one, am eternally grateful.

It is a pity that you didn't include the students who immigrated to Australia, but I understand the small numbers they represent.

My dad still has a fabulous memory. In fact, we are now going through the photos he has from that time and place and writing down the names of people on the back of those photos.

I'll send you photos of this...

I look forward to hearing from you.

Regards, Frances

Thursday 2 April 2020

I jump out of bed and grab my phone and glasses. This is normal behaviour for me. It is probably normal behaviour for all those who have children and grandchildren living overseas. But today, the kids are not my first priority.

I am not disappointed. There is an email from Jeremy Varon awaiting me.

Dear Frances

What an unbelievable surprise and gift your email is! I am so delighted, humbled, and honored. Midst the corona crisis, and days into family isolation, your communication feels that much more special. Scary times.

It's wonderful and amazing that your dad is still alive and still sharp enough to absorb the content of the book and reflect back on the detail of that time. The image of you reading it to him is precious.

Yes, you have it right. Bella started the project; we did a bunch of research together and I did the heavy lift of executing the book. It was enormous work, ten years really. It's both a 'small' story and an infinitely complex story that explores the weightiest of historical and existential themes.

I do regret that I did not talk to David directly. I talked, as you know, to many folks, but not him. It's painful to leave folks out, of course. As I explain in the intro, their absence does not mean that their importance to the student community or the value of their lives was in any sense lesser.

That said, it seems like your dad can place himself in the rich world of the students in Munich that I (painstakingly) reconstructed. Towards the very end, I talk at length about their post-Germany lives, focusing mostly on the cohorts that went to the US or to Israel. I mention Australia only in passing. It would have been so great to talk to at least one person to learn more about what the whole Australian dynamic was like. But alas.

Again, thanks so much. And please keep plowing ahead with the book, if you two have the wherewithal. Each portion accomplished something important. Also to say, I go into detail about some of the absolutely awful things folks experienced during the Shoah itself. It is silly at some level to give a 'trigger warning' to a survivor and his daughter, but those parts are harrowing.

Peace and whatever blessings I can give.

Jeremy

I forgot to mention—the photos are AMAZING! What a treasure trove of history. If the book helps rekindle your father's interest in the pivotal point in his life and history, terrific. I am so touched!

JV

I can't wait to read this to Dad when he comes over later today. I also make sure that I have printed a copy for him.

As predicted, he is excited. His main focus is Jeremy Varon's regret that he hadn't got in touch with him when he was conducting his research interviews.

Friday 3 April 2020

I decide to tell Jayne Josem from the JHC about our private project as a sort of adjunct to the centre's Survivor Connect project. I share with her what we are reading, its importance for Dad, and the restorative effect it is having on him during this uncertain and lonely time. In addition, I send her the email correspondence between Jeremy Varon and myself. Of course, she immediately picks up on the value of our undertaking.

Chapter Five
Surviving Survival: Living with the Holocaust and among
the Germans

Today we read about the psychological wellbeing of the Survivor Students. Their coping mechanisms and their emotional states are discussed. We learn about their responses and attitudes to their losses and suffering. There is much deep analysis. Dad shrugs his shoulders. Again. I have never thought that Dad is a psychologically minded person so his reaction (or lack there-of) to in-depth self-analysis and reflection is not surprising. He doesn't seem to relate to it at all. "I just got on with it. I didn't look behind. I just studied and looked forward," is his predictable (to me) response. He doesn't realise that his reaction, in and of itself, falls within the categories that Varon has identified.

Dad endured the war in the Lodz Ghetto and Auschwitz-Birkenau before he was moved to a labour camp called Friedland, a sub-camp of Gross-Rosen. He certainly 'qualifies' as Survivor First Class. He prevailed under the full brunt of the Germans, from the beginning to the end of the war. However, he feels that he had a lot of luck and "there are people who had a much, much tougher time than I did. I actually think that I didn't really suffer all that much. Sure, I was hungry all the time. I dreamt of fresh bread, butter with radishes on top. But I never starved to the point of being near death." He is referring, not so obliquely, to Mum.

Mum was also a Survivor First Class. But, as was always made patently clear to me, she was in a class of suffering way beyond not just Dad's, but most people's. She endured years in the Warsaw Ghetto, and only survived the ghetto uprising by jumping out of the fourth storey of a burning building. She was rounded up and imprisoned in the Majdanek death camp before spending 18 months in Auschwitz-Birkenau. She endured a death march[12], then internment in Ravensbruck women's concentration camp, and Neustadt Glewe, a sub-camp of Ravensbruck.

Dad's ordeal can't help but be defined by Mum's. How else could it be that he "… didn't really suffer all that much"? A long-life marriage contains many distinct self-understandings. All of this is left unsaid. It doesn't need to be verbalised. But Dad does stress, "I was only one week in Auschwitz-Birkenau. Just one week."

Varon now tackles an issue that I have thought about over the years. How did my parents, in Munich, manage to live among the Germans? What was the texture of their emotions in closely encountering these people day-in and day-out? The Survivor Students boarded in their homes, shopped at the same markets, and attended daily classes with them at university. Dad explains that at university their behaviour resembled what I have called 'polite distancing'. There was civil and superficial interaction. "We said things like, 'Please pass the test tube or the beaker' during pracs. They didn't ask us where we had been the last few years and we didn't ask them."

Such close contact between survivors and the German populace was not so common in the postwar years. Most Holocaust survivors, and other displaced people from a wide range of nationalities, lived in displaced persons (DP) camps established to house, clothe, feed, educate and rehabilitate victims of the Nazis. The ultimate goal was to relocate this ocean of suffering people back home or to provide refuge until new countries for immigration could be found. The UNRRA was responsible for this massive undertaking. However, many other aid organisations also contributed to this effort. Overall, the Jews living in DP camps didn't experience the same intensity of close and intimate encounters with local Germans as the Survivor Students.

I am most interested in what Varon uncovers about this issue in his interviews with Dad's colleagues. So is Dad.

Many Survivor Students expressed serious discomfort studying with the Germans. Resentment bubbled just below the surface. Dad tells me he didn't feel like that. Has he forgotten? After all, these interviews were conducted between ten and twenty years ago. Perhaps their recollections then were sharper than Dad's could be now. But I recall that Dad always

---

12. A death march was the forcible march of prisoners from Nazi concentration camps, away from the encroaching Allies and towards the heartland of Germany. Prisoners, already starved and brutalised, staggered hundreds of kilometres in mostly snowy conditions, in wildly inadequate clothing. Many did not survive the marches and died by the side of the road. Countless others collapsed and were shot by their German guards. Some escaped. A few survived only to find themselves imprisoned in new concentration camps inside Germany.

talked about the German students as if they occupied a parallel universe. He says, "I was focused on getting a job done. That was what I was there for. The study didn't come easily to me. I really had to work long and hard." I know this about Dad, but it is still not a satisfying response.

It seems that Survivor Students built a metaphorical wall against the Germans (always referring to them as a collective) and somehow cordoned them off from their lives. And then, in our reading, we have a shared "Aha!" moment. It is shared because I already know something about the German who breached that metaphorical wall. It feels good to be familiar with part of the 'inside story'. The eight lines Varon has written about German chemistry professor Heinrich Wieland reinforces my Dad's devoted admiration of him and corroborates all that I have heard about him. (As always, I feel guilty that corroboration is needed and is a source of relief.)

I have heard about Professor Heinrich Wieland forever. Why? He was a Nobel Prize winner. Dad has always been chuffed that he was taught chemistry by a Nobel Prize winner (1927). I can't say that I blame him. When I travelled to Munich with Dad in 2009, we saw a small exhibition about the history of the university. Lo and behold, there was an enlarged photo of Professor Wieland in front of a blackboard covered with diagrams and formulas. Dad was so excited. I took a photo of Dad in front of that photo, with his index finger pointing in the same direction and manner as the professor's in the photo. This photo is a prized possession. As is his *Studienbuch* (student book), with Professor Wieland's stamp on it, testifying that Dad passed his exams in chemistry.

There is an additional significant point to the Professor Wieland story. It was known by the Survivor Students that Wieland had been an opponent of the Nazi regime. Dad says, "We knew that he had been against them. We knew that he saved some Jewish students." Dad claims that Wieland's fame as a Nobel Prize winner protected him from reprisals or punishment.

We read that the Jewish Students' Union sent Professor Wieland special greetings and good wishes on his 70th birthday. This is one of the very few examples when the attitude to, 'the Germans' as a single group is disregarded and a particular German is individualised.

***

We are nearing the end of the book. I start thinking about what we'll do next. Our reading project has become central to Dad's everyday life. During this government-mandated lockdown, it's the only reason he has to leave his house. It's the one thing he looks forward to. He comes to my place. I read aloud to him. I figure that we need to continue, but what shall we read next?

Two vocal and involved Survivor Students are Sabina Zimering and Szymek (Simon) Schochet. In fact, Sabina was one of the powerhouses who instigated Varon's research and the writing of his book. Both Sabina and Szymek are friends of my parents. Each has written a memoir. Dad recalls that Sabina gave him and Mum a gift of her book at one of the reunions. Szymek had given them a copy of his book even earlier.

I rummage through Dad's shelves in search of both these books. His bookshelves are in his study and in the garage. I find Sabina's book. Szymek's memoir eludes me. My perusal doesn't take long and I feel a tinge re-emerging of my young adult disappointment at the paucity of the parental 'library'. Books can be found in most rooms in my home. They are treasured possessions. I remember when I consciously, and conscientiously, decided that I wanted to begin my very own library, my book collection. I used to dig around for secondhand books and for those on sale. I salivated whenever I found a bargain and hyperventilated in the '18 miles of books' in the Strand Bookstore in New York. Today, I pay good money for books. I try to support my local bookstore. But sometimes, only an internet search will locate what I am looking for. My heart races when I receive a package from Book Depository.

What will my kids do with all my books? My husband, Steven, and I have always (sort of) joked, "They'll make a very big bonfire." I am grateful that both our sons are intellectual, voracious readers and multi-disciplinary learners. Nevertheless, they don't necessarily imbibe all this scholarship and culture via the paper written word.

Dad and I are both relieved when I discover Sabina's book, even before we have finished reading *The New Life*. We are both comforted to know what we will be reading next and that we will be able to continue our life-affirming project.

***

According to Varon's research from 1999, out of the 282 Survivor Students who could be traced, eight immigrated to Australia. Who exactly were they? Mum and Dad are two of them. Susie and Marion Lieder, lifelong friends of my parents, are another two. Lusia Frydman is another. She studied at the Technische Hochschule, and so was a little removed from my parents' daily lives in Munich. Who are the other three? Dad draws a blank. Out of the five we have identified, only Dad is still alive.

As I read through the list of attendees at the 1995 reunion in Tel Aviv, I come across the name Israel Getzler, and the country he lives in: Israel. In actual fact, Israel Getzler counts as one of the eight Australians. How so? He originally immigrated from Germany to Australia. I went to school with his daughter in Melbourne. Her parents divorced and her father went to Israel alone in the early 1970s.

Dad recalls another Survivor Student who immigrated to Australia but he can't remember his name. For now, anyway. I am hopeful. Dad does recall that he was from the Polish city of Zamosc. He studied pharmacy too, about two years behind Dad. Dad remembers seeing him a few times in Melbourne. Then Dad heard that he moved to Sydney before immigrating to Israel.

We can now account for seven out of the eight Survivor Students who immigrated to Australia: Mum, Dad, Susie Lieder, Marion Lieder, Lusia Frydman, Israel Getzler and the unnamed pharmacist from Zamosc.

Back to Israel Getzler. Dad remembers that he spent the war years with his parents in the Soviet Union. And that he was well educated before the Munich student days. In Munich, he started studying medicine but left for Australia before graduating. Dad tells me, "In Melbourne, he met an old teacher of his. This teacher encouraged him to study history, not medicine." To Dad, this is interpreted as a negative result. To the academic world, however, it was a positive result. I know a little about his scholarly career in Australia due to his book, *Neither Toleration nor Favour: The Australian Chapter of Jewish Emancipation* published by Melbourne University Press in 1970. I read it when writing a paper about Jewish education many years ago. I know where to find it on my shelf. I open it and a yellowed newspaper clipping falls out. The article is a review of his book. What newspaper is it from? At first, I assume it's from *The Australian Jewish News* which has been the local Jewish newspaper for over 120 years. I turn the article over, hoping to find some clues. To no avail.

The book was given to my parents by Israel Getzler. There is an undated transcription: "For Ella and David, my mates *Sheerit Hapleta* days, Israel."

As previously mentioned, *Sheerit Hapleta* means 'the surviving remnant'. I like the 'my mates' part. It's an acknowledgement of them all landing up in Australia. In the top righthand corner of the dedication page is Dad's old stamp. It is faded, but the imprint is still easily read: D. PRINCE, RICHMOND.

In the centre of this page I have stuck my oversized Ex Libris sticker. With my name, Frances Prince, very boldly written on it. I clearly took over ownership of this book. A long time ago.

In Australia, Israel Getzler completed his undergraduate studies in history at the University of Melbourne. He moved to the UK to gain his doctorate at the London School of Economics. Then he took up a position as professor of history at the newly formed La Trobe University back in Melbourne. After his immigration to Israel in 1971, he became a professor at the Hebrew University in Jerusalem. From his obituaries (he died in 2012 at the age of 91) it is patently clear that he became a stellar scholar in the field of twentieth century Russian history with particular interest in the Russian Revolution. His written works are lauded as masterpieces. It seems that the study of history was a most worthy choice for Israel Getzler.

Dad in front of a photo of Professor Wieland, displayed in an exhibition
at the Ludwig Maximilian University, Munich, 2009

During our 2009 visit to the Ludwig Maximilian University, Dad returned
to the lecture theatre where he had spent so many hours studying
pharmacy after the war

Front cover of Dad's *Studienbuch*, study book

2

Eigenhändige Unterschrift des Buchinhabers:

David Prinz

Zur Beachtung!

Das Studienbuch gilt für die gesamte Studienzeit des Inhabers. Das Buch ist der alleinige Studiennachweis bei der Meldung zu den Prüfungen. Es ist also eine wichtige Urkunde, die sorgfältig zu verwahren ist.
Die Ausstellung einer Zweitschrift des Studienbuches ist mit Zeitaufwand und erheblichen Kosten verknüpft.

3

Des Studenten:

Familienname: *Prinz*
Vorname: *David*
Geburtstag: *21.8.05*
Geburtsort: *Lodz*
Kreis oder Provinz pp.:
Staatsangehörigkeit: *Staatenlos*

Schulbildung des Studenten: *Verifikation 12.6.46*
Reifezeugnis des *Städt. humn. Gymn.*
zu *Lodz*
vom *Juni 1941*
Ergänzungsprüfungen:

Sonstige Vorbildung:

8

Hochschule: **Universität München**
Stud.: *Prinz David (Chemie)*
Sommer- — Winter-Halbjahr 19 *46*
I. tes Fachsemester

Lfd. Nr. d Vorl.-Verz.	Name des Dozenten	Genaue Bezeichnung der Vorlesungen, Übungen oder Seminare	Wochenstundenzahl	Unterrichtsgeld RM	An- und Abmeldevermerke der Dozenten Anmeldung (Tag) / Abmeldung (Tag)	Bemerkungen
334	Rüchardt	Einführung in die Physik	4		Dr. Rüchardt	
	Kappler	Ergänz. Vorlesung zur Einführ. in die Physik	1			
	Kappler	Einführung in das physik. Praktikum Kurs B	1			
346	Wieland	Organische Chemie	4		Wieland	
	Prof. Schwei	Analytisch-chemische Übungen	2			

9

Top: Inside cover of Dad's *Studienbuch*

Bottom: Dad's *Studienbuch*, including Professor Wieland's name

Dad riding his bike, Munich, late 1940s

Sunday 5 April 2020

Chapter Six
Pioneers, Not Scholars: The Jewish Students and Zionism

In the years after the war, Survivor Students felt a growing tension between the desire to leave Germany and their aspirations to stay and complete their degrees. This tension played out in the story of my parents. It echoes Dad's sentiment that, on the one hand, he should have stayed a few more years in Germany and studied medicine. (When he is feeling expansive and confident in his abilities.) They also should have stayed so that Mum could finish studying dentistry. Yet, on the other hand, they wanted to leave already.

However, there was another, more profound, tension brewing. Where did one immigrate to? This was not merely a question of choosing the most suitable country. It was beyond the nerve-racking process of applying to embassies of different countries and waiting apprehensively for visas, invitations and sponsorships. My intention here is not to downplay or underestimate these vexed issues. I am referring to the ideological tension of whether to heed the Zionist call to make *aliyah*[13] and participate in the building of the nascent State of Israel. Or not. All other possible countries form the 'not'.

I am conversant with our family trope surrounding this issue. Dad wanted to go to Israel. By the time my parents were ready to emigrate, Dad had graduated with his degree in pharmacy and the State of Israel already existed. (My parents left Germany on 13 December 1949—nineteen months after Israel was declared an independent nation.) They would not have needed to run the blockade of British Mandated Palestine with the risk of ending up behind bars (again) in Cyprus. However, my mother had been adamant. No more war. Period. I have always had the impression that not much discussion took place on this one.

---

13. This Hebrew term refers to the immigration of Jews to Israel. Literally, it means 'ascent.' It reflects the Zionist value of the move to living in Israel from elsewhere as being an 'ascent' or elevation of one's life.

I don't know how other couples negotiated this decision. I just know the end results for some Survivor Students. I know the names of people Mum and Dad visited on their first trip to Israel in 1966. (I can still remember that I resented having to stay at home with my grandmother on the many nights Mum and Dad were out partying.) I know the names of the people they visited when they travelled to the USA. On my first trip to New York, when I was 21 years old, my parents wanted me to ring up their friends, to say hello and to send their regards. I considered these phone calls to be absurd. What was I supposed to say after "hello"? Who were all these people? How did my parents know so many people? The vast, vast majority were fellow Survivor Students.

We read about the various ways Survivor Students supported themselves. Dad tells me that he and his roommate and study partner, Arek Lukrec, registered at the Fohrenwald DP camp.

"What for?" I ask.

"To receive aid packages from the Joint you had to be registered as living in a DP camp. Fohrenwald was close to Munich, so we registered there," he answers. "We sold the cigarettes and chocolate contained in those packages. This money enabled us to pay for things. Most importantly, the funds allowed us to employ a tutor to prepare us for the entry exams to the university. Everybody did this. I didn't invent the scheme," he explains.

The Jewish Students' Union found them housing. This usually consisted of boarding in the apartments of Germans. The Jewish students literally lived with Germans. Together, in the one apartment. Food, clothing, transportation? Overall, it seems that the Jewish Students' Union was the dominant provider. In turn, the Union had to procure these resources. UNRRA, the Joint, and a hodgepodge of other organisations wove a delicate and tense tapestry of material assistance.

I ask Dad whether he ever had a part-time job while studying. His response is an emphatic, "You've got to be kidding!" I ask him to explain his outburst. "I had a lot of catching up to do. I had so many gaps in my knowledge. I simply did not have time." I ask him about Mum. This time, there is a bit of a derisive guffaw. "She also had to study almost non-stop. Also, remember Buba was the chief dentist for the Joint in Munich.

Mum had material support from her mother." I ask whether Israel, Dad's father, who was living in Regensburg during this time, gave him financial assistance. He is silent for a few moments before answering, "From time to time he gave me some money." I ask him whether his father supported him in terms of encouraging him and cheering him on. He answers, "Well, let me put it this way, he didn't discourage me. The truth is that he didn't really know what was going on. He was living in Regensburg. I was living in Munich. He wasn't around to see what was happening in my life."

We continue reading. I am taken aback when we read that the Jewish leadership in Munich had a negative attitude towards our Survivor Students. I had never heard such a thing, from either of my parents. Ever. Dad says he remembers absolutely nothing about this. Has he merely forgotten? Or was he oblivious to the hefty ideological struggles swirling around him?

On one level, the Survivor Students were criticised for studying in Germany, amongst Germans. Full stop. There seemed to be a revulsion towards the mere thought of living, studying and interacting amongst the murderers of the Jewish people. We have already explored how the Survivor Students felt about this. But now we read how other Jews viewed their choices. Dad tells me that he never experienced this criticism in Germany. But he did, later, in Australia. He remembers being quizzed, "How could you study with them? How could you live with them?" It needs to be underscored again that thousands upon thousands of Jewish survivors lived in Germany after the war. However, the vast majority lived in DP camps and had less direct contact with the German population.

There was another layer to this criticism from the Jewish leadership. An accusation of disloyalty directed at the Survivor Students. Disloyalty to the Zionist cause. Instead of readying themselves to build the about-to-be Jewish state, these sturdy and able-bodied youths were sitting in classrooms. Instead of learning agriculture, they were studying maths. Instead of learning to plough and till, they were conducting scientific experiments and memorising formulas.

It seems obvious to me that this friction preceded the question of immigration destination. The disapproval began before many immigration decisions had been made. This push against the choices of Survivor

Students to study in Germany emanated from the strong and influential Zionist ideology pervasive within the Jewish leadership in Europe and Jewish representatives from Palestine. There was a degree of shaming these young people into changing their minds and the direction of their energies. The collective Zionist cause was understood to be greater than the individual's desire to learn, to graduate with a university degree and secure a professional vocation. Undoubtedly, this either/or attitude was an oversimplification. Many Survivor Students did indeed end up making *aliyah* and living in the Jewish state. However, most immigrated *after* they had graduated with university degrees and secured vocations. Dad does not recall this discord. I wish he could. It sounds like a fascinating ideological battlefield.

The defence of many of the Survivor Students to these accusations of selfishness and self-centredness was that they were re-building the 'Jewish intelligentsia' decimated in the Holocaust. They were re-establishing an emphasis on modern education, which they considered integral to Jewish culture. And they made the point that the Jewish state would also need professionals, not only farmers. I can't imagine Dad having such highfalutin ideas about his place in the world, nor about this moniker as an intellectual. This is not Dad's self-image. He is all too aware of how difficult the study was for him. He never pretended to be a scholar. Simultaneously, he always venerated Mum's scholastic aptitude. I grew up with Dad telling me what a talented student Mum was. "So much cleverer than me." As for aspirations to participate in the resurrection of Jewish intelligentsia? Dad laughs at this, "I didn't even know what or who the intelligentsia was. I don't think I'd even heard the word before the war." Perhaps this is where Dad's lower-middle class Lodz background puts him at odds with many of the other Survivor Students. Maybe others could rightly and sincerely have made these claims. Dad never could. Dad never would.

As time goes on, the Jewish leadership pushed or promoted (there are varying attitudes on this) its Zionist agenda onto the Survivor Students in a harsher manner. We read about decidedly underhanded tactics. The students protested to defend their right to study. Dad does not remember any of this friction.

Once the State of Israel was declared on 14 May 1948, the position of the Survivor Students, and all remaining Jewish DPs, altered. Previously, the British Mandate had strict limits on the number of Jews allowed into Palestine. Boats were intercepted and passengers arrested. Many Jews attempting *aliyah* had ended up in an internment camp in Cyprus. But now there was a Jewish state. Welcoming all Jews. Needing all Jews, to help build and defend the country. Our Survivor Students didn't need pressure from the leadership; many felt their own inner pull to participate in the most amazing adventure of the Jewish people in 2000 years. They were Zionists. They supported the establishment of a Jewish state. They celebrated this personally and collectively. However, the vast majority did not choose to immigrate immediately, before completing their degrees. Like many challenging and complex issues, the range of personal reactions, inner turmoil and guilt was vast.

Yehuda Knobler was the Zionist star and standout figure of the group. Dad doesn't need me to read about his decision. Dad remembers clearly, "Knobler went to Israel. He was a real Zionist. If I remember correctly, he was already fluent in Hebrew. He just took off and left. In fact, I think he left even before the State of Israel was declared. He just dropped his studies." I am unsure of Dad's tone. Is it admiration? Ongoing disbelief? I'm not sure. Neither is he. Yehuda Knobler became a professor of organic chemistry at the Hebrew University in Jerusalem. He has a slew of academic publications to his name. I guess he managed to finish his studies in Israel. Dad and I both enjoy reading about Varon's visit and interview with Yehuda in Tel Aviv in 2004. Dad is right. He left Munich in January 1948, a few short months before Israel was established. And he paid a hefty price. He spent time, en route, in a British internment camp in Cyprus. I ask Dad how well he knew Knobler, as he calls him. "Quite well. We were in the same chemistry classes together."

So much to mull over. We could explore alternative lives. We could contemplate different decisions. What if my parents had not gone to Australia? What if my parents had made *aliyah* to Israel? What if they had immigrated to America? In a broad sense, all these options play out in the varied choices made by the Survivor Students.

DIPLOM

Herr David Prinz

geboren am 21. Juli 1925 zu Lodz

der mit Genehmigung des Bayerischen Staatsministeriums für Unterricht und Kultus nach 6-semestrigem pharmazeutischen Hochschulstudium zur

Pharmazeutischen Prüfung

vor dem Prüfungsausschuß in München zugelassen worden war, hat diese Prüfung in sämtlichen in den Prüfungsvorschriften vom 8. Dezember 1934 angegebenen Prüfungsfächern bestanden und am 12. Nov. 1949 das Gesamturteil

»Mit Erfolg bestanden«

erhalten.

Der Vorsitzende
des Ausschusses für die pharmazeutische Prüfung
an der Universität München

o. ö. Universitätsprofessor

Heiratsurkunde

(Standesamt München ___ II _____ Nr. _8̶7̶9̶___)

Der ___Studierende der Pharmazie David P r i n z ,___

_____, wohnhaft ___in München,___

geboren am ___21. Juli 1925___ in ___Lodz, Polen,___

(Standesamt ___Beurkundung nicht nachgewiesen___) und

die ___Studierende der Zahnheilkunde Rachela___

___a l z b e r g___, wohnhaft ___in München,___

geboren am ___14. Februar 1927___ in ___Warschau, Polen,___

(Standesamt ___Beurkundung nicht nachgewiesen___ Nr. _____)

haben am ___21. Mai 1948___ _____ vor dem Standesamt

München ___II___ _____ die Ehe geschlossen.

Vermerke: _____

_____

_____

München _____ den ___21. Mai___ 19 ___48___

(Siegel)

Der Standesbeamte

Dietz

Mum & Dad's civil marriage certificate, Munich, 21 May 1948.
Their Jewish wedding had been celebrated five months earlier
on 23 December 1947

Monday 6 April 2020

Reading the conclusion in Varon's book, Dad and I learn about the gradual, and then not so gradual, emptying of Jews from Germany. The decisions they made swept them out and into new lives in new countries. The majority of Jewish DPs did go to the young State of Israel. Interestingly, the majority of the Survivor Students did not. They mostly ended up in the USA. Completing their degrees seemed to be the first priority for the Survivor Students, immigration was the second, or simultaneous, concern. That was certainly so for Dad. Concurrent with preparing for final exams, he was going through the painstaking paperwork for immigration. These were not easy stresses to balance.

Mum and Dad left Munich, Germany on 13 December 1949. They arrived in Melbourne, Australia on 26 January 1950. Australia Day. This national holiday marks the anniversary of the British arriving in 1788 and raising their flag on Australian soil. In more recent times, Australia Day has become much more controversial with some referring to it as Invasion Day. Of course, 26 January 1788 does not mark Australia's beginnings. The Aboriginal and Torres Strait Islander people are our First Peoples and they have lived in the country a mighty long time. Nevertheless, my parents always considered their arrival to Australia on Australia Day as an auspicious start to their new lives in their adopted country.

Survivor Students experienced challenges in all the countries they immigrated to. Learning a new language and the need to immediately earn a living, were pressing concerns. The solutions varied greatly. The challenge to have their German degrees recognised and to work in their professional fields, differed tremendously. They differed not only between countries, but between regions within the one country. They differed across disciplines. Within the one country, qualifications in one profession were recognised more readily than another. Anecdotally, it seems to me that Australia was the most difficult country of all. The barriers excluding those with foreign degrees seemed higher and more impenetrable than in other countries. This was the obstacle facing my parents.

Dad applied to the Pharmaceutical Society of Victoria for recognition of his German degree about a year after arrival in Australia. I have the original letter of reply dated 2 March 1951.[14]

I am directed to advise that you make further application at the end of the current year; and that, in the meantime, you undertake study with the object of presenting yourself for the preliminary examination of the Board in the subjects of English, British History and Physical Science—the first two subjects to assist you in your progress with the English language—and the third to help as an introduction to our technical terms.

I would suggest that you endeavour to get as good a pass as possible at the examination, which is held in May and November each year.

I try to understand this letter. What is meant by "the preliminary examination"? This does not sound like a step towards the recognition of a degree, but more like an entrance examination into the pharmacy course itself. Was the organisation informing Dad what he must do to gain entrance into the Pharmacy College program? To even be allowed to study a course he has already graduated from? It doesn't sound like there was much recognition for his degree. The British history requirement is laughable from today's standpoint. However, in terms of Australian identity at that time, this was considered an important subject, I suppose. The paternalistic advice that Dad "endeavour to get as good a pass as possible at the examination" was hardly needed given his monumental efforts to gain a university degree with a starting point of only one year of high school education. Dad, at the age of 26, already had a life's worth of endeavour. However, with a wife and child, he could not afford to follow the advice to return to fulltime study. I ask whether he followed up on this letter. Perhaps he asked for a meeting or further consideration? "No. I didn't have the confidence or language skills to do that. I just gave up," he tells me.

---

14. See Appendix D

Dad continued in the job he had begun soon after arriving in Melbourne, at a factory called Granowski's. He worked as a fitter and turner on a lathe, using the skills he had learnt in the ghetto and in Friedland labour camp. Dad worked at Granowski's from 12 May 1950 until 13 March 1952, leaving when the factory ceased offering overtime to employees. Working overtime for higher rates had significantly boosted Dad's wage and my parents had been reliant on this extra income.

He applied to work at Moulded Products, a factory producing plastic household goods. He was interviewed by the foreman and all seemed to be going well until Dad was asked to fill in some forms and came to a question about his religion. Dad had been in Australia—and out of Europe—long enough to know that such a question was not appropriate. The foreman told him that it was no big deal, just a formality, so Dad wrote, "Jewish". The foreman took the forms and disappeared to consult with his boss. When he returned he said, "What a pity, we don't hire Jews." Dad could not believe what he was hearing and demanded an explanation. After further consultation with his boss, the foreman offered the following answer. A Jewish man had worked for the company. Then he left and opened a rival company close by. This is classic antisemitism. A negative experience with one Jewish person tars all Jewish people. However, after Dad protested some more, Moulded Products did end up employing Dad to work on a lathe in the tool room.

There is a funny addendum to this story. One day, not long after he started working there, a man cornered Dad and said to him, "V*as machstu?*—How are you?" In Yiddish. Dad nearly keeled over. They had a conversation in Yiddish. Dad asked him how he got the job, given that Moulded Products had a policy not to hire Jews. The man responded, "A Jew? I told them that I am Armenian."

We have one remaining piece of Dad's handiwork from his time at Moulded Products: a pale green cup. This example of Dad's skill is a much treasured heirloom.

Over three years after Dad's initial application to the Pharmaceutical Board of Victoria he gave it another go. I also have this letter of reply, dated 11 August 1954.[15] It was signed by the same person who had written the letter over three years earlier, the registrar, F.C. Kent. This was an altogether different type of letter. It was certainly not warm and fuzzy. Or even slightly encouraging. But it made more sense and provided a glimmer of hope. The letter explicitly outlined the requirements for Dad to qualify for registration. They were onerous and demanded serious commitment:

(a) *to serve an apprenticeship of three years with a registered pharmaceutical chemist*

(b) *to attend a course of lectures extending over three years... such lectures to consist of a combined 1st/2nd year, 3rd year and 4th year*

(c) *to pass examinations: the College Examination at the conclusion of the 1/2 year course; the Intermediate Examination after completion of the 3rd year studies; and the Final Qualifying Examination on completion of the 4th year course.*

I re-read both letters sent by F.C. Kent on behalf of the Pharmacy Board of Victoria. There are substantive changes. Firstly, they were allowing Dad entrance into Pharmacy College. They were accepting him straight in. It may not read like a compassionate acceptance, but that is exactly what it is. He did not need to sit for an exam in British history to enter Pharmacy College. Phew. Secondly, they were allowing him to combine first and second years so it would take him three years to complete the degree, not four. My parents interpreted this as a godsend. The three-year apprenticeship requirement was crucial for Dad. He would be paid for that work. The family budget relied on it.

The Pharmacy Board of Victoria seemed to have undergone a radical change of approach in the three years between Dad's first application and his second. We discuss what could have accounted for this change. "Maybe, as more and more European migrants came to Australia, they began to think differently about them," Dad suggests. Maybe.

I ask Dad, "What made you reapply? Why did you give it another shot?"

He answers without hesitating. I find it interesting how he can immediately remember some things, but not others. "I was working

---

15. See Appendix D

at Moulded Products, the largest plastics factory in Australia. I was recuperating at home after a hernia operation. That gave me thinking time to reflect on my long-term future. Also, my English had improved tremendously. I was more confident and I had the time to carefully prepare my application." Dad, with Mum's support, committed to becoming a student again.

Dad was set to begin Pharmacy College in March, the start of the 1955 academic year. He was almost 30 years old with a wife and a four-year-old son. He was to serve his apprenticeship with a pharmacist named Bob Wally. Bob Wally holds a venerated position in our family. With good reason. Mr Wally asked Dad if he could begin work earlier than March 1955. In fact, he wanted Dad to start straight away. Dad gave Moulded Products two weeks' notice and started working full-time in Bob Wally's pharmacy, under supervision, in September 1954. He earnt thirteen pounds and ten shillings a week. He tells me this, without prompting. Such a detail is so important to him. Understandably. Once classes started, Dad was to work part-time for Mr Wally and his pay would drop to four pounds and three shillings. In early February 1955, Mr Wally told Dad that he obviously couldn't continue to pay him thirteen pounds and ten shillings once university began. Dad knew this—my parents had budgeted accordingly. Then Mr Wally told Dad, apologetically, that he could afford to pay him ten pounds a week. And that he hoped this was okay. "I nearly collapsed! I thought that maybe I had misunderstood. I couldn't believe it. I couldn't wait to get home and tell Mum. I mean, this was double what I thought I would be earning. It was unbelievable." Dad sounds as excited today as he must have been 65 years ago.

Many years later, after Dad was long qualified as a pharmacist and had his own pharmacy, Mr Wally passed away. Dad got in touch with his widow to offer his condolences and she told Dad how highly her late husband had spoken of him.

***

Back to the Survivor Students. It seems, from our reading, that those who could work professionally soon after immigrating, did so. Those who had difficulties having their qualifications recognised pivoted into other livelihoods. We don't come across anyone who, like Dad, had to repeat most of their studies. Let alone at the age of 30.

The close, loyal and enduring friendships between the Survivor Students are heart-warming to read about. Many shared their greatest joys and deepest sorrows with each other throughout their lives. I can't help but think that the tyranny of distance precluded my parents from maintaining these relationships. Not that my parents didn't have close and intimate friends in Melbourne. They certainly did. But except for Susie and Marion Lieder, Mum and Dad had no close friends from that period.

Obviously, we only know about the Survivor Students who are subjects in Jeremy Varon's phenomenal research project. We can't hear from those who are not party to his questions. Dad and I assume that there must be those who had no interest in keeping in touch with others. There must be those whose whereabouts are unknown. They are off the radar.

There is a photo in the book from the Jewish Students' Union reunion in Boca Raton, Florida in 2000 that Mum and Dad attended. There are maybe 80 people in the photo, which has been taken from a bird's-eye view. They are all looking up at the camera. I spot my mother in the front row. I know that hairdo, that smile, her hand positioning. I know her outfit. I even know those shoes that are only partially visible. She was 73 years old. I can't find Dad in the photo. That's unusual, he likes being in photos. We get out the magnifying glass. Dad pores over the photo, seeking himself out. To no avail.

Varon unearths an uneasiness among the Survivor Students that I have often wondered about: the long-term relationship between those who immigrated to Israel and those who left for America or elsewhere. It seems that this remained a point of tension between these two groups, forevermore. In broad terms, and simplistically, the Israelis among the cohort always felt that those who chose America over Israel took the easier option, economically and possibly emotionally. By immigrating to America, they chose not to play their part in the building and defence of the Jewish state. The American Survivor Students didn't exactly disagree. This fed into their own guilty consciences. I ask Dad about this. He says that he has no idea about these tensions. Why? "I had nothing to do with organising the reunions. I wasn't aware of the friction between the groups when they were trying to get together. My relationships were with individual friends in both places. In America, we caught up with friends. In Israel, we caught up with friends." I ask whether he ever felt any resentment from the Israelis. He answers, "No way. Never. Mum and I felt welcomed. We were greeted very warmly. We were wined and dined. We reminisced about the old days. They seemed more than happy to see us." Fair enough. I decide not to dig for deeper layers as is my usual want.

A reunion was held in Germany in June 2005. Precious few Survivor Students attended; it sounds like the event was a failure. I ask Dad about it. He recalls, "Yes, I remember correspondence about it. Then it just fizzled out." Varon attributes this to the ambivalent feelings of the Survivor Students towards the country that both persecuted and redeemed them.

We finish our monumental reading project. The initial one, anyway. A recent mantra of mine is that we should all meet old people when they were young. I feel that via Jeremy Varon's masterpiece I have almost been able to accomplish this.

Dad holding the cup he made while working at Moulded Products, Melbourne, 2020

Mum is in the front row (second from the right) at the Jewish Students'
Union reunion, Florida, 2000

Reading
Project
Part Two

Tuesday 7 April 2020

Hiding in the Open: A Holocaust Memoir
Sabina S. Zimering
Published by North Star Press, 2001

'To Ella & David, friends from way back. Sabina Zimering, October 2003'

I recall meeting Sabina Zimering in 1998 when I accompanied Dad to the reunion in New York. She was one of the organisers, the *machers*, of the event. She was confident and charismatic. Her husband, Ruben, was also a former Munich student. Sabina had studied medicine. Ruben had studied engineering. I remember asking Ruben, "How did you learn German to a level that enabled you to study at the university?"

He didn't miss a beat when he answered me, "I read the dictionary from beginning to end."

Dad and I begin to read Sabina's memoir.

We learn that she was from a small town in Poland called Piotrkow. Dad stops me after the very first sentence. This does not bode well for our reading project. My Polish pronunciation of Piotrkow is incorrect. This is followed with, "What a hole, a *shtetl*." These two issues will become recurrent interruptions. My Polish doesn't improve and any place in Poland that's not Lodz or Warsaw or Krakow is dismissed as a provincial backwater.

Sabina dives straight into the war. There is no preamble. No chronological backstory. We do however learn about her life before the war as she skilfully weaves it in and out of her war story. Holocaust memoirs are usually divided into 'before', 'during' and 'after'. Not necessarily equally divided, but divided nevertheless.

The family decided to flee east. Away from the Germans, towards the Russians. So they think. They, and thousands of others, Jews and non-Jews. They all thought they could outrun (or outwalk or outcrawl) the

German army. The Germans caught up to them. Sabina and her family turned around, exhausted, and joined the throngs heading back home. We read about their incarceration in the Piotrkow Ghetto with its deteriorating living conditions. Overcrowding, hunger, typhus, arrests, violence. No matter how many times I read about the ghettos in Poland, with their litany of horrors, each individual story has the power to scuttle and fell me.

Dad starts what will become a regular disruption throughout our reading program. "Stop. What date is it now? How old is she now?" I realise that Dad is trying to place himself within the narrative. What was he doing at that particular time? How old was he? When she was here, where was he? This is the first instance of what I think of as a 'search for parallelism'. I suspect that it may be a subconscious game of one upmanship. Who suffered more? Who faced more dangerous challenges? But I quickly dismiss this line of thinking. It is totally inconsistent with Dad's personality. He may be competitive about some things, but not in the realm of the suffering stakes.

***

I get a phone call from Jayne Josem informing me that *The Australian Jewish News* (AJN) is doing a story about JHC's Survivor Connect project. Since Dad was one of the survivor volunteers who has been receiving emails, would he agree to be part of the story? In addition, our own project could be part of the story, if we wish. I know that Dad won't mind at all. In fact, I'm sure he'll love it.

Wednesday 8 April 2020

The first night of *Pesach* (Passover) starts tonight. There isn't really much to prepare and cook. After all, there will only be three for the Passover meal, the *seder*, tonight, and the same three tomorrow night for the second *seder*. Dad, Steven, me. It feels strange. It feels strange for all Jewish people. Enough words have been written about *Pesach* during the time of coronavirus without my additional ramblings. However, I can't quite help myself, and send *Pesach* greetings to family and friends consisting of two contrasting photos. One photo I label '*Pesach seder 2018*'. The tables are overflowing with cutlery and crockery laid out for 22 people. The 2020 version depicts a sparsely set table for three.

***

In Sabina's memoir, we meet three key non-Jewish people quite early on. Sabina's schoolteacher, Mrs Justyna, and her daughters Danka and Mala. The family were instrumental, early in the war, in saving the lives of Sabina and her younger sister, Helka. In fact, they re-met after the war and continued their friendship across geography and generations. When we are first introduced to them, Dad gives a deep sigh. He doesn't need to say a word. I know what that sigh means. No-one helped him. There were no Righteous Among the Nations[16] who hid or fed or aided him in any way. I grew up with this lament. To be fair, the Lodz Ghetto was sealed off virtually completely from the outside world. It was hermetically sealed, as Lodz survivors are prone to saying. There was little opportunity for non-Jews to assist them.

***

Today I receive an email from Rebecca Davis, the journalist from AJN tasked with writing the article about the Survivor Connect project. She would like to tee up a phone call interview with me for next Tuesday. In the diary it goes!

---

16. A title bestowed on non-Jews who risked their lives during the Holocaust to save Jews. Yad Vashem (Israel's national Holocaust memorial) honours these people for their bravery and altruism.

Thursday 9 April 2020

False identity papers, an escape from the Piotrkow Ghetto on the day of its liquidation, separation from parents, aimless wanderings in search of shelter, passing for a Catholic girl, travelling to Germany as a Polish worker: it's all here. All the while, Sabina was looking after her little sister, Helka. None of these perilous escapades could have been even remotely possible unless Sabina and her sister had 'dobry wyglad'.

All Polish Jews are familiar with the term 'dobry wyglad' or 'good looks'. What are 'good looks'? To the innocent reader it implies that someone is pretty or handsome. It infers the positive gains of being attractive. For those in the know, it was a code, not in the beauty stakes, but in the life and death stakes. Having 'good looks' meant that one did not look Jewish. 'Good looks' meant that you could pass as a Pole, that you didn't have the physical characteristics of what was understood to be typically Jewish features. It was the main requisite for successfully hiding in the open as a Polish non-Jew. It wasn't the only criteria but if you didn't have dobry wyglad you couldn't even begin to contemplate this avenue of survival.

Dad and I discuss this. Dad says, "Until we went to Poland together you really didn't understand this, did you?"

I defend my knowledge base. "Yes, I did," I retort immediately, and then I add, "theoretically, anyway." We went on a trip to Poland, together, in 1994. It was extraordinary on many levels. But Dad's comment certainly hit home. Walking through the cities of Poland, whether it be Warsaw, Lodz or Krakow, we both stood out like sore thumbs. I was shocked by the homogeneity of the people all around us. And how different we looked. My dark curly hair and Dad's ample nose? What a combo we were! Neither of us have 'dobry wyglad'.

We continue to read about Sabina and Helka's many narrow escapes and plucky decisions. These are all narrated with a generous coating of fear. Eventually, the sisters ended up in the German city of Regensburg. Coincidentally, this is where Dad, his father and brother lived not long after they were liberated. The girls were set to work in the Maximilian

Hotel. Here were two Jewish girls, passing as Poles, working in a glamorous and elegant hotel that was frequented by the SS top brass. Sabina was a cleaner, Helka a waitress. I am briefly reminded of *Downton Abbey* or *Upstairs Downstairs*. It's like a period piece, but in Germany during the war, the drama was lethal.

Dad is holding his breath. So am I. We know she survives, but the tension is so palpable, we can't seem to be sure. Sabina's book reads like a movie script. It seems so cliched to think that if a film was produced based on this memoir, no-one would believe it had really happened. But neither of us can shake this feeling. And then, a small flyer drops out of the book. Indeed, Sabina's memoir has been adapted, not for the silver screen, but for the stage. It premiered at the Great American History Theatre in Saint Paul, Minneapolis in March 2004. Dad and I are both excited by this. I must have missed this pearl in my initial Googling of all the Survivor Students featured in Varon's study. I Google again. I find that the play attracted critical acclaim and that it was brought to the stage again in February 2010.

Friday 10 April 2020

Towards the end of the war, Sabina exerted extraordinary self-restraint and calm whilst living amongst the Germans. She was like a fly on the proverbial wall. We gain a glimpse into the reactions of Germans in a German city to the impending knowledge that they were losing the war and were about to be occupied by the Americans. We are used to reading first-hand accounts of Jews waiting to be liberated. Sabina saw liberation from the viewpoint of the perpetrators. And she had grandstand seats. The American soldiers arrived in Regensburg on 27 April 1945.

The American military top brass replaced the German senior authorities at the Maximilian Hotel in Regensburg. Gradually, Sabina and Helka revealed their true identities to those around them. It was difficult to procure new identification papers and they were not able to embark on their much-anticipated journey home to Piotrkow until three months after liberation.

This was the trek most survivors undertook as soon as possible after their liberation. Some managed to return home within a few days or weeks of their new-found freedom. Others found that ill-health, transportation chaos, bureaucratic anarchy or a myriad of perilous dangers, prevented them from going 'home'. Polish Jews felt impelled to return to their hometowns to search for surviving relatives as soon as they could. Maybe some of their loved ones were alive?

In Piotrkow, Sabina and Helka found an uncle and first cousin who had survived, and learnt that their younger brother was alive in France. They had already known that their mother had been killed. The death of their father was confirmed. The sisters convinced their uncle and cousin to leave Poland with them and to return to Regensburg in Germany. However, the trip was nearly derailed by Russian guards who suspected they were spies.

***

Dad tells me that his surviving family (his father, brother and himself) went back to Lodz at least three times in the immediate aftermath of liberation, when they were living near the camp of Friedland where they had been incarcerated for eight months. But they did not undertake the trips together. Dad recalls that his father Israel went first, on his own, to Lodz and then returned. Then Dad went, on his own, for the second foray of a week or two. He tells me he went to The Jewish Community Office at 32 Szodmaysker Street. "How on earth do you remember the address?" I bellow in amazement. He shrugs his shoulders. He doesn't remember who went the third time. "Did you find someone?" I ask hopefully.

"Yes, *Cioca* (Aunt) Mala and then, another time, *Cioca* (Aunt) Lola." Two of his mother's sisters.

Then he tells me that walking along Szodmaysker Street, he literally bumped into a cousin on his father's side, Aleck Sladowski.[17] They ran into each other's arms, hugging and crying. Aleck and his two brothers, Heniek (who also immigrated to Australia) and Jusek (who ended up living in Germany for the rest of his life) were also still alive. Heniek and Jusek had

---

17. He later immigrated to Australia and changed his surname to Slade.

survived on Aryan papers. Aleck had been in Auschwitz-Birkenau and a labour camp called Jaworzno, a sub-camp of Auschwitz. One of many. In Jaworzno, he had toiled in a coal mine, as part of the construction of a power plant. Aleck took Dad home to where he was living with his two brothers. Dad can't remember how long he stayed with them, but he does say, "I slept there for at least one night. That is for sure." Also staying with them was another cousin who had survived, Bella Wittelsohn. She took care of the domestics for the three Sladowski brothers. Who was to know then, that in the not-too-distant future, Bella's brother would marry Dad's mother-in-law? Dad hadn't even met Mum yet. That was still about two years into the future.

We arrive to the part of Sabina's story that we have been anticipating. Munich. Her story and my parents' stories are inching closer. They will soon converge. She writes about the Jewish Students' Union, the university entry process, and the provision of material goods. She describes the *bursa*, the dining hall, sponsored by the Joint, where the students met, ate and socialised. We read that this is a place where "many serious relationships, which often led to marriages, sprang up." Including my parents'. Yet again, we read a reference to the place where Mum and Dad met. Yet again, it delights me.

Sabina savours, with breathtaking excitement, the nature hikes and other excursions she participated in with other Survivor Students. Dad looks carefully at photos of these outings that she has published in her book. We have our trusty magnifying glass on standby. He recognises most of the people in them. He has many similar photos. Even I can recognise and name some people who appear in photos in Varon's book, Sabina's book and Dad's own photo collection from that time.

Sabina discusses her medical studies, the economic hardships, the lack of textbooks and the discomfort of being in classes with Germans. Much of this material has been covered in Varon's book, to which Sabina made a significant contribution. We read about her friendship and then growing romance with a man called Ruben. He had his own tragic story. She studied, reunited with her brother, socialised with the Survivor Student group, and her relationship with Ruben grew more serious.

Over time, more and more of the friends graduated and left for other countries. We read that Ruben, recently qualified as an engineer, left for America in September or October 1949. Mum and Dad left for Australia in December 1949. Dad had completed his studies in pharmacy. Mum had not completed her studies in dentistry. Then I read that Sabina did not go with Ruben. She decided to remain in Munich until she had completed her last exams in medicine. I am bowled over by this. To be fair, I know that Sabina and Ruben weren't married at the time (and my parents were) but they were committed to one another, and she stayed on, in Germany, on her own, to complete her studies.

I feel that I'm about to revisit old territory. Re-hashed territory. Why didn't my parents stay on so that Mum could complete her studies? I find that I am jealous, on Mum's behalf, of Sabina. I am jealous that the couple were prepared to separate so Sabina could graduate as a doctor. While I have no clue as to how they arrived at this decision, I am jealous of what I perceive as her determination. For all I know, she may have wanted to dump it all and just go with him and he convinced her to stay and complete her studies. I have no idea.

I am also jealous, on Mum's behalf, of Sabina's lifelong medical career in the USA.

Even though this is a recurring issue for me, reading about Sabina and Ruben's situation does sharpen my frustrations surrounding my parents' decision. Dad and I have discussed this problematic (for me) subject many times before. Why didn't Mum finish studying? Why didn't they wait before emigrating? It's a question I ask again now. It annoys and aggravates Dad. I know I sound accusatory. It seems like a swiping reproach. Dad is exasperated and responds, "We were kids. We weren't experienced. We didn't weigh things up so carefully. The visa arrived, we prepared to leave." This is the oft-repeated refrain I have grown up with. But this time I won't let it go so easily. Dad continues, "We knew we were going to have troubles having our German university qualifications recognised by the relevant authorities in Australia. So, it seemed pointless for Mum to finish. It was better to leave already and begin our new life." This still doesn't satisfy me. Probably nothing ever will. I know that hindsight is amazingly insightful. The 'retrospectoscope' is a wonderfully wise instrument. Then Dad throws in a curly one. "And anyway, I don't think Mum was so thrilled studying dentistry. Don't you think that Buba (Mum's mum, the dentist) had a hand in Mum's decision to study dentistry? You think she was enjoying it so much?" This line of reasoning has never been part of the family narrative until now.

Sabina Zimering (third from the left) and Dad (fourth from the left)
on a Jewish Students' Union excursion

Jewish Students' Union excursion. Dad is standing at the top tier
of the fountain (top left) and Sabina Zimering is second from the left
in the first row of people standing

Sunday 12 April 2020

Today, Dad turns up with Simon Schochet's book! "Where did you find it?" I gasp.

"On the shelf," answers Dad in a matter-of-fact manner. I feel remorse at my ungenerous thoughts about the lack of tomes in my parents' home. Perhaps I had been immersed in my own judgemental thoughts when I could have been hunting down Simon's memoir.

It feels like serendipity that Dad has found Simon's book while we are still reading Sabina's. Again, there is shared relief that our next reading is lined up before we have completed the current reading. We will be able to seamlessly roll from Sabina to Simon.

***

After some time, Ruben left for America. Sabina had never been comfortable with the Germans she had been living with, so she decided to move into a room, recommended by a friend, with much nicer landlords. I feel relieved. She deserved it. She was alone, without Ruben. She was studying so conscientiously and hurdling over one exam after the other. Then, because my eyes skip ahead of my mouth, I see what's coming and all I can say to Dad is, "You won't believe this!!!" I can't get the words out. I'm speechless.

Dad is staring at me. "What is it?" he implores.

I read aloud. "The new landlords, Herr and Frau Stein, an older couple with no children, lived nearby on Brahms Strasse." I know the Steins! I know Brahms Strasse! This is where Mum and Dad lived from when they got married in December 1947 until they left for Australia two years later. The Steins had been *their* landlords!

Sabina continues, "My new room, on the main floor of a good-sized apartment building, proved spacious, bright and well-furnished. Both Herr and Frau Stein showed friendship right away." Dad is incredulous, as am I. I know all about the apartment, the furniture, and most importantly, the kindness and warmth of the Steins. Mum and Dad had always said that they were fine people. I had always grimaced at that statement. In actual fact, Dad had told me that Herr Stein was very fond of him, and that he and Mum were like substitute children for them. I had always dry-retched at that statement. To take it a step further, Dad now says that if he and Mum had stayed on in Germany, he is sure that the Steins would have left them their inheritance! Now I want to throw up.

"Were you the friend who told Sabina about the Steins?" I wonder. After all, the timing fits neatly. Dad can't remember.

Left: Mum looking out the window of the Steins' apartment on Brahms Strasse, Munich. Mum & Dad lived there between December 1947 and December 1949. Sabina Zimering lived in the same apartment not long afterwards

Right: Dad standing below the same window, 2009

Monday 13 April 2020

Sabina finally received her medical degree. She sailed (not too comfortably) to New York where she reconnected with Ruben and, together, they moved to Minneapolis. She reunited with her sister and brother, who had emigrated earlier. As immigrants, they faced a number of challenges as they settled into their new life. After Sabina's medical degree was recognised by the Minnesota Board of Medical Examiners she was required to pass exams, in English of course, to earn her Minnesota medical license. She tried to learn English in numerous ways and in mid-1951 began her medical internship. Her first child was born not long after she completed her exams.

Sabina and Ruben forged a meaningful and fulfilling life. Children and grandchildren followed. Satisfying long-term professional careers were established. Friendships, close family relationships and their own marriage were savoured and enjoyed. We have read a brief sketch of a 'good life'.

Tuesday 14 April 2020

Spoke with Rebecca Davis from AJN this morning…

Feldafing, Simon Schochet
Published by November House, 1983

'To Ella & David, my dear friends, with best wishes and love, Szymek'

Simon (Szymek) Schochet was another of my father's student peers in Munich. But he was of a different ilk. While the vast majority of the Jewish Munich students enrolled in medicine, dentistry, pharmacy or engineering, Szymek studied the humanities. Most students had a practical bent, with a focus on pragmatic, vocational qualifications. Szymek studied history and also, perhaps, journalism. Not so practical, the other Survivor Students thought. "But we said nothing," pipes in Dad. Despite the early scepticism of his colleagues, Szymek did end up having a fulfilling career in academia in the USA. In fact, his painstaking research identifying Jewish officers of the Polish army who were massacred by the Soviets at Katyn during the war, was an important scholarly breakthrough.

Feldafing is a most unusual memoir. It's not about the author's prewar Jewish life. And it's not about his Shoah experience, at least not directly. It opens a few moments before liberation and continues through liberation and its immediate aftermath. The story mostly takes place in the Feldafing DP camp. The displaced Jews of Europe gathered in these makeshift and ad-hoc communities to restore their health and begin to rebuild their lives. Feldafing is about thirty kilometres southwest of Munich in the American zone of Germany.

Feldafing was the first DP camp to be established in Germany. Szymek was there from the very first day. Dad and I are intrigued by this unusual quirk of happenstance. Szymek was one of about 20 men still alive during a death march when their guards, sensing that the war was nearly over, abandoned them and fled from the advancing Allies. These exhausted and starving men were liberated (in this default manner) near a villa and group of other buildings. They were understandably fearful of the very real possibility that Germans were nearby, but none were sighted. After a few vigilant days of watching and waiting from a distance, the surviving marchers stealthily made their way to the buildings. They stumbled upon stockpiles of food and gorged themselves. They suffered from stomach aches caused by overeating after years of hunger. They slept. The next morning, American tanks came rolling in.

Not only was Szymek in the Feldafing DP camp from the time of its establishment, he, in fact, played a significant role its formation and administration. His reasonable grasp of English was important as camp organisers prepared food, clothing, medical care and appropriate accommodation for the unknown number of people who would eventually find their way to Feldafing.

He describes for us how these traumatised, bedraggled, homeless and often ill people emerged from the European inferno and staggered into the camp. Each 'Feldafinger', as he endearingly calls those who arrived, carried a backpack full of secret sufferings and gruelling memories. The reader is provided with vignettes about some of the characters and personalities who inhabited the camp. Through his narrative we are provided a glimpse into the growing efforts to provide shelter, food and education for an ever-increasing number of disoriented people. There was confusion, rivalry and an overlap of services provided by the different aid organisations, including UNRRA, the Joint, and the American military authorities. There was the lack of understanding of what these survivors and refugees had endured. There was discomfort and disharmony amongst some of the inhabitants of this strange artificial 'island' within Germany. There were violent incidents and heart-warming reunions. There were suicides and there were great love affairs. There was slow healing and there was descending despair.

Dad's immediate postwar experience was very different. My father survived with his father and brother. They were a family. They lived together in an apartment in Regensburg. Dad never lived in a DP camp—he is what Szymek calls 'a free liver'. Dad didn't experience the group dynamics, rules and regulations, order and rhythm, that most survivors faced in the DP camps. He didn't witness, in large numbers, the emergence of Jews from the camps, from hiding places, from amongst the partisans and from Russia. He was not a part of the amassing together of the remnants of Europe in such close living quarters.

According to scholarship, by the end of 1946, 94,667 Jews lived in DP camps in the American Zone of Germany. In addition to this number, 4,743 lived in children's homes, 3,490 youths lived on agricultural training farms and 2,758 were either in hospitals or in rest homes. Another 36,427 were spread across many different communities.[18] This adds up to 142,084 in total. Therefore, only about 25 percent of Jews in the American Zone of Germany at this time were 'free livers'.

---

18. Mankowitz, Zeev. *Life between Memory and Hope*, Cambridge University Press, 2008

Simon Schochet (left) and fellow teachers in the Feldafing DP camp

Wednesday 15 April 2020

The postwar world for Jews in Europe, including life in the DP camps, remains an under-researched topic. It is obvious that the catch-all phrase 'the postwar period' is not sufficiently nuanced to capture the rapidly evolving situation. The conditions and experience of camp life during its early formation in May 1945 (when Szymek arrived at Feldafing) was very different only a few months later. The environment and living conditions would continue to change over the months and years as refugees arrived and then gradually moved away. The authorities adapted to the changing needs of displaced Jews as they began to rebuild their lives. The picture is a complex one.

Dad says, "When I was living and studying in Munich, we went to visit Feldafing once or twice."

I ask, "What for?"

"Just to check it out. To see what was going on there," is Dad's response.

"Who is we?" I ask.

"Arek Lukrec, my roommate, my study partner, my closest friend."

Arek Lukrec had survived five concentration camps and been liberated during a death march. (Not too dissimilar from Szymek's liberation experience.) He had no immediate family remaining. Arek was the friend with whom Dad had originally travelled from Regensburg to Munich. Together, they found the student pathway. Dad and Arek studied together for their entrance exams to the Ludwig Maximilian University. They also went on to study pharmacy together. Dad tells me, "We shared everything except underpants. We shared socks, shirts, everything. We shared money." I want to know more. He continues, "He was an excellent student. Just outstanding. He picked up new things so quickly. He was much smarter than me. He could also sit on his *tuches* (Yiddish for backside) for longer than me. I had to stop studying and go to sleep around 11 o'clock. He would study half the night."

Dad and Arek boarded with a German couple, Mr and Mrs Blumburger, and their daughter, for about 18 months until Mum and Dad got married. On our trip to Munich in 2009, Dad and I went to the Blumburger apartment. We stood outside the common entrance to the building. On one side was a vertical panel with each apartment number and name listed next to a buzzer. While I looked at them, trying to figure out which one to press, a young man from inside the building opened the main door to go out. I quickly grabbed the door handle with one hand and Dad with the other, and in we went. Dad was in a bit of a shock. I was exhilarated by the adventure. We were in the building! Dad led me up the stairs to the Blumburger apartment. We stood outside the front door. Dad was unsure what to do next but I had no hesitations. I knocked with the confidence that only a person born into freedom and safety can muster. After a short wait, the door opened. Barely ajar. An older woman peered out at us. Dad, in his impeccable German, explained that he had lived there many years ago and was now visiting with his daughter. All the way from Australia. The door didn't shift. Not an inch. Without missing a beat, Dad mentioned the Blumburgers, his former landlords. Simsalabim! That was the key to the unlocking of the door. It was swung wide open and we were greeted with a huge smile and a hearty "*Welkem!*"

We entered the large apartment and, after exchanging niceties, we were left alone to look around. Dad took the lead, turning right into his and Arek's old room. Roommates literally means roommates. Not flatmates. They didn't share a flat; they shared a single room. It was now lightly furnished for visiting grandchildren. Dad pointed to the spots where his and Arek's two beds were once positioned. Where their little cooking stove and their shared table for eating and studying stood. Then Dad whisked out of his bag an enlarged laminated photo of himself studying in the room. It was an emotional moment.

Dad had co-opted one of my sons to enlarge and laminate a number of photos in preparation for this trip. These were also whisked out at other appropriate times.

Arek stayed in Munich for much longer than my parents. He undertook postgraduate degrees. He must have been one of the last Survivor Students to leave Germany when he immigrated to America in 1953. Dad remembers that Arek had an uncle who was a rabbi in America. I remember meeting Professor Arek (Aron) Lukrec, and his wife, Shulamit, a couple of times. They lived on Staten Island, New York. Arek held both academic and clinical positions in chemistry. He was an advocate for people suffering from mental illness. He relished Jewish literature, classical music and the study of psychology. Arek remained a scholar all his life. Material gains and light-hearted social interactions weren't for him. Arek passed away in 2012.

***

After nearly a year in Feldafing, Szymek moved out of the DP camp and headed toward his life as a Survivor Student in Munich. Soon his, and Mum and Dad's destinies would converge at the Jewish Students' Union.

As we are nearing the end of our reading about Szymek and Feldafing, Dad suddenly says to me, "I nearly drowned there." I neither know what he is talking about nor what prompted this revelation. He explains, "Near Feldafing was the beautiful Lake Starnberg. We were on one of our outings, a Jewish Students' Union excursion." I want to know exactly who was there. Dad remembers only Szymek Schochet. However, he says, "What I will never forget is the fear, I thought I was going to die. We were on a boat on the lake. I jumped into the water and started swimming around. And before I knew it, the boat was gone. It was far away. It became very cold where I was. I don't know if I was in a cold spot in the lake or whether it was my panic. I screamed and waved and yelled. They must've heard me or seen me or something. Luckily they came back for me." Lucky indeed.

Szymek passed away in 2011.

Dad studying in the room he shared with Arek Lukrec, Munich, late 1940s

Dad in the room he had shared with Arek Lukrec. He is holding a photo of himself taken in the same room in the late 1940s, Munich, 2009

Simon Schochet with Mum & Dad, New York, 1985

Friday 17 April 2020

The AJN article made the front page! Dad is a minor celebrity. How strange to see our private project become public property. But I did, after all, invite the attention.

THE
Australian Jewish News

Melbourne edition 4361. $3.80 (including GST)

Friday, April 17, 2020 - Nisan 23, 5780

SURVIVOR CONNECT

'WE NEED HOPE TO SUSTAIN US'

REBECCA DAVIS

"THERE is a big difference in being isolated now and being in the concentration camp," reflects 97-year-old Shoah survivor Phillip Maisel.

"In the camp, few people cared."

Born in Lithuania, Phillip was a prisoner at a hard labour camp in Estonia and later other concentration camps across Nazi-occupied Europe.

Speaking to *The AJN* from the isolation of his Caulfield home ahead of Yom Hashoah, which begins on Monday evening, an upbeat Phillip gratefully thanked the Jewish Holocaust Centre (JHC) for its newly launched program 'Survivor Connect'. The initiative is a response to the coronavirus crisis, and sees the profiles of each JHC survivor posted online, allowing community members the opportunity to reach out to them with a special message. The letters are emailed to the JHC which then has volunteer messengers relay the notes on to survivors.

"We need our survivors to know that their stories are still having an impact, even while they are not able to talk directly to an audience," shared JHC museum director Jayne Josem.

"This will make them feel valued

Mel Raleigh with her zeyde, survivor Tuvia Lipson before isolation.

during this period of isolation and will give them hope for the future. Right now we all need hope to sustain us."

Phillip has been a volunteer at the JHC for more than 25 years, responsible for filming thousands of survivor testimonies. Prior to the COVID-19 pandemic, he was still working three days a week at the centre. Since its closure, he has received a few letters – and "it was very, very encouraging".

"Now, somebody cares. Before [during the Shoah], nobody heard us," told Phillip, who remembered, "Then, when we went to bed, we had to hope that we would get up the next morning and now, it is just the opposite!

"These acts adds meaning to life, because there are many disappointments in life – particularly when you are 97! Life can be very difficult, but this has helped a lot."

95-year-old Auschwitz-Birkenau survivor David Prince has also received letters as part of the JHC program. One was penned by CEO of Kathmandu and Rip Curl, Xavier Simone, who heard David speak at the JHC some time ago.

"We all got a kick out of that one!" shared David's daughter, Frances Prince.

But beyond the initiative, the COVID-19 threat has seen David and Frances come together on another unexpected project.

Immediately after the war, David and his late wife Ella were among a select group of 400 Jewish students who were given access to a university education in Munich. Fortuitously, Frances discovered a book about the group just before lockdown. And so, as part of their isolation ritual, every afternoon David lays on the couch, closes his eyes and Frances reads to him for a couple of hours.

JHC survivor guide David Prince sorts photos from his post-Shoah student days in Munich.

"It's been more than beautiful. It's astonishing," she told.

"As I am reading, he is saying, This is the story of my life. This is the life that made me."

And the exercise has stimulated David's memory, as he suddenly recollected many people and details long forgotten. He brought out his old photos which now cover the dining table. After reading the daily portion, together they pore over the photos. David remembers details, and Frances takes notes.

"I am recalling people that I

have not thought about for many years. This recollection of youthful times is marvellous," explained David.

"The afternoons spent with my daughter, take away the loneliness and boredom of being in isolation. All my activities are cancelled, I can't see my few remaining friends. I think I would have spiralled into a depression without having these afternoons to look forward to."

Frances concurred, adding, "I've been given this gift of time with my dad that I would not have normally had.

Phillip Maisel giving his survivor testimony at the 2008 Yom Hashoah commemoration.   Photo: Peter Haskin

"I keep saying to myself, in the future, I'm going to look back on this time and say, how lucky I was."

Isolation has seen a shift in communication between Mel Raleigh and her adored grandfather, Auschwitz survivor Tuvia Lipson.

The retired JHC guide is a resident of Emmy Monash, and since regulations have tightened, Mel has not been able to visit the zeyde she calls her best friend.

"But we are lucky to FaceTime twice a day," she told, continuing, "and he has also received a couple of letters through the initiative".

One note read, "Tuvia Lipson, at this difficult time for me, you have inspired me with your will and resilience."

Reflected 94-year-old Tuvia, "I feel very proud to know someone is thinking of me and I don't know them. A lot of us survivors have been through hell and back, been through good times and bad times.

"One thing I can tell you. I live until now, and the reason why? Because I'm always looking forward. I never look back.

"I hoped for a better tomorrow, and a better tomorrow always came."

For more information on the project, visit jhc.org.au/survivor-connect/.

Front page of *The Australian Jewish News*, 17 April 2020

Sunday 19 April 2020

Dad and I have a well-established routine. It has become the highlight of Dad's day, perhaps even the highlight of his present life. How do I know this? He tells me so. Often. His many activities—including speaking to school students at the Holocaust Centre, going to hydrotherapy classes, and playing bridge—have been cancelled during the pandemic. He has few friends left. He no longer drives. He is not online. I fear for his mental health. Our reading project is the best way I can think of to alleviate Dad's boredom, loneliness and inertia. My brother takes care of all of Dad's physical needs. He does the shopping, attends to medical requirements, and runs the errands. I have the far easier role: sitting, reading, talking.

Dad arrives at my place every afternoon at 2pm. I can hear his walker lumbering over the gravelly pathway to my front veranda. I open the door and our ritual begins.

Due to the coronavirus pandemic, we do not greet each other with a kiss or a hug. I have thought much about those who live alone during these times, bereft of any tactile contact with another human. There are so many different types of human physical touch, ranging from sexual intimacy to a perfunctory handshake. There is much in between that defines the texture of different relationships. I hope that once this crisis is over, I will never again take for granted even a light-hearted kiss on the cheek when meeting a friend.

We make our way to the lounge room and get comfortable. I usually have a cup of tea, with lemon and one sweetener, ready for Dad prior to his arrival. It will have cooled to an appropriate temperature by the time he is comfortably settled. I don't usually join him in a drink as I am sufficiently fuelled with coffee by this time of day.

As I begin our daily reading, Dad's eyes close. They open and turn to me when he wants to contribute an opinion or interpretation. Most welcome are the segues into his own life. For me, they are the main game. It is his memories that I am truly seeking.

Our reading project has become too important to both of us to stop now. But what will be our next book? We have read all the Munich memoirs on our bookshelves.

In fact, unbeknownst to Dad, I have ordered two new books that I found on the internet. However, due to reduced air freight capacity, Book Depository and Abe Books warn me that there will be significant delays. I can't wait for them to arrive in order to select our next book. That is when I have my brainwave. Maybe we can spend our time together reading Shoah memoirs. I am up for it, but is Dad? I don't reveal to him this 'great plan' of mine. I think that maybe we'll go memoir by memoir and see what transpires.

My bookshelves groan under the weight of Shoah memoirs. Which should I suggest to Dad? I bring out a few random books, tell him a little about each one: whose memoir it is, where they were from, a broad sketch of their Shoah experience. I can see he is tuning out. His eyes are glazing over and he is losing interest, rapidly. What should I do? It dawns on me that he needs some sort of 'skin in the game' to really get interested and engaged. I have another brainwave. I show him memoirs of people that we know, or knew, or have some connection with. I strike gold!

***

Hiding Places: A Mother, a Daughter, an Uncovered Life
Diane Wyshogrod
Published by Excelsior Editions, 2012

'For Frances—It's an honor to share my story with you; you have devoted your life, after all, to the transmission of our people's story, in all its power, poignancy and beauty, to so many. May we and our families continue to share smachot and naches together in the years to come. Love, Dina.'

Dina (Diane) Wyshogrod is a close friend, originally from New York, but now a long-time resident of Jerusalem. Dina is married to Chaim Zlotogorski, the nephew of our closest family friend, Sula Rozinski.[19] (You really do need some familiarity with the Polish language to get your tongue around 'Wyshogrod', 'Zlotogorski' and 'Rozinski'.)

We met Dina and Chaim in the mid-1980s when my husband and I lived in New York. Then they made *aliya* in 1991. Coincidentally, we were spending that year in Israel and literally bumped into them when one of their sons and our son attended the same kindergarten. We continued to occasionally catch up on some of our many family trips to Israel. Since 2015, this on-and-off connection has solidified into a firm, fast and enduring friendship as we spend increasing amounts of time in Jerusalem.

Dina and Chaim were among the founders of the Children of Survivors organisation in New York in the late 1970s. They were Holocaust 'activists'. All four of their parents were survivors: three from Poland and one from Hungary. None are alive any longer.

Dina is an experienced clinical psychologist and a pioneer in the practice of mindfulness. Her book is a joint project belonging to Dina and her late mother, Helen (Lutka) Rosenberg Wyshogrod. Dina brings her analytical and probing mind to the work. Interspersed with her mother's story, Dina writes about her own childhood, American life,

---

19. Sula passed away during our reading, not of this book, but of the next one. It really would be too spooky if she had died while we were reading this one.

Israeli life, all laced with reflective analysis together with searches for meaning and understanding.

There is a genre of Holocaust literature that could perhaps be entitled 'once removed' memoirs. However, this book is not 'merely' a recounting of someone's else's narrative, it is also the story of the telling of the story, including how Dina convinced her mother to allow her to publish the book. We read how Dina encouraged and cajoled her mother to go further and deeper into the details. It is also a reflection on how a daughter absorbed the suffering of her mother. It is a diary. It is an exploration of inter-generational bonds and parental influences. It is all these things and more.

Monday 20 April 2020

Zolkiew, Lutka's hometown in south-eastern Poland, is now in the Ukraine. Of course, my pronunciation is all wrong. Again. And again, Dad begins his small-town snooty litany. "What a hole, a *shtetl*." We read of the significant number of Jews who were professionals. We read of their access to the cultural delights of nearby Lvow. (Now called Lviv.) As we read, I comment that it doesn't sound like such a *loch* (Yiddish for 'hole') to me. "Maybe you're right," Dad reluctantly acquiesces.

Lutka's father was a pharmacist. This is sure to grab Dad's attention. His eager and instant affinity with other pharmacists is deep-seated. Even though her father was a pharmacist before Dad was even a glint in his parents' eyes, the affinity is perpetual, transcending time and space. Dad's pride in, and gratification from, his profession is infinite. It has been my blessing to grow up witnessing a parent take such enormous pride, interest and delight in their career. Not that I counted this blessing when I was a child. But I am convinced that I absorbed it subliminally.

The description of Lutka's childhood in Zolkiew reinforces my understanding of the diversity of prewar Polish Jewish life. In my teaching of Jewish history, I have always emphasised the tremendous range of

Jewish lifestyles. There can be no generalisations when it comes to prewar Polish Jewry. The assortment of Jewish societies and communities was endless. I am aware that when a survivor describes his or her family life before the war, they are describing a particular, personal milieu.

We read about Lutka's charmed childhood. She was born in 1925. So was Dad. That makes it easy for him to place himself within the narrative. He doesn't need to do his stop-and-start interruptions: "What year is it again? How old is she?" He doesn't need to search for experiential 'parallelism'. Lutka was an only child. We learn about her parents and extended family members. She was educated by nuns at a Catholic primary school. We enjoy reading about her childhood.

I ask Dad to tell me about his Lodz childhood. I already know bits and pieces. I am hoping for some new snippets. "Start with school," I suggest. Maybe a framework will help order his memories. He began at the Fajnhaus School at 26 Zawadska Street. He lived at 17 Zawadska Street. A short walk. This private Jewish school, founded by Lithuanian Jews, operated according to the Litvak tradition which is known for a certain intellectual approach to Jewish learning and a specific Hebrew pronunciation in prayers. Dad loves displaying his knowledge of this Litvak enunciation. However, to the unfamiliar listener, it is nearly impossible to discern from any other rendition.

Then, after grade two, Dad went to the state school at 21 Wolczanska Street. State school number 123. Dad explains, "This was the best school that was close to us. What do I mean by 'the best'? I'm not talking about the quality of the teachers, but the quality of the kids. There were less *lobbuses* there than at the other nearby school my parents considered." 'Lobbuses' is the plural of 'lobbus', the Yiddish word for a little rascal or cheeky, mischievous kid. "A better class of children were at my school," Dad concludes. He went to school six days a week from 8am to 1pm. He remembers the name of the principal. Pan (Mr) Lewkowicz. I am thrilled when he adds, "I remember where his office was in the school." Even though it was a state school, every single student was Jewish. Every teacher, bar one, was Jewish. This is what it meant to be a Jew in Lodz before the war. As an addendum, Dad says, "Next door to our school was the Hochsteinover Girls' School. This was a very poshy school."

This is an appropriate segue into Mum's schooling in Warsaw. She went to a very 'poshy' school. The Perla Wubinska Jewish School for Girls. Her mother and her aunts had all gone to the same school. This was the *alma mater* of the women in the extended Gringlas family. My mother's Jewish history teacher became very famous. He was Dr Emanuel Ringelblum, the Jewish historian who instigated the *Oneg Shabbat* underground archive that recorded virtually all that is known about the Warsaw Ghetto. Many years ago, when I was studying all about him and telling Mum about his amazing contribution to Jewish history, she laughed uproariously. She told me that he was the worst teacher she ever had. He couldn't address the class without his spittle flying over all the girls in the front row. The girls behaved disgustingly, doing their utmost to ridicule this great scholar. I came to the conclusion that, as an academic, Emanuel Ringelblum had to supplement his income by teaching these spoilt Jewish girls. Recorded history and private memories don't always coalesce.

Back to Dad. I wonder about his Jewish education. I understand it was possible to have a Jewish life by merely inhaling the Lodz air, but even in that intensely Jewish milieu, a child needs some formal instruction. Dad tells me that a tutor came to their home about twice a week to teach him and Uncle Heniek Modern Hebrew and the prayers.

Dad's one precious year of secondary school took place at the Szwajcer School. Its full formal name was Gimnazjum Oswiecenia Kultury I Oswiaty. Google Translate tells me that this means 'Junior High School Enlightenment of Culture and Education.' What an imposing and ambitious name. Dad thinks that 'Szwajcer' may have been the name of the founder. Dad explains that high school lasted four years. The final two years were called a lyceum. "We had the usual subjects: maths, Polish, geography, history and Hebrew."

I love the fact that Dad considers Hebrew one of the 'usual' subjects on par with maths and geography. This is a value that I share with Dad. I have always considered the study of the Hebrew language, for my own children, to be equally important as all their other subjects.

Dad continues, "We had a choice between English and German. I did German. I can't remember if that was my decision or that of my parents. It ended up being a good decision because of my later studies in Munich." This reinforces my opinion that Dad's facility with languages is extraordinary. Learning German for one year, in Year 7, somehow assisted him to study at the Ludwig Maximilian University. Most impressive.

Dad tells me about his German teacher at the Szwajcer School, Fraulein Dr Schochter. When I ask whether she was Jewish, he answers, "Of course!" As if she could have been anything else. Dad tells me he knows one other person who would also remember her.

"Who on earth is that?" I ask.

"Wolf Deane." Wolf lives in Melbourne and is one of the survivors who participates in our annual Lodz Ghetto Commemoration which takes place every August at the Jewish Holocaust Centre in Melbourne. I am part of a small multi-generational committee that has been organising the memorial event for the last fifteen years or so. Wolf attended Szwajcer School in the same one year as Dad. But he was in the English rather than the German language stream. Nevertheless, "I am sure he would remember Fraulein Dr Schochter," asserts Dad. Wolf's son, John Deane, is also on the Lodz Ghetto Commemoration committee.

The Szwajcer School was about a 20-minute walk from home. Today, the building is part of the University of Lodz. I know that my uncle Heniek went to a different school. I ask Dad about this. It was a state school called Kupieckie Gymnasium. This translates as 'salesmanship'. Dad says it was sort of a business school. "It was very hard to get into." I'm not sure if he is referring to scholastic difficulty or Jewish difficulty. He clarifies that it is the latter. He continues, "There were six Jewish kids in his year, including him. That was it." Then Dad whispers, "My father had to use '*protectsia*' to get him in." The term '*protectsia*' refers to accessing connections who can pull strings for you. A strict number of Jews were allowed entry into this school, so my grandfather had to pull in favours to get his son enrolled. The whispering? I guess you never know who might be listening.

I love trying to pronounce the Polish words in all these books: places or people or particular foods. Dad corrects me after each attempt. I don't seem to get any of them right. And that's after growing up hearing Polish daily. *Szodmaysker, Wolczanska, Oswiecenia, Oswiaty, Kupieckie*—they all defeat me.

I know Dad's standard description of his youthful activities. It is part of his regular testimony to students at Melbourne's Holocaust Centre: "What were 14-year-old kids doing? Hanging around other kids, skating in winter, soccer in summer, running 400m and 800m races, indoor gym and chatting up girls." This last activity always gets a snigger from his young audience.

Today I ask, "What else did you do?"

"Collected stamps," he answers. I already know this too. And then he adds, "I tried to learn the trombone, the small alto trombone. There was a school orchestra. I tried out for it. I have no musical talent." He looks at me with a twinkle in his eyes, "But I loved walking around with it, in its special bag. I carried it as if I could play it. I was a show-off with the alto trombone I couldn't play." This is today's little gem.

And then all childhood ends. The first day of September 1939. Germany invaded Poland. Both Lutka (in Zolkiew) and Dad (in Lodz) were 14-years old. Zolkiew, in eastern Poland, was occupied by the Germans for only a week. Then by the Russians. This carving-up of Poland had been determined by the secretive Molotov-Ribbentrop Agreement between these two mighty powers. Not until June 1941 did the Jews of Zolkiew encounter the Germans again. Dad says, "They had two more years of schooling than us." Lodzers lived under German rule from the beginning of the war. There is a long list of reasons why it was better to live under the Russians than the Germans during that two-year period. (Not that it was a proverbial picnic under the Russians.) However, it is his curtailed education that Dad is lamenting to me. I am not surprised. He frequently bemoans the fact that he had only one year of secondary schooling before the war.

Tuesday 21 April 2020

And then, of course, the Germans did return, attacking their former allies, the Russians. It was 22 June 1941. Endless constricting decrees, the closure of schools and violent outbursts, including against Lutka's father, began immediately. The ghetto was established. The Judenrat was formed. This was the Jewish council ostensibly set up to be the intermediary between the Germans and the Jews. In reality, it was a hapless one-way relationship, as the Judenrat was forced to carry out the Nazis' orders against their own community.

In one episode we read how Lutka was scared for the safety of her dog. I say to Dad, "Sounds like Mum and Bruta, eh?" Mum's beloved dachshund ran away while the family was moving into the Warsaw Ghetto. Smart dog. My standard joke is that maybe a dachshund could survive on the Aryan side. Bruta had *dobry wyglad*.

Wednesday 22 April 2020

I ask myself why I chose this book. It's not as if Dad really knew Lutka Rosenberg Wyshogrod. I don't think they even met. Perhaps our close friendship with Dina and Chaim is enough. This, together with the fact that Chaim is the nephew of our closest family friend, is more than enough. Perhaps the fact that it is a mother-daughter endeavour attracted me. After all, we are on a father-daughter endeavour. I think I need Dina to psychoanalyse me.

Thursday 23 April 2020

Today, we meet (so to speak) Emil and Maria Lozinski, the unintentional saviours of Lutka and her parents. They are not as purposeful in their actions as Sabina Zimering's protector, the teacher, Mrs Justyna. They also come from a completely different echelon of Poland's highly stratified society. They become saviours almost by default. Emil Lozinski was an elderly retired railway official known by Lutka's father because he used to hang out at the pharmacy. There had already been a roundup and deportation from the ghetto and rumours were circulating that there would soon be another. Lutka's father asked Mr Lozinski if they could hide at his place "for a day or two" in order to avoid the next roundup. We read how Lutka and her parents stealthily escaped from Zolkiew Ghetto and made their way to the Lozinski home.

***

In the midst of recounting of her mother's story, Dina tells us that in 1994 she first proposed to her family that they take a trip together to Poland, and then onto Zolkiew (now in the Ukraine). Coincidentally, 1994 was the year I undertook my first trip to Poland with Dad. Just him and me. I can't recall how it all came about. (It was only 26 years ago, yet I am expecting Dad to remember details of events that took place between 75 and 90 years ago. Hmmm.) Mum and Dad had gone to Poland the year before. Mum, very reluctantly. It had been Dad's idea. As perhaps was inevitable, Mum fell apart at Treblinka, and they made a precipitous departure from the country.

However, Dad had not seen all the places he had wished to visit and wanted to return. And soon. It was July. As a teacher, I had two weeks school holidays at that time. We could squeeze it in. It took some organising to get the boys looked after during my absence. I was 36 years old; Dad was 69. Who was to know then that this would be the first of my many trips to Poland? That within the decade I would be at the forefront of taking Jewish Year 11 students from Australia to Poland to participate in

March of the Living (MOTL)?[20] Amongst a multitude of roles, I prepared intricate itineraries, liaising back and forth with central MOTL planners. From 2002 until 2009 this was a significant part of my life. Back in 1994, I was not such an expert on Polish itineraries.

Back to Lutka. Life in the cellar at the Lozinskis'. Emil and Maria Lozinski's short-term commitment to hide the Rosenbergs for a few days morphed into the perilous risk to all their lives as the Polish couple continued to provide Lutka's family with shelter, food, water and the means to survive for the long term.

The Russians arrived. Liberation. My attention is always primed for that moment and those immediately after. Lutka and her parents tentatively emerged from their hiding spot. They met up with a few other surviving Jews. They didn't need to return to their hometown of Zolkiew—they had been there the whole time. Submerged. "When is this?" Dad needs to know. It's part of his 'Where was she? Where was I?' parallelism way of thinking and contextualising. It was May 1944, I tell Dad. He just looks at me. No words are necessary. He was one whole year away from liberation. He was still in the Lodz Ghetto. His mother was still alive. The liquidation of the ghetto, Auschwitz-Birkenau and the Friedland concentration camp were still ahead of him.

Lutka and her parents remained in Zolkiew for over a year. They had a roof (not a floor) over their heads. There was some work. Food. Social gatherings with the few other remaining Jews. With the re-drawing of maps, Zolkiew became part of the Soviet Union and former Polish citizens were allowed to leave. Lutka and her family promptly departed.

We go forwards (and backwards, I suppose). In 1995, Dina went on her long-anticipated trip to Poland and Zolkiew with her parents, her brother and a group of former Zolkiewians (I made up this word). Dina is a wonderful chronicler. The trip was a personal family odyssey, but they were part of a commemorative group experience too. This is always

---

20. March of the Living is an international Holocaust education program. It consists of a week in Poland visiting sites where Jewish communities once thrived, areas where the ghettos existed and the remnants of concentration camps. Educational sessions, commemorative ceremonies and survivor testimonies form the major components of the program. The timing of the program is centred around Yom HaShoah (Holocaust Memorial Day) in April each year.

an intricate balancing act. There can be tension between a family wanting to remain close together, exclusively, during their much-awaited private pilgrimage, and the scheduled group program, to be shared with others. On March of the Living, there is a similar dynamic. Participating family members, who are accompanying survivors, want to huddle together for their private moments, as well as share family memories and testimonies with the larger group. I have seen this scenario played out many times. During MOTL participating survivors and their families generally manage this dual role well. They know that a significant purpose of the survivor is educative, to be shared with the whole group. Personal family time can always be squeezed in. In addition, many young people are proud to share their grandparents, who garner rock-star status on the trip. Nevertheless, I am grateful that my first trip to Poland was totally personal. Just me and Dad.

Friday 24 April 2020

I adore the many photographs that Dina has included in her book. They aren't necessary to authenticate her words but they do animate them. Enabling us to put faces to names helps to bring people back to life. So to speak. The elegance, the fashion, the ornaments, the backdrops. They capture moments in place and time. But it is the faces, the expressions that, in my mind, immortalise these people. I can't get enough of the photos. Both those from long ago and those that are more recent.

Our family has precious few prewar photos from either side. From Dad, we have the grand total of three. These remain in our family's possession because Dad's Ciocia (Aunt) Fela (sibling number four) immigrated to Argentina before the war with her husband, Mr Milgrom. She must have taken the photos to Argentina with her or they were later sent to her from the family in Lodz. I check with Dad. He tells me that Ciocia Fela left Poland straight after he and Heniek were born. So we ascertain that she was sent these family photos later.

Dad (right, with the beauty spot) and his twin brother, Heniek (left, with the ringlets), in late 1925. They are seven months old. Positioned on a sheepskin rug, on a bench of some sort, and dressed in identical outfits. What's with the suspenders holding up the long sock that is peeking out from under Dad's shorts? Identical outfits but very different hairstyles.

Dad's father has written on the back of the photo: "As a memento, we offer you this photo of Dawidek and Heniek. (From the) clan of Israel Princ."

Twins Heniek & David (Dad) Princ, Lodz, late 1925

In this photo the twins look about two years old so it's likely about 1927. It's a lovely nuclear family photo. Mum, Dad and sons. The boys are wearing identical outfits and now have similar hairstyles.

Frymet & Israel Princ with Heniek & Dad (on the right), Lodz, 1927

Purim Seudah, March 1928. This Purim Seudah, the traditional feast that takes place during the Festival of Purim, was celebrated with Dad's mother's side of the family, the Klejnbaums.

Dad and Heniek are the little ones sitting on their father's lap.

The Klejnbaum clan consists of eight siblings, from eldest to youngest: Regina (married to Hersh Gdanski); Wolf (married to Bella); Frymet Chaya (my grandmother, married to Israel Princ); Fela (married to Mr Milgrom, whose first name has been forgotten); Lola (married to Moshe Pluzny); Esther (married to Yankel Dimant); Mania (married later, during the war and had a child); Mala (unmarried at this time; later married Salek Ajzner just before the war). And their various children, Dad's first cousins. This photo is displayed in the Jewish Holocaust Centre in Melbourne.

Sitting, left to right:

Hillel (surname unknown) (a second cousin of Dad's)

Wujek (Uncle) Moshe Pluzny (Dad saw him in Auschwitz-Birkenau. They talked.)

Ciocia (Aunt) Esther Klejnbaum Dimant

Wujek Yankel Dimant

Ciocia Mala Klejnbaum

Israel Princ (Dad's father)

Heniek Princ (Dad's brother)

David Princ (Dad)

Ciocia Regina (Rivka) Klejnbaum Gdanski

Standing, left to right:

Szlamek Klejnbaum HaCohen (Wolf and Bella's son, the first grandchild in the family. Later, they had a daughter named Mala who died on the last day of the war.)

Ciocia Lola Klejnbaum Pluzny

Ciocia Mania (married later during the war and had a child; surname unknown)

Wujek Wolf Klejnbaum HaCohen (the only son in the family of eight children)

Ciocia Bella Klejnbaum

Frymet (Frania) Chaya Klejnbaum Princ (my grandmother, after whom I am named)

Sura Mindla Pluzny Klejnbaum (Dad's grandmother, 'Babcia', she was taken from the Lodz Ghetto to Chelmno, September 1942)

Mordechai Klejnbaum HaCohen (Dad's grandfather, born in 1866, died of natural causes in 1938 and was buried in the Lodz cemetery. I have visited his grave a number of times.)

Wujek Hershel Gdanski

After the war, Ciocia Fela (the keeper of the three family photos) immigrated from Argentina to Israel. Ciocia Mala and Ciocia Lola survived and also immigrated to Israel. Fela and Lola lived together there. Dad, Heniek and their father also survived. All the rest were murdered during the Holocaust.

The Klejnbaum family celebrating Purim.
Heniek & Dad are sitting on their father's lap, Lodz, March 1928

Sunday 26 April 2020

Dad brings over a photo, a single image, taken in 1928. This photo is from his father's side of the family. We now have four photos in the Prince family collection. It is a beautiful, staged photo of three little children sitting in an open-top car, one behind the other. The child in the front is the 'driver'. Has this been taken in a photographic studio? Or at some sort of fun fair? These three serious, but sweet, children are Dad's first cousins: Moniek, Lutka and Lutek Kalman. Dad wrote on the back of the photo long ago. They are the children of Dad's father's sister, Regina Kalman (nee Princ). Her husband was Salomon Kalman.

Dad recorded each cousin's Polish and Yiddish names: Moniek (Mosze) born approximately 1919–1920; Lutka (Liba Lea) born approximately 1924–1925; Lutek (Lajb) born approximately 1928–1929. All lived in Lodz and were deported with their parents to the town of Konin in 1939, before the ghetto was established.

Dad tells me that the family had moved to Lodz from Lubraniec, 130 kilometres north-west of the city, about five years before the war. They had a dairy shop, selling cheeses, yoghurt and the like, at 24 Cegielnian Street. The shop faced onto the street and the family lived in an apartment behind. The eldest child in the family, Moniek, had been an apprentice electrician. The middle child, Lutka was closest to Dad's age, and he liked hanging out with her and her friends. He recalls that she went to a non-Jewish school next door to her apartment called Jadwigi. It was considered a very good state school and there were no fees. Dad does not remember much about the other child, Lutek, who was about four years younger.

He tells me that he remembers the day the family disappeared. "Please explain," I implore. I have heard bits and pieces of the story before, but don't have a grasp of the whole picture.

Dad sighs and begins, "This all happened before the ghetto." This could mean anytime between 8 February 1940, when Jews were ordered to start moving into the ghetto, and 1 May 1940 when the ghetto was 'closed'.

Dad's first cousins: Moniek, Lutka & Lutek Kalman

With all the Jews inside. From the way the story unfolds, I surmise that the events took place after mid-November 1939. Why? The initial order to wear the Star of David was delivered at that time. I have narrowed down the timeframe. I think.

This was a confusing interim period. The war had begun, but the Jews had not been moved into the ghetto yet. Of course, they didn't know it was an interim period. Only in hindsight can historical time periods be delineated. School had stopped and kids didn't have much to do. Dad, at 14, went almost daily to his cousin Lutka's place to socialise with her and other kids. He tells me that he lived a ten-minute run away. How does he recall such a precise detail? There was a curfew. Jews had to be off the streets and in their homes by 5pm each evening. He always made sure to leave their place at 4.50pm to be home by 5pm. An important 10 minutes. A crucial 10 minutes.

Dad remembers clearly. "I said goodbye to my Kalman cousins at 4.50 pm, as usual. The next day, I go to their place, as usual. And what do I see? Their apartment behind the dairy shop has been sealed up. Boarded up. No-one can get in. No-one is there."

I ask, "Was it just their place? Or surrounding apartments too?"

Dad continues, "Only their place. No-one else's. I can't remember whether I asked a neighbour or a neighbour just told me, but I was informed that the whole family had been taken away."

We sit in silence. Then Dad continues, "Later on, we did find out what happened. In the same apartment building where the Kalmans lived, 24 Cegielnian Street, there was a family, I think Opatowski, who also lived there. They owned a fur shop on Piotrkowska. (The main street in Lodz.) This means that they must have been quite wealthy. Anyway, my cousin Moniek, who was 19 or 20 years old, was friendly with this family's daughter. We were told that the furrier, Opatowski, got Moniek to deliver a winter fur coat to a customer who lived outside Lodz, in the countryside."

I interrupt, "Was he paid? Was it a favour? Do you think he did it because he liked their daughter?"

Dad is annoyed with me, "I don't have a clue!" This is all beside the point, I know, but I like details. Moniek was caught not wearing the mandatory Star of David. He may also have broken the 5pm curfew. "Was this on his way to take the delivery? Or on the way back?" Dad does not know. It seems that Moniek was escorted home and the whole family was taken away. Regina (nee Princ) Kalman, Salomon Kalman and their children Moniek, Lutka and Lutek. Dad says, "We never saw them again. But we did get a letter from them after about two weeks. They wrote that they are now living in Konin." (Coincidentally, this is the hometown of the ever-present Engineer Alexander Piekarczyk.) What happened to them in Konin? We don't know. But I do know that by July 1940, Konin was *Judenrein*.

In this letter, the last communication from the Kalmans, Dad's family were informed that Moniek, the would-be fur courier, was not with them in Konin. He had been kicked to death, earlier, at the police station.

Monday 27 April 2020

Today Dad comes over with yet another photo. It is sepia: grainy and faded. Now we have a second photo from Dad's father's side of the family. It was taken in 1928. I ask Dad where such a photo would have come from? Who had it? How did it get to us? Neither Dad nor his brother nor his father had any photos with them in the Lodz Ghetto, Auschwitz-Birkenau and Friedland. Dad shrugs his shoulders; he doesn't know. It looks like a celebration, with 27 family members crowded around the dining table. The men wear suits with ties. The women are dressed up. Bejewelled and coiffed. I wonder what the special occasion could have been? There are no clues.

Who can we identify? This is definitely the time to retrieve the magnifying glass. I recognise my grandfather, Israel Princ. We can't seem to see my grandmother, Frymet Chaya in the photo. I say to Dad, "She is probably chasing her three-year-old twins!" He agrees.

Wittelsohn family gathering, 1928
Israel Princ is in the back row, fourth from the left

Dad thinks that some of the people are the Wittelsohn cousins, Leon, Szaja, Bella and Aaron. Unbeknownst to any of them, over two decades later, cousin Szaja Wittelsohn would end up being a 'double relation' of Dad's. But more on that later. Dad wonders whether the only child in the photo could be Bella's son? Dad's points out another Wittelsohn cousin, Shmuel. Dad says, "He was a well-known champion cyclist. He went to Palestine. Then he came back." Not a good move. And then Dad identifies another Wittelsohn sibling. A sister, Chayka. So now we have Leon, Szaja, Bella, Aaron, Shmuel and Chayka.

For me, one of the upshots of this project is that I can now change my internal refrain with regards to only having three precious and priceless prewar Prince photos, to now having five. I have nearly doubled my inheritance.

From Mum's side of the family, we do not have such riches. In fact, there are no stand-alone photos of her original nuclear family. Not even one. What does exist has been sliced and spliced out of other photos. And then enlarged many, many times. There are two photos in this sad non-collection. One is of Mum's maternal grandfather, David Ber Gringlas. The large, black kippah and beard attest to his religiosity. He is wearing a suit jacket, shirt and tie and is staring into the camera lens. No smile. Serious. The other photo is of his son-in-law, Mum's father, Izak Salcberg. The photo of Izak is very blurry. His features are difficult to discern but he looks like a 'modern' man compared to his father-in-law. He is clean-shaven and doesn't appear to be wearing any head-covering. His hair has been brushed or slicked back, emphasising a widow's peak. He is also looking straight ahead with the beginning of a smile. These are my Buba Rosa's father and her husband. The two men she loved and who loved her. Her father was murdered in Treblinka. Her husband in Majdanek.

Dad raises his hand to stop my talking. He is trying to remember and tell me something. All at the same time. "I have some other Warsaw photos. Somewhere at home." If he was quicker on his feet, I would urge him to go and get them. Now. However, he is well-settled and comfortable. I need to wait another day.

My great-grandfather, David Ber Gringlas, date unknown

My maternal grandfather Izak Salcberg, c.1920s

Tuesday 28 April 2020

Dad brings over six Warsaw photos from Mum's family. The problem is that most are not labelled. And there is no-one to identify them. The people in the photos are nameless. Do they count as family heirlooms if we don't know who they are? Their value seems greatly diminished in their anonymity. The photos that are labelled contain their own mysteries. There are two photos of the same young man. They are both originals. Zygmunt Rosenberg. Never heard of him. On the back of one, in Polish, is written, "Dear Grandpa in Eretz (Eretz Yisrael, Palestine) From Grandson Zygmunt. February 1933."

On the back of the other photo is written "Z. Rosenberg." A sticky note is attached, in Dad's handwriting. He has translated the Polish into English. In addition, he has identified the grandfather as David Ber Gringlas, Mum's grandfather. I know that David Ber (and his second wife) immigrated to Palestine in 1932. So, the date of the photo, February 1933, makes sense. But I don't have a clue who this grandson, Zygmunt Rosenberg, could be. The surname Rosenberg is totally unfamiliar. I do know that Buba Rosa had at least one sister, whose married name was Czamarka. She had studied dentistry at the University of Warsaw together with my buba. So, who is Rosenberg? Was there another sister who married a Rosenberg?

Coincidentally, while contemplating this unknown relative, Mum's cousin in Israel rings Dad to see how he is faring during these strange times. To my shame and embarrassment, I had totally forgotten about Mum's only first cousin, Ada Motilsky (nee Gringlas). Buba Rosa and Ada's father were siblings. She must be in her early or even mid-80s by now. I have only been in sporadic contact with her over the years. I feel guilty about this and I have no excuses. The last time I saw her was at my son's wedding in Jerusalem over five years ago. Given that I have been to Israel three times a year, every year since, I have proven to be a somewhat deficient family member. Here I am obsessing about dead family while ignoring the last remaining close relative alive.

I ring Ada. She is delighted to hear from me. We have a catch-up type of conversation in Hebrew. Then I ask her about her father and my buba's other siblings. I am mindful that Buba was the only one to survive. I can tell that Ada's memory isn't as sharp as it once was. She is momentarily confused. Perhaps a surprise phone call with unexpected questions about the distant past is a bit too much. Maybe I should have eased into this type of conversation. My impetuous impatience has thrown her. Nevertheless, I do get results. Not entirely satisfactory ones. But results, all the same. I am enriched by our conversation. I have more information about Mum's family and I have reconnected with Ada. I am not mercenary. I sincerely feel delighted that I am back in contact with her.

Zygmunt Rosenberg, possibly Mum's first cousin, Warsaw, 1933

There is my buba, Rosa; she had a sister, Rachela Czamarka. And there was a third sister, Rivka. Did she marry a Rosenberg? Ada can't remember. The brothers are Ada's father, Mayer, as well as Daniel, Avraham, Joseph and one more, whose name she can't remember. These riches, though far from complete, will suffice for now.

The second photo totally intrigues me. I am fixated with it. I can't quite work out why. It is an original photo of a small family of three. On the back it is dated 1934. The three people are Rachela Czamarka, her husband Bernard Czamarka, and their daughter Dziuto. Rachela, my buba's sister, was also a dentist. There is a resemblance between the sisters. Bernard is a successful businessman who owns a factory manufacturing nails. How old is Dziuto in the photo? Maybe ten years old? That would make her about three years older than Mum. I wonder whether these first cousins played together? The Czamarka family poses in front of an ornamental garden feature. They are well-dressed. Bernard's white trousers and white shoes, buttoned-up white shirt, fitted blazer with a white handkerchief peeking out of its pocket, strike me as especially sophisticated and debonair. The family is on a holiday in Truskawez. Another of those endless European sanitorium places for 'taking' the mineral spring waters to cure everything and anything. This seems to have been a popular spa destination for middle and upper-class Poles. Today, it is in the Ukraine and is still spruiked as a spa destination.

The three unsmiling faces stare out of the photo. Why are they so serious? Little Dziuto? Initially, I empathise with her. What a boring holiday. Then again, maybe they have an entertaining children's program. So there goes her excuse. Maybe the cameraman takes so long that their initial smiling demeanour has been worn away by the time he clicks the shutter button.

What were they like? What happened to them? We don't know. In addition, I am left with two mysteries. Mystery number one: how could Buba Rosa name her daughter, my Mum, Rachela, when that was her sister's name? It's weird. I am used to Ashkenazi families having cousins with the same, or similar, names. They are usually all named after a venerated forebearer. But to give your daughter the same name as your

Buba Rosa's sister, Rachela Czamarka, with her husband Bernard
& their daughter Dziuto, Truskawez, 1934

living sister? Even if the first Rachela in the family had passed away a long time previously? Mystery number two: on the back of the photo, in pencil, is the Hebrew word, עזרה. This means 'help'. The noun, not the verb. Who wrote that? When was it written? Why? My imagination begins to run wild. But I rein it in.

***

We return to Lutka. And Dina's narrative, her reflections and re-imaginings. The way she dips in and out of different voices and genres captivates me. Her writing style is gripping. I enjoy multi-layers and multi-narratives. From Zolkiew, the family went to Katowice, also in Poland. They found some family members there and decided to stay. It wasn't easy. Lutka returned to school. Dad strongly relates to Lutka's pursuit of an education, but it was a short-lived experience for her. She was just one month shy of completing her high school diploma when the family had to move again. Under Russian rule, leaving Poland was now illegal. It was risky and took careful planning. The family hoped to eventually settle in America. Meanwhile, they travelled (taking a very long route, it seems) to Germany. Near Munich.

Now we are back in familiar territory. Postwar Germany. The American Zone. The displaced persons' experience. Lutka and her parents lived in the Gabersee DP camp. I have not heard of this one. Dad has. The family remained there for three-and-a-half years under the impression that they would be leaving for America at any moment. It does not sound like a very fruitful time for Lutka or her parents. From what I have read and heard, other DP camps were hives of activity, vitality and education. Not so Gabersee.

Wednesday 29 April 2020

Today, we read a most unexpected episode. And it relates to my parents. It sounds like it was profound at the time it happened and at the time of its re-telling. I don't know its long-term impact on Lutka but I will ask Dina at some stage. It reads like a 'sliding door' moment. What might have been. The path not taken. The alternative life. For us, this is momentous. My parents took that 'one chance at a real education'. Lutka did not.

Lutka found out about the possibility of entering the university in Munich. She travelled to the city to sit the all-important *Verifikations-Kommision* (Verification Commission) exams. As she sat in the waiting room, applicants who had taken the exams before her came out, loudly complaining of the tough subject matter and the difficulty of the questions. She lost her nerve and left. I want to scream and shout at her, "Go back! Go back! Give it a go!" I can't help but wonder whether Mum and Dad may have been amongst those complaining applicants. I hope not. I don't want them to have contributed to Lutka's loss of confidence and resultant non-sitting of those exams.

Eventually, Lutka and her parents sailed over the seas to their new life in America. We read about the family's early days in New York. New beginnings are tough for all immigrants. They built a life, slowly but surely. For me, a highlight of the closing part of the book is the designation of Emil and Maria Lozinski as Righteous Among the Nations by Yad Vashem.

Lutka passed away in 2007. My friend, Dina, has truly honoured her mother.

Thursday 30 April 2020

I present Dad with our next memoir:

From Hell to Salvation: Surviving the Holocaust, Willy Lermer OAM
Published by the Jewish Holocaust Centre, 2017

'To my respected friend, David. Regards Willy'

Willy Lermer was not part of our family landscape. He was a survivor guide volunteer at JHC. Dad also has been a survivor guide. Since 1997. This has entailed spending one day a week addressing school students about his childhood in Lodz and his Holocaust experience. These youngsters come from all over the city and even further afield. The school program is a jewel in the crown of the JHC. It reaches 23,000 students per year. According to feedback, meeting, seeing and hearing the testimonies of survivors is a powerful and memorable experience. Dad always said he would volunteer there once he stopped working full-time. And that is exactly what he did. He is a man of his word.

I met Willy in the early 2000s while preparing educational sessions for March of the Living students. His name was on a roster of survivors available to talk to the students in preparation for our program in Poland. Willy's warmth and eloquence when telling his story was riveting. I was privileged to hear him a number of times over the years.

Willy was born in Krakow. In his book, he spends only a few pages describing his prewar life. His memoir focuses directly on his wartime experiences. I find myself hankering to know more about his childhood. I am captivated, as always, by the richness and diversity of Jewish life in Poland before the war.

Nearly every page of this memoir makes us gasp. There were so many decisions, twists and turns. So many forks in the road when Willy opted for what seemed to be the more dangerous path. He took risks, weighed up his chances and acted daringly upon his calculations.

Dad is reacting to Willy's story in a way I have never seen before. He seems to be amazed and (perhaps reluctantly?) admiring of Willy's audaciousness and courage. "We did nothing," is accompanied with a shrug of the shoulders. By this, Dad means that he and his family in the Lodz Ghetto did what they were told to do. They lived in the straight and narrow. They obeyed all pronouncements in the hope that by being productive and useful to the Germans, they would survive. They trusted in the assurances of Mordechai Chaim Rumkowski[21] (the controversial leader of the Jewish council of Lodz) that this was the best bet for the inhabitants of the Lodz Ghetto. Dad now wonders about his family's lack of... something. Is it brazenness? Is it heroism? Is it initiative? Are these qualities he now finds deficient in his own family narrative?

I remind him of his boldness in Auschwitz-Birkenau. The quick thinking that resulted in him getting out of that cursed place with his father and brother. When the call for metal workers rang out across the fields of thousands of men in September 1944, Dad grabbed Israel and Heniek and put up all their hands to demonstrate that they were indeed metal workers. They were chosen, but unsure for exactly what. It was then, on their way *out* of Auschwitz-Birkenau, that they faced a selection. Selections upon arrival are well known. But they faced a selection upon departure. My father's intuition told him to lie about his and Heniek's ages. To this day, he can't explain what motivated him. He told his brother quickly, "Let's change our birth dates. I'll make myself older and you make yourself younger." They were twins. He had no idea that being twins in Mengele's Birkenau was not a good thing.[22]

---

21. Mordechai Chaim Rumkowski was known as the chief elder of the Lodz Ghetto who ruled the ghetto in a despotic manner. In an attempt to save the Jews of Lodz he turned the ghetto into a manufacturing factory, producing an almost endless array of goods needed by the Germans. He hoped by being so useful to the Germans, the Jews of Lodz would be saved.

22. Josef Mengele, also known as the 'angel of death,' was a German physician who conducted medical experiments in Auschwitz and had a particular interest in twins. His experiments included the unnecessary amputation of limbs, deliberately infecting one twin with a deadly disease or injecting their hearts with chloroform. When one twin died, he would kill the other to allow for post-mortem comparisons.

We read about Willy moving into the Krakow Ghetto. He describes the wide array of strenuous work allocations meted out to him. He weaves in stolen moments with members of his family. He was sent to Plaszow to Auschwitz-Birkenau to Sachsenhausen to Dachau. Willy outlines for us one stroke of luck after another. It is hard to breathe and read at the same time. Dad had known that Willy had been in a number of camps, but reading the details of his escapades is another matter. "Unbelievable," says Dad.

The war ends. Liberation. This is another feature of Holocaust memoirs that fascinates me. Where was the survivor liberated from? By whom? What happened immediately after? What happened not so immediately? Emotions? Thoughts? Is it possible to even articulate such things?

American soldiers liberate Willy from Dachau on 29 April 1945. Dad was liberated from Friedland by the Russian army on 8 May 1945. "The very last day of the war," he says, as always. Willy goes on to describe that he was so sick, he could not fully appreciate his freedom. I remember from his talks to students that he weighed 38 kilograms. Given that he was 180 centimetres tall, it is understandable that his recuperation took months of attentive medical care. Willy considered 29 April 1945 his second birthday.

Dad's moment of liberation was preceded by two days of uncertainty. The *obersturmbannfuhrer* of Friedland camp, standing with his deputy and underlings, addressed the inmates. Dad can't recall exactly what was said, but he certainly remembers what was not said. "There was no goodbye, no apology, no nothing. However, we were warned not to run away." The most important aspect of this event was that these Germans were no longer wearing their SS uniforms, but their Wehrmacht uniforms. They were dressed like regular soldiers. "We all noticed this at once." The camp authorities shed their genocidal guilt and fled.

The 500 or so prisoners were dumbfounded. Over the next day or so, about 20 German civilians from the town of Friedland came to the camp. They informed the inmates (or semi-inmates at this stage?) that the Russians were close. They came bearing food. Dad burst out laughing. "What is so funny?" I ask.

"It became the joke of the camp. One of these Germans brought us an umbrella."

"What for?" I ask.

"That's the joke. It made no sense. It was so ridiculous," he chuckles.

Then, on 8 May 1945, the Russians arrived. My grandfather, Israel Princ could converse with them. This doesn't surprise me. After all, Lodz had been part of Russia prior to Poland's renewed independence in 1918, and Israel had been born in 1894.

Dad, his father, and brother walked out of the camp and wandered around the town of Friedland. They returned to the camp to sleep. After all, they did have beds in the camp and the local German civilians provided food for them. They did this backwards-forwards shuffle for about a week. They, and many other former camp inmates, then helped themselves to one of the empty, abandoned German houses nearby. They actually took over two houses, side-by-side, and the three of them moved in with other Jewish boys from their camp and Jewish girls from Halbstadt, a female camp nearby. What a share house, I think. It seems that my grandfather became the instant parent of a number of young people. They lived this way for three to four months.

One of the young men, Moniek Goldfeier, who later immigrated to New York, played an important role in my life many years later. When Steven and I, then aged in our twenties, lived in New York in the mid-1980s, Moniek and his wife Angie became sort of stand-in parents. They were not intrusive or meddling, they just kept an eye on us. They invited us to their home every major Jewish festival, took us to fancy (for us) dinners at Upper East Side restaurants, and regularly called to see how we were. I wonder whether, during that time, Moniek thought about the role my grandfather had played in his life. It is now too late to ask him. He passed away a few years ago.

Interestingly, Willy and Dad were in Munich at the same time, in the late 1940s. As were thousands and thousands of others. Their paths did not cross until just before my parents left for Australia. However, they must have been in each other's orbits earlier. Willy worked for the all-important American Joint Distribution Committee, one of the most

Dad working on a lathe, Munich, late 1949

Top: Dad (far right) sitting next to Willy Lermer at the Jewish Holocaust Centre, Melbourne, 2011

Bottom: Moniek Goldfeler, me, Angie Goldfeler, Dad, New York, 1998

crucial aid organisations in the lives of the postwar community of European Jewry. It was housed in the same administrative building as UNRRA and other essential service providers. Dad, like other stateless Jews in Munich, needed access to these services. In my mind's eye, I imagine him at a counter, across from Willy, figuring out how to best eke out a life for himself.

After Dad had graduated and was preparing for immigration to Australia, he asked Willy for a favour. Dad believed his most valuable skills were those he had acquired as a metal turner in the Lodz Ghetto. However, he had not worked on a lathe machine for over five years and he wanted to brush up on his handiwork to be ready for immediate employment in Melbourne. He approached Willy, who was working in the transportation department of the Joint, and asked if he could work for a short period of time in the repair garages on a lathe machine. "I needed to be assured that I still knew how to do this type of work," explains Dad. I wonder how Willy received this request. "He had no hesitations whatsoever. He gave me overalls and my own lathe machine. I was there one week. And no, I had not forgotten my skills," Dad says proudly.

Decades later, when Dad and Willy re-met at the Jewish Holocaust Centre in Melbourne, Willy informed Dad that he had known Mum's mother in Munich. She had been his dentist. Since Buba Rosa was the chief dentist for the Joint, it was logical that he could access her professional services.

Willy Lermer, who touched the hearts of thousands of Australian school students, passed away in 2017.

Friday 1 May 2020

What shall we read next?

I go to the shelves again, to the section of Shoah memoirs. I have them grouped together, but randomly. However, I now realise that I could make a sub-category of memoirs written by people we know or have a connection with. I present Dad with four such books. All four authors are known by our family, some better than others. All four had immigrated to Melbourne after the war. He oohs and aahs. He looks at the photos in them all—before the war, after the war—and is indecisive. How will he make up his mind? I give a little push… "Remember Guta's wonderful testimony at the Lodz Ghetto Commemoration last year?"

"Yes! Lodz!" I suspect the fact that Guta is from Lodz, rather than her superb oratory, is the clincher.

And so we begin.

There Will be Tomorrow, Guta Goldstein
Published by Makor Jewish Community Library, 1999

Guta spends about half the book writing about her prewar childhood in Lodz. She is in no hurry to reach 1 September 1939. I am relieved.

Dad seeks clarification a number of times, "When was she born? How old is she?" Again, he is trying to match up his story with another's. Guta is five years younger than Dad.

I am moved by the way Dad relates and reacts to Guta's vivid recollections and descriptions of her Jewish childhood in Lodz. He knows every street she names, every park she mentions, the lullabies and songs, foods, summer holiday locations, names of schools and books.

At the noting of Guta's address at 92 Pomorska Street he gesticulates with a wave of his hand that this is far from where he lived. "Oh, that was on the other side, near where Judy's family lived." Judy is my mother-in-law. With his eyes shut, the streetscape is right in front of him.

It seems that summer vacations in the countryside were a staple of the prewar Polish Jewish lifestyle. Growing up I heard stories about how mothers and their children would head out to cottages, packed to the hilt with supplies, and how fathers would join them for Shabbat and the weekends. Children revelled in the fresh air, the rivers, the forests, the freedom, and adventures with other kids. This annual escape from a bustling city permeates many recountings of a Polish-Jewish childhood. Guta's is no exception.

When she writes that in the summer holidays of 1938 her family went to the village of Wisniowa Gora, Dad comments, "Yes, some people went there, it was very close to Lodz. Our family liked to go further away for our holidays." I go to Google Maps to see how far Wisniowa Gora is from Lodz. Dad is right. It is a mere 20 kilometres.

"So where did your family like to go?" I ask.

Dad recalls holidaying at a town called Wikno, near a larger town called Ujazd. "I remember a Jewish grocer in Ujazd. That was an unusual occupation for a Jew. Occasionally, at other times of the year, he would deliver specialty food items to us back in Lodz." The only Wikno I can find is nearly 250 kilometres from Lodz. I can't help but think what a *schlep* that must have been for his father. Dad says, "No! That would've been impossible! You've got the wrong place." I return to Google Maps. Same result. I now try the nearby larger town of Ujazd. That is 52 kilometres from Lodz. Sounds more like it. A more manageable Friday afternoon and Sunday evening train trip for Dad's father during those summery months of July and August. What happened to Wikno? Maybe it went the way of Brigadoon[23] and disappeared in the midst of time. These Jewish summer bungalow communities were dotted all over the parts of Poland with significant Jewish populations. I guess that Poles now go to these places to enjoy horse riding, hiking and canoeing, as the Jews once did.

Dad then tells me about another type of holiday he went on with his mother when he was much younger. They went to Ciechocinek, a popular spa or resort town where visitors would 'take the waters' for what was believed to be health benefits. He remembers that the facility they went to was on Lipowa Street. Visitors would arrive after attending a doctor's appointment to obtain a prescription for the appropriate water treatment, of which there were a variety of options and combinations. Dad describes the two rows of baths with fifteen baths in each row. Two of these were three-quarter sized baths for children. He would sit in one of these while his mother took her prescribed treatment in an adult-sized bath. I have to admit that I find this scene a little disconcerting.

***

Guta tells us about her grandfather who "taught Modern Hebrew at Katzenelson's". Dad comments, "Ah…a very good school." She writes about the books that she loved including *Serce (Heart)*, by Edmondo De Amicis which she read many, many times. "So did I," chimes in Dad. I wonder at what age Dad read this European children's classic. He thinks and says, "It was sometime between the ages of 10 to 13." This is not the

---

23. Brigadoon is the name of a legendary Scottish village in the musical and film of the same name. This village would appear for only one day every 100 years. It would disappear and be non-existent the rest of the time.

first time I have heard Dad mentioning *Serce*. He continues, "I remember speaking to Kuba about the book. He wondered whether it was still in print and available." Kuba is my husband's late uncle. An unusual man and an original thinker. As a Polish patriot, he had been a soldier in Anders' Army.[24]

I think I have an English copy of the book. I find it and show it to Dad. He thinks Kuba would have given it to him, and he must have passed it on to me. Sounds like the most likely scenario. But Kuba also loved giving books as presents to us and our kids and there would always be an inscription from him on the front page in his florid European script. In this copy of *Serce*, there is no inscription so I draw the conclusion that Kuba did not give it directly to me.

What is this book that children growing up in Poland loved to read? Firstly, it's not a Polish book at all. It's an Italian book much loved by Italian youngsters. Published in 1886, it really is a book from another time, written in the format of a diary of a young boy. I start reading it, to myself. It is a charming and captivating book of morality tales set across a range of socio-economic strata. Emphasis is placed on the school. Teachers, students and parents are the key characters and the stories provide valuable life lessons. In its essence, it's a book about ethical behaviour and living an honourable life.

Discussing *Serce* with Dad, he tells me about a teacher in his last year of primary school, 1938. "Mr Abramson was a very strict teacher; kids were very obedient. This was on the last day of primary school. You need to understand that everyone was going in a different direction the following year. For some, it was the end of their schooling altogether. For others, like me, it was going to a new school, a high school. On that last day of school, when everyone was saying goodbye to each other, Mr Abramson cried. We just couldn't believe it. He looked at us all and cried."

---

24. Anders' Army was the unofficial name of the Polish Armed Forces under the command of Wladyslaw Anders. It was formed in the Soviet Union and then made its way across parts of the Middle East. It fought under British command in the Italian Campaign.

Sunday 3 May 2020

Dad and I continue to read about and enjoy Guta's detailed portrayal of a Jewish childhood in Lodz. I am intrigued by her ability to find her younger self's voice and emotion. Her tender love and protection of her younger sister, Munia, are heart-warming. The premature death of their mother, of pneumonia, at 37 years of age, is heart-breaking. She tells us of her father's re-marriage and her love for her stepmother. We learn about her enthusiasm for school and particular teachers.

And then, inevitably, we reach 1 September 1939.

We read about the German invasion of Poland and the occupation of Lodz. We read about the endless anti-Jewish edicts that are slowly smothering the life out of the Jews of Lodz. We read about the growing food shortages and the order to wear yellow armbands. Against this backdrop, we learn something about the conversations, emotions and decisions taken by the adults around Guta.

And then, there was the directive to move into the area designated to form the Lodz Ghetto in part of the city known as Baluty. As Dad tells his always-captivated student audiences at the Jewish Holocaust Centre, "This was the oldest, poorest, shabbiest part of town." Guta's family had to find a place to live within this small congested area. So did Dad's family. Luckily for them, Dad's aunt, Ciocia Mala, already lived in Baluty.

Ciocia Mala was only eleven years older than Dad and was his favourite aunt. I have always imagined that she was more like an older sister than an aunt. Closer to his generation than his parents'. Ciocia Mala had recently married Salek Ajzner. As a young married couple, they could only afford to live in a less than salubrious part of the city. In this case, Baluty. So, when the Jews of Lodz were forced to find accommodation in the new ghetto, Dad and his family moved out of their rather lovely apartment on Aleja 1-go Maja and into Ciocia Mala and Wujek Salek's place.

After the war, Dad's three remaining aunts, Fela, Lola and Mala immigrated to Israel. I remember elderly Lola from my first trip to Israel. Mala married Avraham Pluzny, her second cousin, and they had one child, a daughter named Mina. I met Mala a number of times. She doted on me; I don't think she could quite believe that her little 'Davidek' (David) had children of his own.

There is a moving addendum to this story. In 1986, while living in New York, I attended a Jewish education conference in Washington DC. I was sitting in one of the break-out sessions, in a large circle of about 20 people, and we were going around the circle introducing ourselves. I don't recall what I said when my turn came around, but of course, as an Aussie, I sounded different to everyone else. Then, from directly across the other side of the circle, a woman asked, "Are you any relation to David Prince?"

I nearly fell off my chair. Her attire, including her wig, identified her as religiously observant and she spoke in a mixed Israeli-American accent. "I am his daughter," I responded. All eyes in the room were shifting from her to me and then me to her.

She said, "I am Mina, Mala's daughter, your father's first cousin." In unison, everyone in the room gasped. We ran to each other, hugged and cried.

Mina, born in Israel, had married a cantor, Baruch Shifman. They accepted a posting in South Africa and then another in Columbus, USA. Baruch is an accomplished, well-known and admired cantor. Mina is a Jewish educator. They have lived in Columbus for many decades now. They have children, grandchildren and many great-grandchildren.

Me with Dad's aunt, Ciocia Mala, Israel, 1984

Monday 4 May 2020

Back to the ghetto, with Guta. We read about the congested living conditions, impossibly unhygienic communal toilets, shrinking food supplies, freezing winter weather, and total isolation from the outside world. Guta tells us about the awful impact of these conditions upon her family and those around her. Starvation, illness and death surrounded her. Dad looks at me at sporadic intervals, shrugs his shoulders and says, "Yes, that's how it was."

Eventually, both parents died and Guta and her sister Munia were moved to a part of the ghetto known as Marysin. This was considered a good thing. Originally a children's summer camp, it had become a type of orphanage located on the outskirts of the ghetto. There was a perception that Marysin was a semi-rural haven set apart from the ghetto. When Guta speaks publicly about her war experiences, she always dedicates significant time to Marysin. She describes the wide variety of Jewish homes that the children came from. We hear about the girls she became friendly with—their personalities, interests and talents. Inevitably, starvation, cold, illness and death followed these children to Marysin.

Little Munia contracted meningitis and died. She was just seven years old. Dad and I look at each other. We cannot go on for today.

Tuesday 5 May 2020

We read how Guta's aunt whisked her away from Marysin. Just in time. Only a few hours later, all the young children were deported. This is why it is important for Guta to speak about the friends she had in Marysin. She is their only memorial.

All who survived the Lodz Ghetto remember a week in September 1942 that became known as the 'szpera' (pronounced 'shpera'). It haunted and traumatised all who were there. Every street and every building was suddenly blockaded and the entire population was told to assemble for a selection. Anybody who looked too old, too young, or too sick was separated and taken away, as we now know, to the Chelmno death camp. The remainder were told to return to their homes. So home they went. Some without a mother, some without a father, some without their children.

Dad describes the scene, "Stop! Don't move. The ghetto came to a standstill. Big trucks, big heavy Germans with dusty boots and thick goggles. We had to come down and stand to attention. All the Jews stood about 50 metres from trucks lined up. We didn't know what the trucks were exactly for but we certainly had a gut feeling that it was not good to be put on one." It is known that 16,000 Jews were deported from the Lodz Ghetto to Chelmno during the *szpera*. Dad continues, "During that event I lost my nana and cousins." Guta was hidden in various places by her aunt during the multiple selections that took place during the eight days of the *szpera*. Somehow, she avoided being found during any of them.

The Lodz Ghetto was transformed into a massive production machine. The range and huge numbers of goods manufactured for the Germans is beyond belief. The production of undergarments, furs, leather goods, carpentry, metalwork, brushes, shoes, electrical goods and more, was generated by an army of Jewish slave labourers. Guta describes her difficult work in a straw factory that produced 'overshoes' to be worn by the German soldiers on the Russian front.

I ask Dad to tell me about his work in the ghetto. I know the broad outline but I am hoping to elicit some new snippets. He tells me that when school finally closed in the ghetto, his father went to an engineer named Rak to organise a job for him. His brother, Heniek, was already working at the electrotechnical shop. Rak agreed to also take Dad on. Dad and Heniek worked on a lathe. They had to rewind electrical motors. He explains, "We were repairers. We were not producers. We didn't make anything, we just fixed things. I was good with my hands."

I ask, "What work did your mother do?"

He tells me, "She worked at Klugman's. They made carpets out of rags." This is a new snippet. "We had the very same jobs until the ghetto was liquidated and we were sent to Auschwitz-Birkenau."

Life (and death) in the Lodz Ghetto continued. Guta, with her aunt caring for her, endured ever-worsening conditions. Other girls in the ghetto experienced the same dire circumstances. Nevertheless, I am heart-warmed reading about their friendships.

By August 1944, Lodz Ghetto was the last ghetto remaining in Europe. All the others had been 'liquidated'. The term 'liquidated' in Holocaust parlance meant removing all remaining inhabitants from a ghetto. In practice, it meant murdering any Jews still alive. In some places, Jews were transported into nearby forests to be shot, en masse. More often, they were transported on cattle car trains to death camps.

Today, we read about the liquidation of the Lodz Ghetto and the deportation of Guta to the death camp of Auschwitz-Birkenau. She describes the horrendous cattle car journey, the disorientation and horrifying violence upon arrival, and the wrenching separation from beloved family members. This journey is all too familiar to me. It was Dad's journey, a mere two weeks later. It was the journey of nearly everyone from Lodz who had survived until liquidation. I read. Dad is silent.

I ask Dad whether he wants me to stop. Maybe he needs a break from yet another re-animation of his own experiences. I can't really imagine what he is seeing with his closed eyes, stretched out on the couch. He misunderstands the intention of my question. He opens his eyes, raises his sleeve a little to look at his watch and says, "No, it's ok, we've still got more time."

We read on. Dad interrupts me to recount the arrival of his intact nuclear family to Auschwitz-Birkenau. This is a most familiar story to me. But today, I hear a new twist. They (Dad, his brother and their parents) arrived at the entrance ramp where they received a most brutal reception. They were in complete shock. Ferocious bellowing accompanied the vicious emptying of the cattle cars' human cargo. Dad grimaces and continues, "Sheer hell broke loose. *Raus! Raus!* (Out! Out!)." This is part of the well-practised testimony that he imparts to students who visit the Jewish Holocaust Centre. I have heard it often, yet it has the power to demolish me every time.

"It happened so quickly that I couldn't really understand what was going on," Dad resumes. He is referring to the chaotic, fierce and hasty separation of himself, his father and his brother, from his mother. They were sent to the right and their mum, linking arms with their elderly neighbour, Mrs Frankel, was sent to the left. Dad says, "You know, my mum was three years younger than my dad. She wasn't old. She may have been able to survive Birkenau." Then, a new discussion point emerges. It's not, in fact, entirely new to me. I have thought about it before but have never dared to bring it up with Dad. This time I do.

"Do you think that if she wasn't arm-in-arm with elderly Mrs Frankel, and assisting her, she may have been selected to live, at least at that early stage?"

Dad stops for a moment, looks at me, and says, "Probably." We agree that her kindness may have come at the ultimate price.

Guta writes about her six weeks in Auschwitz-Birkenau in gut-wrenching prose. The deprivations, cruelty, starvation and constant fear. The seemingly never-ending *appel* line-ups and counting. These *appel* line-ups were a feature of virtually all the concentration camps. Twice a day, morning and night, inmates were ordered to assemble in open areas, spaced apart. Rain, hail or snow. The number of prisoners present had to match the number recorded in the camp records. Survivors describe the many hours they spent in this formation in agonising terms. It is hard to believe that the camp personnel were so innumerate that counting was the only purpose of this brutal routine.

I have to say again that I love reading about the close friendships that seem to sustain Guta. Dad didn't have these. After all, he was there with his father and brother. They sustained each other.

We follow Guta as she is transported out of Auschwitz-Birkenau to Bergen-Belsen. It didn't take her long to adjust to the conditions and rules of this new camp. We read about the diseases that killed people in such conditions. Diphtheria, typhoid, typhus, tuberculosis. The prisoners were really dying of extreme hunger, lack of decent sanitation and hygiene, overcrowding, exposure to the elements, lack of medical care, overwork and physical exhaustion. These are the prerequisites for disease to take hold. Dad turns to me and says, "You know, I can't explain it but I never got sick during the war. Never. Not even once. Not a cold, not a cough. Nothing." We are both truly amazed.

After ten weeks in Bergen-Belsen, Guta was transported to a work camp in German Saxony near a village called Mehltheuer. I ask Dad if he has heard of this place. He has not. I am always astounded by just how many camps there were. Again: appalling conditions, hard labour, starvation, rations and cruelty. A watchman, an older German man, showed unprecedented kindness and snuck food to Guta and her friend.

I ask Dad, "Do you remember anyone showing such unexpected kindness to you?"

"No," is his disappointed response.

Guta was finally liberated by the Americans on 16 April 1945. She was fifteen years old.

The book ends. We are hankering for the 'after' story. Dad says, "Nu, what happened next?" I inform him that Guta has written a sequel, *Towards the Future: A Memoir*, published in 2018. I guess we'll just have to read that too.

Wednesday 6 May 2020

Who (not what) shall we read next?

Now that we have agreed that reading about people we know is rather compelling, I present Dad with a few options. None of these authors are alive anymore. They were all born in Poland and ended up living in Melbourne. Dad finally makes his choice.

Six Million and One: My Survival in Poland During the Nazi Occupation
Martin Lane

Details of publication unknown

T he year of publication is not written in the book, anywhere. This is a bit of a mystery. I like to know when each book was written. I take the year of publication and subtract a few years to approximate the period of the actual writing. I am interested to know how many years have lapsed between the experience and the time of writing. Is there a common broad age group when an author decides to put pen to paper? Are there conclusions to draw? Probably not. As I said, it just interests me.

So, I search on the internet for Martin Lane's memoir. There are two entries. The first entry I find is on Amazon UK with publication date 1990. This is a different edition to mine. Then I find it listed on Eric Chaim Kline Bookseller, which is a member of the Antiquarian Booksellers' Association of America. That sounds right. The description—hardcover, blue cloth binding—matches my edition. But it also states that the text is in Yiddish and the publication date is 1973. This is a surprise. Did Martin write an earlier version in Yiddish, publish it in 1973 then translate it into English for its 1990 publication? Sounds plausible. However, my edition of his book is hardcover with blue cloth binding, but in English. It sounds like I have a hybrid of the two publications. In addition, as far as I know, Polish was Martin's first language, not Yiddish. This is to remain a (minor) mystery. It won't keep me awake at night.

Who is Martin Lane? I remember him and his wife Klara as acquaintances of my parents. Klara Lane, vivacious, elegant and a dedicated WIZO volunteer[25], is much more vivid in my memory than Martin. He was one of the older friends of my parents. In fact, most of our family friends were older than Mum and Dad. I didn't notice it that much until significantly later, when they started getting sick and dying.

---

25. WIZO or Women's International Zionist Organisation is dedicated to raising awareness and funds to improve the status and lot of women and children in Israel. It was founded in 1920.

I have no recollection of Mum and Dad ever socialising with the Lanes on their own, but always together with the Feuers, who were closer friends of ours and relatives of the Lanes. (Klara Lane and Janek Feuer were brother and sister.) Both couples were childless. So too, were other couples we knew including the Kahanes and the Kellers. Before IVF and widespread access to fertility treatment, were they merely among the statistically infertile? Or were they somehow rendered infertile by medical experiments from Auschwitz? Perhaps it is growing up in the milieu of survivors that I even think like this.

The deciding factor in choosing this memoir is the fact that Martin Lane was from Warsaw, where Mum was born, and therefore a nod to my mother's experiences, and not just my father's. I suspect Dad will not be as captivated as he is by the Lodz memoirs. Stories set against the backdrop of his childhood city seem to be spellbindingly engrossing. Warsaw? Not so much.

The clincher is the fact that Martin once told my parents that he remembered Mum's parents wheeling my mum in her pram when she was a baby, in the late 1920s. That was a rare connection to my mum's childhood.

We are settling into our usual positions on my spacious couch when Dad says, "Maybe we are masochists?"

I say, "Who?"

He replies, "Both of us." We laugh and begin.

I knew that Martin Lane was older than my parents, but I didn't realise by how much. He was born in Warsaw in 1901. No wonder he could clearly remember my grandparents wheeling Mum, born in 1927, around the parks of the city.

His account of youthful activities in Zionist organisations and the Maccabi sports club are reminiscent of the lives of Jewish children in Melbourne. However, those similarities end abruptly when he joined the Polish army at the age of 17. He became an officer. He was awarded medals. Later he studied banking and held a senior position in an international banking company in Warsaw. I enjoy his portrayal of Warsaw as a sophisticated European capital for middle-class and upper-class Jews. This is the world of my maternal grandparents, Rosa Gringlas and Izak Salcburg. In fact, Martin lived at 23 Panska Street. Mum lived at 93 Panska Street.

Dad comments that Martin had a full life before the war. He was an adult, aged 29 years, in 1939. At 14 years old, Dad was still a kid.

I turn the page and see a photo of the Tlomackie Synagogue. It gives me a jolt. It is so familiar. Also known as the Great Synagogue of Warsaw, its architecture is grand and aristocratic. As is written in Wikipedia, it "… served the acculturated elite of Warsaw's Jewry". But it is no more. It was blown up by SS commander Jurgen Stroop on 16 May 1943, as his final act in the destruction of the Warsaw Ghetto. I show the photo to Dad. No need for words. We both know that my mother's parents, Rosa and Izak, were married there in 1924.

I gasp when we read that Martin got married in 1934 to a woman called Halina Maizel. Who is she? Martin's wife is Klara. It hits me like a thunderbolt. Halina was his first wife, Klara his second. Klara was, what I term, his 'replacement' wife. I ask Dad whether he knew that Martin had been married before the war. He answers that he didn't. But, of course, it makes sense. As Dad had said earlier, Martin had a full life before the war.

I am fascinated by this phenomenon (what else to call it?) of 'replacement' families. I know precious few of them. My parents and most of their friends were too young to have had spouses and children before 1939. Even their older friends, by a few years, would have been too young.

As I ponder this Halina/Klara combination, I unpack its implications. How would wife number two have felt about being the 'replacement' wife? Is it possible to be jealous of a forever young, martyred first wife? Perhaps, if the couple both lost first spouses it may be easier. Who knows. Then I start drilling down. Maybe it's possible to psychologically cope with being a 'replacement' spouse, but how about 'replacement' children? What does it mean to be the second family of one or both of your parents? Did they grow up seeing themselves as a 'replacement' for the murdered child? Did they share the same name of the 'lost' child? Or did their parents search for an entirely new name, disconnected from the past? When hugging and kissing them, were their parents thinking of that other child? Did those parents even tell their 'new' family about their 'old' family? There are many layers to explore. All I know for sure is that none of those old enough to have had prewar families are alive today.

In our reading, we arrive, once again, at 1 September 1939. The German invasion of Poland, its aerial bombardments and sheer terror resonate with me. Martin's descriptions of Warsaw echo Mum's depictions. Same time; same place. Martin was 29. Mum was twelve. To her dying day, Mum was scared of thunder and lightning. A legacy from precisely this time. I will never forget, when I was about ten years old, during a thunderstorm, I found Mum cowering and shaking in the narrow space under the bathroom vanity.

Tlomackie Synagogue, Warsaw, 1910.
My maternal grandparents Rosa & Izak married there in 1924

Thursday 7 May 2020

Martin writes about his decision to travel eastwards to flee from the Germans. He and tens of thousands of others. Martin describes the desperation, chaos and frightened stream of humanity hoping to escape the invading Germans. After a time, it became obvious that the Germans were catching up with them and that their attempt to flee was futile. He decided to return home to Warsaw.

The litany of horrors begins. There were multiple and never-ending edicts, enforced by violence and fear of violence. In November 1940, the Jews of Warsaw were forced into a specific part of the city designated as the ghetto. Overcrowding, food shortages, lack of medicine, gruelling working conditions took their toll. Then Jews from surrounding towns were also forced into the Warsaw Ghetto exacerbating the appalling conditions. Hunger, sickness, terror, death escalated relentlessly. Of course, I can't help but imagine my mother in this scene.

Martin recounts the suicide of Adam Czerniakow, head of the Warsaw Judenrat (Jewish council). Czerniakow was an engineer and happened to be a friend and associate of Mum's father, also an engineer. In the ghetto, he lived in the same street as Mum and her family, Elektralna Street.

Martin writes about the deportations from the Warsaw Ghetto to the Treblinka death camp, starting in mid-1942. This was when Mum lost her little brother, Samuel, or Mulo for short. She often talked about him being snatched away and forcibly taken to the *umschlagplatz*. The *umschlagplatz* was the rounding-up area where Jews were gathered before their train journey, squashed in cattle cars, to the death camps. The scenes described by survivors are horrendous in their brutality and sheer terror. Mulo was just ten years old. Mum never got over his murder.

Martin discusses the ambiguous (to say the least) role of the Jewish police in the ghetto. They became an integral part of the German genocidal apparatus. Jews who joined up, certainly in the early stages of the war, could not have been aware of their ensuing diabolical role. (I assume that it was not explicit in the job description.) They ended up, wittingly or unwittingly, complicit in the destruction of their own people.

Dad reminds me that while in the Lodz Ghetto, he wanted to join the Jewish police. He had reasoned that he could earn extra food rations for his family. His parents absolutely forbade him. He has been forever grateful for their adamant admonishment.

Martin was assisted by the son of his family's former caretaker. He took Martin out of the ghetto and into his home on the 'Aryan side' where the family fed, washed and sheltered him. He recovered somewhat from his bedraggled starved state and then returned to the ghetto to find Halina. They escaped from the ghetto together and returned to the caretaker's home where they were hidden. They lived in constant fear. So did their hosts.

Martin devotes a separate chapter—albeit a short one—to the vexed topic of attitudes of Polish people to Jewish people. The title of this chapter 'Poles and Jews' contains the nub of the issue. The implication is that Poles and Jews are separate peoples. The premise under which I operate in the interfaith space today is that Jews and non-Jews are all Australians. We acknowledge the many different types of Australians and we embrace and celebrate our differences. The complex Polish positing of identities, nationhoods and belongingness was a completely different story. It was not only a lack of unity that permeated Polish society. Not only that separate groups lived side-by-side. Separate but equal would have been a profoundly different reality. The voices that promoted and practised antisemitism overwhelmed those who wanted a more inclusive society. These pre-existing attitudes and actions, official and unofficial, reached a crescendo during the war. They turned out to be the difference between life and death for part of Polish Jewry.

This dangerous divide has been hinted at in the earlier memoirs we have read. Martin, however, discusses it head-on. He acknowledges the wide discrepancy in the treatment of Jews by their Polish neighbours during the German occupation. After all, we have read about Sabina and Helka Zimering helped by Mrs Justyna and her two daughters, Danka and Mala. We have read how Lutka Rosenberg Wyshogrod and her parents were saved by Emil and Maria Lozinski. In our current story, Martin and Halina were hidden by the caretaker and his family. These Jews owed their survival to the brave actions of non-Jewish Poles. In other occupied countries the penalty for hiding or helping a Jew may have been a beating or imprisonment. In Poland, it was immediate death. And everyone knew it. These heroic saviours risked their lives to rescue Jews.

However, the underbelly of this issue is those Poles who were so hostile to Jews as to actively turn them over to the Germans and certain death. Their complicity in, and contribution to murder is the sticking point for Jewish people. It is one thing to not assist Jews. This is perfectly understandable. Not preferable, but understandable. The death penalty was a powerful restraining deterrent. Mum always appreciated the predicament of the Poles. She used to say that if the situation were reversed, she didn't think she would have been prepared to risk her life and the lives of her family members to save others. I appreciated her honesty. However, there is a gigantic leap across a moral gorge between not endangering oneself to save others and proactively seeking out Jews to assist the Germans in their genocidal mission. Aiding and abetting the Nazis cannot be overlooked. Better to be a bystander than an accomplice.

Dad remembers an episode that a survivor friend in Melbourne recounted to him. The war had recently ended and this friend returned to his hometown of Krakow. Shortly after arriving he bumped into a classmate from his prewar schooldays. A non-Jewish Pole. They were pleased to see each other. The classmate was excited to share an experience with Dad's friend. He gushed forth explaining how, during the war, he had saved the life of a Jewish classmate of theirs. He had been walking along a main street in Krakow and two Gestapo officers happened to be walking in front of him. Just then, he saw the Jewish classmate on the other side of the street. With great fanfare he announced that he decided not to notify these Gestapo officers that the lad across the road was Jewish. And thus, he had saved his life.

I have no doubt this topic will resurface in other memoirs. It is omnipresent and insidious in the memories of Polish Jews.

***

The Warsaw Ghetto revolt took place from 19 April to 6 May 1943. Martin, at this time, was in hiding on the Aryan side. He watched the uprising from the outside, quite literally. Martin witnessed the machine gun fire, incendiary bombs, cannon blasts and engulfing flames that signified the last embers of the Warsaw Jewish community. My 16-year-old mother and her parents were in the ghetto. Mum jumped out of the fourth-storey window of a burning building, landing on the debris in the street below, thankfully without as much as a scratch. Her parents also survived the liquidation of the ghetto and the small family were subsequently rounded up and transported to the death camp Majdanek. After the separation of men and women, my mother and grandmother never saw my grandfather again. A few years later, my grandmother bumped into a man who told her that my grandfather was not immediately sent to the gas chamber but remained alive in the camp for at least some time.

Friday 8 May 2020

Today is the anniversary of the end of World War II in Europe. The anniversary of the day Dad was liberated from the Friedland labour camp in Upper Silesia, Germany.

I told Dad yesterday that I would not be reading with him today. He was silent. I have shopping and cooking to do for Shabbat. Winter is approaching and Shabbat starts early. Also, the Covid restrictions have eased and my house cleaners are allowed to return for the first time in weeks. I have arranged for them to clean Dad's home as well. He is anxious lest they move any of his papers and other paraphernalia. I am not sure if I am doing the right thing, having three strangers in his house in the middle of a global pandemic. I decide that hygiene and cleanliness are crucial. Luckily, the weather is sunny and I send him off for a walk and then suggest that he sit at my place until the cleaners leave.

Later on, Pauline Rockman, co-president of the JHC, and her partner, Avi Paluch, pop by for their weekly check-in visit with survivors who volunteer at the centre. Thankfully, there are a number of survivors still 'on the payroll'. Pauline and Avi are doing their much-appreciated rounds.

When the cleaners leave, Dad asks hopefully whether maybe we could do some reading today. I apologise that I am too busy—I only have about three hours left to cook for Shabbat. I am certain that he remembers that I had said I would not have time today, but I guess he thought he might give it a shot anyway.

Sunday 10 May 2020

Martin formed a little group of fugitives with his wife Halina, his sister and brother-in-law, and another two unrelated people. They scrambled about to different hiding places on the Aryan side of Warsaw. The Jewish side no longer existed. Amidst the chaos of the Germans and the Russians firing at one another, they scurried from one deserted ruin to another. They often escaped just moments before the Germans set fire to the wreck of the building where they had been sheltering.

Then, in August 1944, the Warsaw Uprising began. As intense street fighting raged between German soldiers and Polish resistance fighters, Martin's group scampered from one dugout to the next. Foraging for food became more and more difficult; they began to grow weak and fall ill.

On the one hand, I want a break. On the other hand, I want to go on. After nearly every page I say to Dad, "I need to stop for a little while. It's too much." He acquiesces each time, happy with whatever I decide. But then I find myself re-starting. It's that familiar revulsion-compulsion urge experienced by many people immersed in reading about the Holocaust.

We continue. Bridges were blown up, pavements ripped up, burning buildings collapsed. The German air force dropped bombs and the German army's tanks ploughed through what remained of the streets. Our amazing six continued to hide amongst the ruins of Warsaw.

"This is unbelievable," says Dad. He says this at least once or twice during every book. I think Dad's sense of feeling 'ordinary' is deepening. In earlier memoirs, whenever the protagonist was bravely proactive or made daring split-second decisions, I would hear the refrain, "I did nothing." I intuit, yet again, a sense of self-defined timidity or pangs of perceived submissiveness. He feels twinges of inadequacy. How can anyone equal Martin's 'extraordinary' struggle to defy the murderous intent of the Germans? I'm not sure what to make of Dad's need to measure up. I remind him that every individual's fight to stay alive was unique. And after all, three out of four of Dad's nuclear family did survive. "I suppose you're right," he responds meekly.

While Martin and his brave entourage burrowed and buried themselves in rubble, the Polish resistance movement surrendered to the Germans. It was October 1944. The Jews hiding in the devastated debris of Warsaw were still at risk of being discovered, both by Germans and Poles. There were so many close calls. They were terrified and starving. At one stage they did not eat for 12 days.

And then, about a month later, the beloved wife of Martin's youth, Halina, died. I gasp out loud. Dad slaps his thigh. We are in shock. We shouldn't be, but we are. We know that Halina must die for Martin to marry the delightful Klara. By now we both need a break.

Monday 11 May 2020

As the freezing Polish winter approached, Martin and his surviving companions began to sink into despair and depression. Hyperalert and in continuous fear, they continued their relentless search for new dugouts and scraps of food. And then, finally, the Russians marched in and liberated Warsaw. It was January 1945.

After hospitalisation and convalescence, Martin went to live in Lodz. It seems that Lodz, besides being Dad's hometown, became the most important transit centre for Jews in postwar Poland. A gathering place for the remnants of the Jewish people. Jews trickled in there from different directions. They came from the Soviet Union, out of hiding from throughout Poland, out of the camps.

Our reading venture began during the postwar years in Germany. What's with Lodz positing itself as the meeting place of Jews? Dad tells me that, firstly, unlike Warsaw, Lodz was still standing. In addition, the returning Jews quickly formed organisations to assist themselves and others like them. We discuss the time lag between the end of the war and the arrival of large numbers of Jews to the American Zone of Germany. Perhaps many went to Lodz first and then onto Germany, either to the DP camps or as 'free livers'. Everything is more complicated than it at first appears.

Martin was not one of those Jews who went to Germany. He left Poland for Paris and then immigrated to Australia. He does not write much about his life in Australia. I feel relief knowing that he will meet and marry the charming Klara.

Tuesday 12 May 2020

Survivor's Tales, Dr Lidia Eichenholz

Published by iUniverse, 2004

Today we begin Lidia Eichenholz's memoir. This is the Lidia who Dad thinks introduced him to Mum in the Jewish Students' Union cafeteria. This book is one of my internet finds. It becomes apparent, early on, that it's not really a memoir, but a collection of 'memoiresque' vignettes. At first it feels disjointed and fragmented. We have become used to recollections recounted in chronological order. We have enjoyed getting to know our protagonists, their families, friends and lifestyles. Descriptive autobiographical details have enabled us to build a narrative around each of our survivors.

However, this book is a series of short, seemingly disconnected sketches of events from Lidia's life. It is not as accessible as the other writings we have been swept up in, and reading it feels like something of a chore. After the first few pieces I begin to think that each has been written independently of the others, that the stories were never intended to form a wholistic treatise.

Dad and I discuss this different approach to writing and once we acknowledge what seems to be Lidia's intention, we can appreciate each separate 'tale' on its own merit. Through her disparate short sketches, we piece together something of her life. Having said that, we are disappointed that only a few pages have been devoted to her student days in Munich. After all, this is why I went searching for her on the internet and ordered her book in the first place.

We are not really getting to 'know' Lidia.

Thursday 14 May 2020

In a tale entitled 'Hope', set after the war, Lidia hints at later disappointments. I try to guess them. And then, in a short tale, "Life is not predictable," she writes, "there was a divorce, my health failed me, and I lost my son to his father." I gasp.

We are both feeling sad and flat when we finish Lidia's book. I want these survivors to be compensated in some way for what they endured in their earlier lives. When they write about a wonderful spouse, gorgeous children, adorable grandchildren, close friends, satisfying careers, meaningful voluntary roles and exotic travels, I am thrilled. I don't try to weigh up these reparations in any formulaic way. Nevertheless, I feel relieved, in a simplistic sense, that life turned out okay for them. Not so much with Lidia.

Sunday 17 May 2020

Who shall we read next? We return to our familiar Melbourne survivors. Dad peruses a number of memoirs. He says, "You choose."

I say, "No, you choose."

"Ok, let's start with a thin book," he decides. We laugh.

Out of the Ashes: How I Survived Lodz Ghetto, Auschwitz-Birkenau and Torgau Lager in Germany, Tova Tauber

Published by Makor Jewish Community Library, 2011

Tova participated in the 2017 annual Lodz Ghetto Commemoration. I have already mentioned this memorial event that takes place on the last Sunday of every August and described my role in its organisation. We aim for a short—one hour—dignified commemoration which includes lighting six memorial candles, reciting prayers, displaying original photos, music, poetry and prose. The centrepiece of our program is the testimony of a survivor. And we always end with the resounding *Partisan's Song* sung in Yiddish and *Hatikvah* in Hebrew. Each year we search for an innovation. Perhaps a new book has been written. A new song composed. Maybe a Lodz story has been unearthed or never-before-seen photos have emerged. Or perhaps someone who has never spoken before decides it is time to participate.

Tova was one of the latter, convinced by her son to speak. They stood on the stage together. She read a poem by her brother, the late Avraham Cykiert, a well-known Melbourne Jewish playwright and poet. Her son read an extract from her book. I still have that particular section marked with a sticky note. In 2017 there was an audience of maybe 150 Lodz survivors, their children, grandchildren and even great-grandchildren. Tova passed away the following year.

Dad seems more talkative during today's reading than he has been over the last few sessions. I wonder if it's because we're back on familiar and solid ground, the city of Lodz.

Reading the very first paragraph, we laugh. Tova writes that she and one of her sisters had blue eyes. It was said that they were "throwbacks to the Russian tartars". She adds, "It was a bit of a joke."

Dad says, "We used to joke that if someone had blue eyes or were very tall, that they were a throwback to the Cossacks." It is as if the three of us are somehow having a stifled laugh about the rape of Jewish women from long ago. What have we come to?

Tova tells us a little about the small villages her parents were originally from. I expect Dad to have heard of them. He hasn't.

"How come?" I ask.

He is aggravated with me. "Do you know every single town from Melbourne to Bendigo?"

"I know quite a few," I respond defensively. He rolls his eyes at me. I thought the rolling of eyes was my prerogative. I guess not.

"You can't even compare. Transportation, travel, communication, internet. Ha! What did we know?" he retorts before adding his usual comment about small towns, "A hole of a place. A nothing." It sounds even more derogatory in Yiddish. "A *loch.* A *gonirscht.*"

Continuing her description of prewar life, Tova mentions that Lodz had no sewerage. Dad interrupts, "Wrong! Parts of Lodz, the newer parts, did have sewerage. We didn't, but if you went past Piotrkowska Street, on the other side and then turned left, there they did have sewerage." Like always, whenever he describes the Lodz landscape his eyes are shut and he indicates with his hand the path you need to follow to get to the area he is describing. He then adds, "Our cousins, the Wittelsohns, who were quite well-off, lived at 48 Przejazd Street in that area. I think that they had sewerage."

I am moved by Tova's attempt to describe her mother. "I can still recall my mother's face, but not clearly." Without thinking, I blurt out, "Do you remember what your mum looked like?"

There is silence. Then Dad says, "I'm not sure." He goes on to describe her in ways that I have heard before. He has fallen back on familiar tropes. But he does add, "In the years immediately after the war, I thought about her a lot. Everywhere I went, I stared at the faces of women who could be my mother's age. I kept thinking that maybe I'll bump into her on the streets." Not much chance of that when, upon arrival at Auschwitz-Birkenau, she was directed to the left, arm-in-arm with Mrs Frankel, their elderly neighbour.

Wednesday 20 May 2020

We learn about the coffee and confectionary shop on Brzezinska Street that Tova's parents owned. Even I know Brzezinska Street. It was in the Baluty, where later the Lodz Ghetto would be formed. It is familiar to me because this is the same street where Dad's Ciocia Mala and Wujek Salek lived, and where Dad's immediate family moved to when the ghetto borders were announced. Their address was 30 Brzezinska Street. "What number Brzezinska was the coffee shop?" Dad asks. Tova doesn't tell us.

The war started. Here we go again. Dad has much to say. It is not directly related to anything Tova writes, but, I think, it is a reaction to our accumulated reading. "Why didn't we try to get out of Poland?" he shakes his head. "Mum had a sister in Argentina. I don't remember any discussion, at any time, about going there, or anywhere else. We had a Blue Box[26] in the house, but Palestine wasn't discussed. Maybe, if I had been a few years older I would've had more say in the family. Maybe, I could've forced the issue." This is an attitude I have never encountered from Dad before. In my opinion, it is more than vivid hindsight fuelling this sentiment. The build-up of our reading about proactive and daring endeavours at escape is having an impact on him. Perhaps it is a way of self-excusing the passivity he sees in himself. He sighs and we continue.

Tova describes the destruction of the many synagogues in Lodz. In particular, she mentions the Wolborska Street synagogue. Dad mishears me or my poor Polish pronunciation misleads him. He cries out, "Wolczanska Street synagogue!"

Then it's my turn to get confused. "Yes, that must be it. She's writing about 'our' shule!" I exclaim back. The 'our shule' bit just pops out of my mouth. Why is it *our* shule? This is indeed where Dad's family went to synagogue. It was at the end of their street. The Wolczanska Street synagogue was popularly known as the Litvak shule because its founders were Jewish merchants from Lithuania and Lithuanian Jews are called

---

26. A Blue Box is a charity box that Jewish families and organisations had in order to donate money to assist in the building of the Jewish homeland. This form of fundraising began in 1901. It demonstrates the dedication of Jews to Zionism.

Litvaks. It was constructed between 1899 and 1904 with a magnificent edifice. The Nazis burned the synagogue down in November 1939 and the rabbi was ordered to personally tear up the Torah scrolls. In March 1940, the remaining walls were demolished.

There is now a partially empty block where the synagogue once stood. Some of the land has been built on. The last time I was there was in 2009 with Dad, my then 16-year-old younger son, and about 100 other young Australian Jewish students on the March of the Living. There was no plaque or signage. Just Dad standing on the block, passing around enlarged photos of the enormous structure that once graced the area. I'll never forget Dad's opening words to our large group: "You are standing on consecrated ground." We looked down. All we could see was dirt and rubbish.

Reminiscing about that trip, I go to my study to retrieve one of the enlarged photos that Dad had made and laminated. And then, Dad says, "Spell out for me the name of the shule she wrote about."

"W-o-l-b-o-r-s-k-a", I slowly spell.

He responds, "Ah, the Wolborska shule. That was somewhere else." I guess it is not our shule after all.

Our conversation is prompting more childhood memories. Dad says, "I love synagogue choirs. I always have. As a kid in Lodz, on Friday nights I would go to the synagogue on Zochodnia Street just to listen to the choir. That synagogue was called the Vilker Synagogue. This wasn't our family's shule, but it was still close to home, maybe a five to ten-minute walk." Here we go, yet another synagogue in the crowded Lodz synagogue landscape. I stop Dad for a moment to check Google Maps. The walking distance from where this synagogue once stood to where Dad's family lived is a six-minute walk. He continues, "I went on my own." I wonder about his father or brother. "No, it was just me."

"How old were you when you were doing this?" I ask.

"From about the age of ten. I kept going until the war broke out when I was fourteen," he answers. He describes the scene: "The conductor was in the middle. There were about 20 men and boys in the choir, standing in a U shape." Dad's hands are on the move. "On this side were the sopranos. On that side were the altos. These were the boys. Their voices hadn't broken yet. Behind them were the men." Dad sighs. "It was such beautiful *chazanut* (prayer singing). I loved it."

He starts to sing some of the Shabbat Friday night prayers. I'm afraid that the Prince family has not been endowed with melodic voices. He continues, "A friend of mine from primary school, Heniek Koswoski, sang in that choir. I remember the conductor very clearly. He had long hair. That was very unusual for the time." I recall that whenever a guest *chazan* (cantor) or liturgical choir comes to Melbourne, Dad always wants to attend. He is usually excited for weeks before the performance. I have always known this. What I hadn't known was that this enthusiasm began in the Lodz synagogues of his childhood.

Dad is humming some familiar liturgical tunes. Then he opens his eyes and says, "You know what? I remember the name of the *chazan* of that shule. Raskin was his name." These spurts of memory thrill me. He continues, "I bumped into him after the war in Munich. He was on the other side of the road but I recognised him immediately and crossed over to introduce myself. I said to him something like, 'You don't know me, but I went to your shule every Friday night.'"

Tears are welling up in my eyes. "How did he react?" I ask.

"He embraced me," Dad answers. We don't know *chazan* Raskin's war story. I can only imagine his emotions when meeting this young man, barely out of his teens, who remembered and appreciated his lost life.

Dad adds, "I think he immigrated to America and became a *chazan* in a big city. Maybe Philadelphia?" I start Googling and find an advertisement for "High Holy Days" at the Seagull Hotel at Miami Beach for September 1971. It announces: "The Famous Lodz Ober Cantor LEIB RASKIN Formerly of Mt Eden Center Bronx, N.Y. Will Officiate." I think we have found him. Dad's concluding words about him are, "Maybe 25 or 30 years after I met him in Munich, I remember reading in the *Australian Jewish News* that the famous *chazan* Raskin had died."

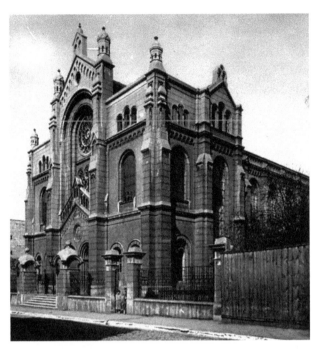

Top: Wolczanska Street Synagogue, the synagogue Dad's family attended in Lodz

Bottom left: My younger son, Noey Kolt & Dad, on the site where the Wolczanska Street Synagogue once stood. March of the Living, Lodz, 2009

Bottom right: My older son, Gali Kolt & Dad, outside Dad's home (1936–1940), Aleja (Avenue) 1-go-Maja No.7, 2006

Wednesday 25 May 2020

Tova outlines the work that was allocated to people in the ghetto. This triggers Dad to tell me about his father's first job in the ghetto, cleaning bricks from destroyed or partially destroyed buildings and stacking them, ready for re-use. It was miserable work. One day, the chief building engineer, Szper, who my grandfather knew before the war through his work as a building draughtsman for the city of Lodz, spotted him. He instructed my grandfather to come to his office the next morning where he gave him a new job working on plans for the ghetto. I do wonder what they were building; I figure something was being done with all those clean, stacked, used bricks.

Dad attributes his father's survival through the years in the ghetto to this stroke of luck (one of many). There are three basic reasons. Firstly, he was able to work indoors, out of the elements. He was warm and as comfortable as possible in the circumstances. Secondly, he was no longer doing heavy manual labour, with all the risks and added burdens of hard physical work. Thirdly, he was able to somehow sneak out with pieces of timber in his bag. Their family would then trade that timber for bread and vegetables. Dad explains, "As strange as it sounds, things were easier for us in the later stages of the ghetto because of my father's new job."

As an aside, Dad adds that chief building engineer Szper was a convert. "In or out?" I ask. In other words, did he convert *into* Judaism? Or did he convert to Christianity *out of* Judaism?

Dad looks at me like I'm an idiot. "Who would convert into Judaism? Of course, he converted out. How would he get a job as the chief building engineer of the city of Lodz otherwise?" I do feel a little naïve. He may have converted *out*, but to the Germans, he was still *in*, and ended up sharing the fate of the rest of the Jews of the Lodz Ghetto.

Wednesday 27 May 2020

Tova writes about Mordechai Chaim Rumkowski, the controversial head of the Judenrat. As an aside, she mentions a play that her brother, Abraham Cykiert, wrote about Rumkowski called *Emperor of the Ghetto*. It was written and performed in Melbourne in the 1990s. I remember it well. When teaching the Holocaust to Jewish high school students, I would take the whole year level to see it. The acclaimed Australian actor, Alan Hopgood, *became* Rumkowski in this one-man play. It was a riveting performance that captured the ambiguities and the strongly divided opinions and emotions that Rumkowski elicited from Lodz survivors.

We read that Rumkowski had believed that Hans Biebow, the German chief administrator of the ghetto, would save him and his wife and adopted son from Auschwitz. When Rumkowski asked that his brother and family could also be saved, Biebow refused. Both brothers and their families were placed together on the train to Auschwitz-Birkenau.

Tova writes this as important historical information for her reader. Dad witnessed the event in real time. He remembers the scene as if it happened yesterday. It took place at 16 Jacuba Street.

"What's that? Where's that?" I ask.

Dad responds, "It was a *ressort* where German uniforms were made by ghetto inmates." In ghetto parlance, a *ressort* is a slave labour factory. I know this, but I didn't always. I tell Dad that when I was young and Mum talked about going to 'resorts' in the Warsaw Ghetto, I was confused.

"I wondered how Mum could be relaxing by a swimming pool while she was starving," I confess to Dad.

He looks at me in wonder and says, "Hmm, yes, I can see how you could've thought that."

Back to Rumkowski and Biebow at the *ressort* on 16 Jacuba Street. Dad tells me just how close he was to them. "As close as I am now to the end of this room."

I gasp and add, "I guess you had to be, otherwise you wouldn't have been able to hear them."

Dad continues, "I saw and heard them arguing. Rumkowski's brother was standing behind him, as the argument went backwards and forwards. I remember Biebow yelling, 'Why should he stay here?'" Dad remembers that after a while Rumkowski turned to his brother and said, "Let's go together." And so, their fraternal fate was sealed and off they were sent to Auschwitz-Birkenau. Dad, with his parents and brother, were transported to the same destination a mere two days later. The very last transport from the Lodz Ghetto to Auschwitz-Birkenau. The last remaining ghetto in all of Europe had been liquidated.

The *ressort* at 16 Jacuba Street played a role for Dad's family at this time. About 500 Jews were to remain in the ghetto after its liquidation for the euphemistically called purpose of 'cleaning up'. They were required to sort through every room in every apartment in every building, collecting items that could be of use to the Germans. These belongings of the murdered Jews of Lodz were sent to Germany.

Dad's small family of four was supposed to be part of this group of 500 (which eventually grew to over 800 people), ordered to stay at 16 Jacuba Street until the last transport had left and to be spared Auschwitz-Birkenau. Not to be spared death, but death at Auschwitz-Birkenau. "How come you were part of this group?" I ask.

Dad says, "I remember distinctly what happened. We (Dad, Israel and Heniek) were working in the *ressort*. Our boss, Weinberg, who was head of the electrotechnical department, gathered all those who worked there, and their families, to be the ones to stay behind and 'clean up'."

I jump in, "So what happened? Why didn't you stay behind?"

Dad goes on, "We ended up sleeping there, in the *ressort*, for only one night. Some 'toughs' came in, some low-lifes, maybe like mafia. They threw us, and others, out of the building and took our places. And so we were put on the next, the last, train to Auschwitz-Birkenau." This is a new story for me.

Sunday 31 May 2020

Today we read about the deportation of Tova from the Lodz Ghetto to Auschwitz-Birkenau. Here we go again. I gulp for air. I know what's coming—in broad strokes anyway. But, as always, it is the individual's experience that is so powerfully absorbing.

Tova, her little sister and mother, remained indoors hoping to evade the latest roundup. When she thought the coast was clear, Tova poked her head out of the front door to see if her father was returning home. She was spotted and they were nabbed. They were transported by truck to the train station and from there onto the cattle cars to Auschwitz-Birkenau. Both Dad and I appreciate her honesty and expression of the guilt she would forever carry. Tova knew that the fate of her family was not her doing, but, she writes, "I feel guilty because I accelerated it."

Tova describes the line-ups and separation from her mother and little sister upon arrival. A starvation diet, the futile hope of finding her father and her other sisters whom she believed had also been sent to the extermination camp, sadistic overseers, sickness, time spent in the hospital and an encounter with Dr Mengele. She endured two months of daily terror and cruelty.

And then she was transported to a work camp in Germany named Torgau. Neither Dad nor I have heard of this one. Tova worked twelve-hour shifts in the ammunition factory. Again, conditions were appalling. She writes, "It was marginally better for us than Auschwitz." Auschwitz is like the benchmark of all camps. Every Holocaust experience seems to be compared to it.

Tova was liberated from Torgau on 25 April 1945. American soldiers were welcomed. Russian soldiers were feared.[27] Tova fled and made her way into the American Zone of Germany. She spent some time with a rag-tag group of other Polish Jewish survivors in an abandoned home of Germans. Sounds like Dad's immediate post-liberation experience. Through sheer luck she found her brother, Abraham, and together they

---

27. Russian soldiers had a frightening reputation for drunkeness, theft and rape.

went to Switzerland to recuperate. There, they joined a group of young people learning agricultural skills to prepare for their futures in Palestine. This tug to participate in the Zionist cause was powerful. Most survivors considered it, even if they eventually emigrated elsewhere.

Tova completes her memoir with a few stand-alone, poignant short episodes from her later life. She writes about her arrival in Australia and finding out, a few years after the end of the war, that she has one surviving sister, Mirla. We learn about her marriage to George, who managed to flee Austria not long after Germany's annexation of the country in 1938. He spent the war years in the British West Indies. Tova recounts their family life, George's illness and his eventual death. She augments her memoir with a number of deeply personal reflections and acknowledges that "life can be lonely at times". Nevertheless, Tova has many constructive lessons to impart to her readers concerning the importance of a positive attitude and continual engagement with life.

While reading this concluding section, I hope that I am channelling some of Tova's positive energy to Dad. I think I fail. All he says at the end is, "I too know what it's like to be lonely."

Tuesday 2 June 2020

One of our long-awaited memoirs is delivered today. Dad has made it his job to bring in my mail. I haven't checked my mailbox for months. That would deprive him of one of his few remaining errands during this lockdown period when government restrictions are curtailing our usual daily activities. Dad brings the package in. He has no idea about the contents. I tell him that this package is for us and unpack the book excitedly. It was written by Emanuel Tanay, one of Dad's Munich colleagues.

Passport to Life: Autobiographical Reflections on the Holocaust
Emanuel Tanay

Published by Forensic Press, 2004

T his memoir seems hefty to me. The book is thick and the writing is
small and closely-spaced. For me, this is a positive sign. It signifies
that we will be well occupied for a few weeks.

I remember meeting Emanuel Tanay back in 1998 at the Munich
student reunion in Upstate New York. He was a distinguished-looking
and charismatic man. I knew he had studied medicine in Munich and
that he became a psychiatrist in USA. He was also one of the organisers
of the reunions and edited the short-lived newsletter that the Survivor
Students produced during the 1990s. He features prominently in *The New
Life: Jewish Students of Postwar Germany* by Jeremy Varon (our original
project). He also appears frequently in Dad's Munich photos, especially
the images of their out-of-town trips. Therefore, I am not surprised to
learn that he was the leader of the first Jewish Students' Union excursion
in the summer of 1946.

Interestingly, Emanuel started his student career in the field of
political science. He viewed those who studied medicine negatively. In his
own words, "We in the social sciences… viewed medical students with
disdain. They were parochial, preoccupied with passing examinations."
Nevertheless, he did change direction, dramatically, and ended up
enrolling in the medical faculty. It seems that he, like the majority of the
Munich students, eventually took a more practical approach geared to his
future livelihood.

On the first page of his memoir Emanuel writes, "The Holocaust and
forensic psychiatry have been the twin poles of my life. My professional
life was, for the most part, devoted to the study of people who had killed
someone; people who wanted to kill me dominated the early part of my
life."

I feel that a person who describes their life in this manner will indeed
have written a hefty book.

Emanuel Tanay's love for America, and what he sees as American liberal values, shines through from the beginning and, as we will find, permeates throughout his memoir. Emanuel passed away in 2014. I imagine that he would have been turning in his grave during the Trump era.

Interestingly, he has some strong opinions that go against the grain of mainstream thought in the study of the Holocaust. He expresses these with confidence and certainty. This makes for compelling and thought-provoking reading. For me. I am not so sure about Dad. I am not sure he is picking up on all the nuances. I feel rude and more than a little obnoxious, but I do test this out now and then. I am right. Sadly. I can't quite figure out if this is because Dad is drifting off for a catnap here and there, or whether he is only partially focused on the content and just enjoying hearing my voice as I read to him. Or is it simply that he isn't understanding all that I am reading? I am saddened by this realistic possibility. The dilemma I now face is whether to re-read and then explain certain ideas and opinions that Emanuel expresses. Or to leave it alone and mull through these in my head. On my own. I end up cherry-picking and doing both.

Sunday 7 June 2020

Emanuel's hometown was Miechow, a small town about 40 kilometres north of Krakow. Emanuel's parents were the two dentists in town. The two doctors and the two lawyers were also Jews. Dad and I laugh together.

Miechow. "A *shtetl*. A hole," is Dad's predictable opinion. Being a Lodzer, and therefore a city slicker, makes Dad a snob. This is a repeat of his opinion about other Polish places—other than Lodz or Warsaw or Krakow—that we have encountered during our reading. I think it's funny that he can be a snob about a community that no longer exists. This is also reminiscent of my mother's Warsaw snobbery about Dad coming from the industrial city of Lodz. When they argued, she would often fling that accusation at him.

Monday 8 June 2020

Today is cold but sunny. We sit outside to catch some wintry rays. We keep shifting our seats, trying to follow the sun.

***

Describing his education in a Polish (non-Jewish) school, Emanuel refers to the epic poem *Pan Tadeusz*, written by the nation's greatest poet, Adam Mickiewicz, in 1834 and memorised by every Polish school student to this day. Emanuel writes the first words, "Lithuania, my fatherland." Dad doesn't miss a beat and recites the whole first stanza in Polish.

> *Litwo! Ojczyzno moja! ty jesteś jak zdrowie;*
> *Ile cię trzeba cenić, ten tylko się dowie,*
> *Kto cię stracił. Dziś piękność twą w całej ozdobie*
> *Widzę i opisuję, bo tęsknię po tobie.*

> O Lithuania, my homeland! Thou art like health;
> Only he can truly appreciate thy worth
> Who has lost thee. Now I see and sing thy beauty
> In all of its glory, because I long for thee[28].

I love moments like these. I try to figure out exactly why. The recitation makes Dad youthful; the decades seem to disappear in the telling. There is also something exciting about the corroboration between the written word and Dad's recollection. I am proud of Dad's memory. He hasn't lost it yet—phew. Does the writing somehow authenticate Dad's memory? Is there something about the combination of voices that point towards a picture of a Polish-Jewish childhood that once was?

Dad tells me about an altercation he had with a Lithuanian man who worked in the same factory as him in Melbourne in early 1950s. This 'new Australian' (as immigrants were sometimes called at the time) insisted

---

28. Translation by Christian Kasparek, a Scottish-born writer and translator of Polish descent. Wikipedia en.wikipedia.org/wiki/Pan_Tadeusz

that Adam Mickiewicz was really a Lithuanian poet and that his name was Mickiewiczus. Dad countered that no, he was, in fact, Polish.[29] It was as if the fierce multi-ethnic and national identity issues of the nineteenth and twentieth centuries had entered Granowski's Engineering Factory in Richmond, Melbourne. Dad says that this fellow would have been happy to continue the 'discussion' outside. My Dad? Not so much. Another new story for me.

Emanuel evocatively describes his childhood in Miechow with his parents and younger sister. It was filled with love, culture and privilege in a relatively small Polish town. The intellectual refinement of his parents and their integration of a proud Jewish and Polish identity paint an idyllic picture. They were known and respected by all. Prewar Polish Jewish life was indeed diverse.

Then everything changed. The Germans invaded. Emanuel's family, like so many others, made a dash eastward before turning around and returning home when it became clear that the Germans had outflanked them.

The Miechow Ghetto was delineated. Emanuel celebrated his *bar mitzvah* a few days before the Jews were ordered to move there.

"Tell me about your *bar mitzvah*," I ask Dad.

He describes what he can remember of the joint *bar mitzvah* he celebrated with his twin brother Heniek in April 1938. "It took place at home. Not in the shule. The Sefer Torah (Torah scroll) was brought to our place. The shule was at the end of our street, so it wasn't a big deal. It was just the family. The aunts, uncles, cousins too. I remember that my (maternal) grandfather was very emotional. He actually died not that long afterwards."

As twins, I wonder how the various Torah and other readings were divided between the brothers. Dad tells me that he chanted the section called the *Maftir*, the last section of the weekly reading from the Torah. And he did the *Haftarah*. This is a section from the Book of Prophets that has a link to the particular Torah reading of a particular week.

I ask, "Who was your *bar mitzvah* teacher?"

---

29. Adam Mickiewicz was brought up in a Polish-Lithuanian milieu in the first half of the 19th century when Russia ruled over the Polish and Lithuanian homelands. Both Poles and Lithuanians claim him as their national poet. He wrote in the Polish language.

I don't expect him to remember but he does. "It was Mr Landau. He lived at 64 Piotrkowska. He originally came from a small town called Czortkow. It was in south-west Poland in those days."

"So, if you did the *Maftir* and the *Haftarah*, what did Uncle Heniek do?" I wonder, out loud.

"I don't remember," Dad says sheepishly.

The Judenrat was established. We are both fascinated by Emanuel's lack of ambivalence about the role of the Judenrat in Miechow, and all Judenrate (plural). It seems that Emanuel isn't ambivalent about much. This is one of his strongly held opinions that goes against the more conventional interpretations in Holocaust scholarship. It is one that I know Dad will engage with. Emanuel is adamant that ambiguity at best, and criticism at worst, of the actions of these leaders is misguided and mistaken. He is unreserved in his lavish praise for Judenrat leaders. Unequivocally, he credits these leaders with doing the best they could in near-impossible circumstances. Amongst Holocaust academics, the role of the Judenrate is a much discussed and vexed issue. Their role as would-be saviours or damned collaborators are two extreme positions. Most respected scholars are nuanced in their approaches. They distinguish between Judenrat leaders in different ghettos. They ponder the 'choiceless choices' they were forced to make. They also distinguish between the first generation of such leaders and their successors, who are usually seen as less suitable. They study different scenarios and the variety of responses. This is complex stuff.

We think that perhaps Emanuel is extrapolating his observations about Miechow to his opinion about all Judenrate. And then Dad says, "You know what? I bet that his dad was one of the communal leaders. And therefore, he would've been on the Miechow Judenrat."

"You're right", I respond. We know his parents were the only two dentists in town. And the only two doctors and two lawyers in town were also Jewish. Once they were all shoved into the ghetto, who would be on the Miechow Judenrat? In most ghettos, it was the professionals who formed the leadership. This is not mentioned in Emanuel's memoir. It is our guesswork. No more.

As Dad leaves to return to his home around the corner, he thanks me, as he always does. Today he adds, "The hours with you give me life."

Tuesday 9 June 2020

Conditions became increasingly challenging and precarious in the ghetto. However, Emanuel and his family were sort of protected, for a limited time anyway. The chief of the Gestapo in Miechow would summon his father to play chess with him on a regular basis. He also provided dental treatment for at least a dozen Germans. And then the deportations began. The family, with the assistance of Polish friends and acquaintances, evaded a major deportation. They returned to a shrunken ghetto, diminished both in its physical area and its number of Jews.

Emanuel's parents secured false identity papers for him and sent him out of the Miechow Ghetto. He had *dobry wyglod*. He did not have what is considered to be 'typical' Jewish features. This was a good start, but it took much more to stay alive. So began 14-year-old Emanuel's terrifying odyssey over the next three years or so.

He spent about a year in a monastery as a young novice, frantically cramming in an abridged, but sufficient, familiarity with Catholic doctrine and prayers. He was constantly on guard. Anything he said or did might give him away. He endured sexual abuse, by the person who was supposed to be his protector. The falsehood of his life took a mental and emotional toll. When one of the priests began to grow suspicious, he decided to leave the monastery.

Dad stops our reading to tell me about a family friend who had spent part of the war hiding in a convent. He told Dad that every night, if not a few times a night, a different nun would enter his room to have sex with him. He was in fear for his life. I assume he was scared the nuns would discover that he was circumcised and denounce him as a Jew. "No, no, you don't understand," says Dad. "He was so exhausted from these nocturnal engagements that he wanted to refuse some of them. But he was scared that perhaps the ones he refused would get so offended they would denounce him." I am speechless.

After leaving the monastery, Emanuel found refuge living with a Polish man. He took on a new identity as the man's nephew and assisted him in his smuggling operations. His life was endangered for so many reasons. There were countless close calls requiring him to move to new places and much-anticipated clandestine meetings with his mother and sister. This reads almost like a 'Boys Own Adventure' book. Emanuel was bold and daring, enterprising and quick-thinking. The single but all-important factor that prevents this from being 'merely' a dangerous and heart-palpitating saga, is Emanual's writing style. It is dense and detailed. An overlay of self-reflection, search for meaning, and analysis adds to its weightiness. After all, this is the memoir of a psychiatrist.

Wednesday 10 June 2020

Emanuel Tanay heads in a direction that I knew he would, sooner or later. He bluntly and openly addresses the challenging topic of Polish-Jewish relations during the war. His own survival narrative included both Poles who protected him and Poles who were ready to turn on him. His war experience was a tightrope balance between these two opposing forces. One meant instant death. The other, a chance at life. Like other memoirists, Emanuel fully appreciated the dreadful suffering of the Polish people under German occupation. They were conquered, persecuted, imprisoned and murdered in significant numbers. But did they—some? many?—need to denounce Jews? He didn't expect heroism. But he did expect decency.

This divisive and uncomfortable topic has been raging since the end of the war. Scholars characterise it as an issue of competing memories and narratives. The debate can be bitter and rancorous, and it certainly includes an emotive competition in the claims of suffering. I have been immersed, personally, in this issue for a long time. I have studied and researched it. I have incorporated this topic in March of the Living educational sessions for students. I have organised Australian Jewish young people to meet with Polish Christian young people, in Poland. I have railed against those in the Australian Jewish community who espouse views that Poland is nothing but a 'Jewish cemetery'. I have protested against attitudes that smear all Poles with a uniform antisemitic brush and influenced the thinking of others. I have presented papers on this topic at conferences, including at Yad Vashem. In 2017, I even became a co-recipient of the Henryk Slawik Award, bestowed by the Australian Society of Polish Jews and their Descendants (ASPJ) for my "long standing contribution to enhancing relations between Jewish and non-Jewish Poles both in Australia and Poland".

I have had partners in dialogue. Polish people who haven't shied away from the ugliness and hurt of this issue. We have met and talked with open minds and hearts. Many Polish people are prepared to confront, head on, this dreadful past. Unfortunately however, the present Polish government has outlawed any whiff of an accusation that Poles played any role in the murder of their Jewish compatriots.[30] It is frightening to think that if I had written this in Poland in 2018, I could have been arrested. The role of Poles during the Holocaust is an ongoing issue. However, stifling honest discourse and attempting a whitewash of history undoes the slow, careful and sensitive progress that has been made.

***

We seem to be taking longer to read this memoir than the earlier ones. Partly because we are spending fewer hours reading together. As the numbers of new coronavirus cases come down, Melbourne is 'opening up' more and more. Life is creeping back to normal—or, rather, advancing forward to the 'new normal'. There is more that I need to squeeze into each day, that I *want* to squeeze into each day. There is more on my mind and on my plate. I try explaining this to Dad. However, his world has not altered one iota. None of his activities have resumed. Nor are they likely to in the near future. After all, his age group is the most vulnerable. I have started guiltily pushing our starting time from 2pm to 2.30pm. And then to 3pm.

---

30. In 2018 the Polish government made it a criminal offence to accuse Poland of complicity in Nazi war crimes. The law was amended so that it was no longer a criminal offence, but it is still a possible civil course of action.

Thursday 11 June 2020

Emanuel hatched a plan to escape from Poland to Hungary, which had not yet been occupied by the Germans. He led his mother, sister and childhood girlfriend in this audacious escape. Through mountains and valleys, with some trustworthy and some not-so-trustworthy people smugglers, they crossed borders evading guards and police. They made it to Budapest.

The Hungarian place names are much more difficult for me to pronounce than Polish ones. Admittedly, there seem to be fewer letters in each word and fewer 'scz' combinations but my total lack of familiarity with the Hungarian language renders me a corrupter and mutilator of this difficult tongue. I say to Dad, "I know what I am saying is all wrong, but not even you can correct my Hungarian." He smiles in agreement.

The lull in fear that the little group experienced was interrupted in March 1944. The German army marched into Hungary and occupied its former ally. Anti-Jewish ordinances were introduced. For a while Emanuel managed to hide his family in plain sight. During an attempted escape with Jewish underground members, he was arrested by Hungarian border guards and incarcerated in a notorious prison. They were turned over to the Gestapo. We read about escapes, reincarcerations and imprisonment in a concentration camp. We meet a myriad of larger-than-life characters.

In the midst of our breathtaking reading, Dad says, "I should've written things down years ago. There is so much I can't remember anymore. Why didn't I write it down? Was I too stupid or primitive to do so?" My opinion? He was too absorbed and preoccupied with his work. He was busy establishing himself and providing for us, his family. However, I don't believe it was merely the hunger for a decent livelihood that drove him. Dad was one of those lucky people who loved his work. It was an all-encompassing life.

One episode we read today stands out for its far-fetched implausibility. I re-read it aloud to Dad a few times. Emanuel refers to a time when he was incarcerated in Szeged, a major city about 175 kilometres south-east of Budapest. Adolf Eichmann was visiting Gestapo headquarters in Szeged and Emanuel was tasked with washing his car. His black Mercedes. Dad and I are both speechless. What is there to say? We know that truth can be stranger than fiction. How much more so when it comes to the Shoah.

Friday 12 June 2020

Emanuel expresses yet another staunch opinion that runs contrary to mainstream Jewish Holocaust scholarship. Do I share it with Dad? Do I write about it? I decide to do both. While in the Foe Street prison in Budapest, Emanuel met Peretz Goldstein. They were incarcerated together. I know that name—Peretz was one of 37 Jewish parachutists from the Yishuv (Jewish community) in Mandatory Palestine who were dropped behind enemy lines by the British Armed Forces. While Emanuel describes their intense discussions and growing friendship, I know that Peretz will not survive. He will die in the Oranienburg concentration camp in March 1945.

Hannah Szenes (pronounced 'Senesh') is the most famous of these incredibly brave young Jews who parachuted into Europe to assist anti-Nazi forces. We learn that she was held in the floor below Emanuel and Peretz in the Foe Street prison. We know that she also will not survive. She entered the annals of Jewish history as a courageous and daring heroine, as well as a talented writer of poems. Every Israeli child learns about Hannah Szenes. She is a model of daring nerve.

Emanuel did not question the personal courage of the Palestinian Jewish parachutists. In fact, he admired them for their incredible bravery. However, he did criticise the whole parachute project undertaken by the Jewish leadership in Palestine. He claimed that the presence of these parachutists endangered the lives of Jews like him. Those under arrest in Hungary. Due to their association with the parachutists, Emanuel's group was accused of being spies for the British Armed Forces. Emanuel went further. He refuted the view of Israeli academics that Hannah Szenes had a positive psychological impact on the Resistance. He claimed that, at the time, next to no-one even knew about them or their mission to help save some of the remaining Jews of Europe. In truth, most of the parachutists were indeed apprehended soon after their arrival in Hungary.

I need to think carefully about all of this. In my education and in my own teaching, Hannah and her fellow parachutists have been lionised as the most courageous of heroes. While they were not particularly successful in their mission, in their status as Zionist emissaries coming to save the Jews of Europe, they are giants. This is part of the Israeli narrative. I like to think that as a Holocaust educator, I taught with nuance and the presentation of different viewpoints. I now realise that perhaps I was nowhere near as nuanced as I believed.

There is one more personal addendum to this matter. In 1991, when I was studying at Yad Vashem, one of the parachutists of 1944, Reuven Dafni, addressed the group. He had actually parachuted into Yugoslavia with Hannah Szenes. He told us that Hannah crossed the border into Hungary and he was instructed to wait for her in Yugoslavia for three weeks. If she didn't return, he should assume she had been captured and leave. He ended up waiting for six weeks. She had indeed been captured.

While reading Emanuel's strongly held views, I feel somewhat traitorous to Reuven Dafni.

Sunday 14 June 2020

We begin today's reading with the war ending in Budapest. Like in most other testimonies, liberation for Emanuel is a mixed and complex experience. I am looking forward to reading Emanuel's 'after' narrative. For one thing, it brings us closer to his Munich student days and thus the convergence of his story with that of my parents. In addition, I feel drained by the tension of all his near-misses, risks, dangers and vulnerabilities. I mention this to Dad. He says, "So how do you think he felt?"

With his usual daring and ingenuity, Emanuel managed to get to Munich. No mean feat. Together with his mother and sister, he moved into a DP camp near Munich called Deggendorf DP camp. I have not heard of this one. Dad says, "Helenka Ball and her mother, Mrs Wolkovitch, were there." Helenka and her husband, Szymek, were family friends of ours in Melbourne. Helenka was from Lodz too. I knew that her father had been a barber in a building across the road from where Dad's family lived on Zawadska Street. Dad continues to tell me that after the war he went to Deggendorf to visit them. He adds, "I think Mrs Wolkovitch wanted to match me up with Helenka." I've never heard this one before.

Later, Emanuel and his small family were sent to Landsberg DP Camp. This place I do know. It has been well-documented. Also, my mother-in-law went to school there. Emanuel was most unhappy with their living conditions and extricated them from Landsberg, in order to live independently and freely in Munich. They moved into the home of a German woman in the district of Schwabing.

"Ah, that's the other side of the railway station. Uncle Heniek lived there too," pipes in Dad. I have never thought to ask Dad what happened to his brother Heniek in the years after Dad moved to Munich to study. I have been so engrossed in my dad's narrative that I have not asked about his twin brother. Until today. Dad tells me, "Heniek moved to Munich not all that long after me. He thought that maybe he would also give study a shot. He started electrical engineering at the Technische Hochschule."

I interrupt to ask, "That means that he must've sat and passed the Verification Commission exams, no?"

"I suppose so," responds Dad.

I know that Uncle Heniek did not end up studying in Munich, so I inquire, "What went wrong?"

Dad is quiet for a little while. He is collecting his thoughts and his words. Maybe his emotions too. "The course was too difficult. For engineering you needed high-level maths. There was simply too much to catch up on. It was one of the most difficult courses of all."

"So, what did he end up doing during those years?" I wonder.

"Willy Lermer (whose book we have recently read) got him a job working for the Joint. It was office work. Administration of some sort."

We are told that Emanuel's mother got a job as a dentist in the

Foerenwald DP camp. I wonder to Dad, "Maybe she knew Buba?" This is at the time my grandmother, Dr Rosa Salzberg[31] was the chief dentist for the Joint in Munich. Dad shrugs his shoulders. We'll never know.

Like Dad, Emanuel registered at Foerenwald DP camp, but lived in Munich. Like Dad, he needed to receive care packages so that he could sell the goods and scratch out a source of income.

Emanuel mentions a ski trip to Garmish-Paterkirchen. Dad says, "That's where we went on our honeymoon." I already know this, but I love hearing it. Admittedly, I find many of Dad's repetitions a little grating, but never this one. The thought of my parents young, in love, and on their honeymoon warms my heart.

We read about Emanuel's sister, Olenka. We learn that she had a troubled life and died prematurely in her early forties. I feel gutted. I need a break from reading. It's a reminder of how I felt when reading about Lidia Eichenholz's less-than-satisfying postwar life.

Monday 15 June 2020

Dad and I are both excited when Emanuel begins to write about his student days. Some of his story is familiar to us from Jeremy Varon's *The New Life*, the book that started us on our reading journey. But there are new revelations as well.

Halinka, Emanuel's love interest, applied to enter the UNRRA University in Munich to study pharmacy in 1945. Dad did not arrive in Munich until 1946. At this stage in our reading, we don't know if Halinka was accepted into the course, or, if she was, whether she transferred to the Ludwig Maximilian University when UNRRA University closed. Dad says, "There was a Halinka doing pharmacy in the semester ahead of me. I think she committed suicide later, in Israel. What's her surname?" There is no surname. Could it be the same Halinka? Later, we discover it is not Emanuel's love interest who committed suicide. I am relieved.

---

31. Salzberg is the German spelling of Salcburg.

Not long after that, Emanuel was accepted to study political science at the UNRRA University after falsely stating that he had already matriculated. Dad did the same later. As did Mum and hundreds of others. Emanuel describes the foundation of the Jewish Students' Union by Jozef Silverman in December 1945. He was there when the organisation was established.

I say to Dad, "No wonder he was involved in creating those alumni newsletters all those decades later. No wonder he was central in organising the American reunions and is one of the key people in Varon's study."

Dad agrees. "Yes, he was there from the very beginning." Dad arrived in Munich just a few months later. The Jewish Students' Union accomplished a lot in a very short period of time.

I muse, "I think he has a sense of ownership. Not in a possessive way. But he's proud of all that they achieved."

We read about the outings of the Survivor Students. We find out that it was Emanuel who organised the excursions. He appears in every single one of Dad's outdoor group photos. He is reasonably easy to identify with his signature glasses and boyish looks.

The Zionist establishment hurled criticisms at the students. Jeremy Varon addresses this issue at length in his book. In summary, the students were branded as selfish and judged for placing personal aspirations ahead of the collective Jewish people's aspiration for a homeland. It was felt that their energies should have been directed towards the Jewish State-to-be and not their goals of self-improvement and professional qualifications. Emanuel is strident in his rather militant role in combatting these critics and their negative attitudes to the Survivor Students and their endeavours.

Emanuel engaged a tutor to prepare for entrance exams to the 'proper' university, Ludwig Maximilian University. He paid the tutor in cigarettes and then, when he realised that the fellow was seriously hungry, food was added to the transaction. Dad pipes in, "Our tutor ate like a horse!" I knew that Dad and his roommate, Arek Lukrec, also hired a tutor to ready them for the same set of gruelling exams. The Verification Commission exams. I knew that they had a high opinion of her. But I didn't know that she ate with them. Let alone how much she ate.

Emanuel's mother remarried. Emanuel lets the reader know that this man lacked his father's looks, education, refinement and charm. I have already ruminated on 'replacement' spouses while reading Martin Lane's memoir. Except, back then, I didn't ask Dad about the second marriages of my grandparents. Now I do. I start with his father, my grandfather, Israel. We called him by a mash-up of the Polish word for grandfather, *dziadek*. The '*dz*', for an English speaker, sounds like a 'j', so phonetically the word sounds like 'jadek'. Somehow, in my family, that got shortened to 'Jaja' which is what we called my grandfather. The next generation—my and my brother's children—also call my dad 'Jaja'. My brother's grandchildren call him what sounds like 'Judge', a shorter version of 'Jaja'. So, it seems to have lasted a few generations. When our Israeli daughter-in-law refers to Dad as Jaja, I smile inwardly. It's such an unfamiliar term to her, but over time it has come to sound almost natural.

My jaja, Israel Prinz[32] did not remarry in Germany. But he did, in Melbourne, in 1955. To a woman, also a survivor, whom we called Buba Chana. Grandmother Chana. What did we know about her? Not much. She had been briefly married before the war and her first husband did not survive. She came from a small town called Zabludow, somewhere near Bialystok. That's about it. I ask Dad about how my grandfather met her and whether he had been out with other women beforehand. I draw a blank. Dad simply doesn't know. He explains, "We didn't talk about such things. Dad just came to us one day and informed us that he was getting married. We had never met her. We were not invited to the wedding." I am taken aback. Dad continues, "I know that sounds strange to you. But that's just how it was. It wasn't appropriate for us to be there. And also, it wasn't a big deal of a wedding. There was a rabbi, witnesses, I suppose, and finished. They were married." Where? Who was the rabbi? Who else may have been there? Dad has no idea. I ask him to go back into his treasure trove filing cabinet with the old-fashioned green dividers and see what he can, almost literally, dig up on the marriage. Perhaps a certificate, or something. We draw a blank.

32. Prinz is the German spelling of Princ.

I remember Buba Chana. She was a large woman, both in physique and character. I recall her warmth, her broad smile and full laugh. She used to tell Dad and my uncle Heniek that she loved them as if she had given birth to them herself. This isn't new information for me. But dwelling on it now, I am blown away by the depth and generosity of such a statement. True, they weren't young children and she didn't have to live with them and bring them up. In addition, since she never had children of her own, they didn't have to compete with anyone else (alive or dead) for her affection. Nevertheless, this statement is mind-blowing. I, for one, cannot imagine loving any children as much as the ones I gave birth to. Except for grandchildren. My children's children. That's how Buba Chana felt about us.

In the 1960s, Buba Chana and Jaja lived in the inner-city suburb of Brunswick where a once-substantial Jewish population was in decline. This was quite far from the more salubrious Jewish suburb of Caulfield where we lived. As a consequence, we didn't see my grandparents regularly. They certainly weren't a daily fixture of my childhood. We did, however, regularly celebrate Jewish festivals at Buba Chana and Jaja's home. They didn't travel on the Sabbath or Jewish festivals as they were religiously observant, so we would go to them in Brunswick. I felt their warm-heartedness from the first minute we arrived. There was a certain old-world European heaviness in their flat, materially evidenced by the furnishings and ornaments. It was like stepping back in time. Buba Chana's first language was Yiddish, so while she certainly understood and spoke Polish, my parents would conduct the conversations in Yiddish out of deference to her. Perhaps this is how I seem to have a semi-dormant and subliminal understanding of the language. Whenever I am exposed to Yiddish, I surprise myself with how much I can comprehend.

Buba Chana & Jaja Israel Prinz, Melbourne, c.1960

Tuesday 16 June 2020

I ask Dad about his father's level of Jewish observance. It seems that he became more religious after the war than he had been before. Dad confirms this, but tentatively. "Yes, my dad was *frumer* (more religious) in Germany, in Regensburg, than we were when I was growing up. But we had been quite traditional back in Lodz." In other words, Dad rejects the binary description of being either religious or not religious. His prewar family home sounds similar in its level of religiosity to many families I grew up with. It was a Jewish life that comfortably incorporated Jewish rituals without the burden of too many religious strictures. I wonder, aloud, if Dad knows why Jaja became more rigorous in his Jewish observance at this stage of his life. Was it related to beliefs about God? A search for meaning? A sense of a new beginning? Dad doesn't know.

"How would you describe your relationship with your father, here, in Melbourne?" I ask.

Dad is silent for a while before answering. "We spoke on the phone about every second day. I dropped into his place after work when I could." And then the guilt seeps out. "I should've spent more time with him. I didn't look after him enough." I wonder whether he feels that now that he is receiving care, or whether these sentiments reflect his feelings from that time. I verbalise this to Dad and he answers unequivocally, "both".

I vividly remember the morning after Buba Chana died. I was ten years old. I woke up to find my bedroom door closed which was most unusual. Then I heard wailing and crying. I recognised that these frightening sounds were from Jaja. Unbeknownst to me, Buba Chana had collapsed and died late the night before. This was my first encounter with death. However, as was common for the time, I did not go to her funeral. Over the following year, my grandfather was plagued with ill-health, operations and hospitalisations. I recall difficult visits and stress in the family. There were emotional discussions between Mum and Dad and my uncle Heniek and his wife, my aunt Fela. Medical decisions and convalescent arrangements were the main topics of conversation. In between, Dad was busy working in the pharmacy and was deeply involved at his Masonic

Lodge. It was a tense time. Then my grandfather passed away. I was eleven years old, considered still too young to attend a funeral. Jaja was 75 years old when he died. Of course, my brother and I thought he was a really, really old man.

What about the second marriage of Mum's mother, Buba Rosa? Dr Rosa Salzberg (nee Gringlas) married Szaja (pronounced 'Shaya') Wittelsohn, in Germany. My parents were their *shadchanim* (matchmakers). Szaja was my paternal grandfather's first cousin (Szaja's mother and Israel's mother were sisters). Dad says about this wedding, "It wasn't a big event. No fiesta. We weren't there. It just took place." I am curious to know when they married. I find an official German certificate of marriage dated 29 September 1950. The problem with that date is that my parents were already long gone by then. They left Germany in December 1949. And Dad remembers there being a wedding, even if he and Mum weren't in attendance. In addition, as he tells me, "I remember them living together. It's not like today, if they weren't married, they wouldn't be living together." This is a certainty. The only explanation is that the Jewish marriage ceremony took place much earlier than was registered with the German civil authority. I find a photo that might confirm my instincts. Buba Rosa and Szaja are dressed very formally. Looking at the camera but with their bodies towards each other. Next to Szaja is a woman and next to Buba is a man. On the back of the photo, in Polish, is written, "My dear children….With our witnesses, Toni and Huger." I don't recognise the handwriting but I do recognise Dad's smaller script in the bottom righthand corner, "Szaja & Nanna's wedding." I don't know why he calls her Nanna and not Buba. No-one ever did. I am making the (not large) leap that this photo was sent to Mum and Dad in Melbourne after the civil wedding on 29 September 1950. In addition, in traditional Jewish weddings, there must be two male witnesses. Therefore, I deduce that this is a photo of their civil wedding ceremony.

Civil wedding of Buba Rosa & Szaja Wittelsohn, with their witnesses,
Munich, September, 1950

Heiratsurkunde

(Standesamt München ___ **II** ___ Nr. *1568/1950*)

Der ___ Kaufmann Szaja W i t t e l s o h n,

israelitisch ___, wohnhaft ___ in München,

geboren am ___ 27. Februar 1898 ___ in ___ Lodz, Polen,

(Standesamt ___ Beurkundung nicht nachgewiesen ___ Nr. ___), und

die ___ Zahnärztin Rosa S a l t z b e r g, geborene Grünglass,

israelitisch ___, wohnhaft ___ in München,

geboren am ___ 20. Oktober 1903 ___ in ___ Warschau, Polen,

(Standesamt ___ Beurkundung nicht nachgewiesen ___ Nr. ___)

haben am ___ 29. September 1950 ___ vor dem Standesamt

München ___ **II** ___ die Ehe geschlossen.

Vermerke: ___

___

___

München ___ den 29. September 1950.

(Siegel)

Der Standesbeamte

[signature]

___

geb. bez.

Quitt. Nr. 56977.

1./49. 30' 0155

Civil marriage certificate for Buba Rosa & Szaja Wittelsohn

Who was Szaja Wittelsohn? He was born in Lodz in 1898 but had been living in Germany before the war. He had been married and divorced. He fled to the Soviet Union and survived the war there. When he returned to Munich, he owned a fur business. Long ago I claimed the single remaining clothing hanger from his business. I considered it a 'cool' ornament for my home. I still do.

On the smooth, shiny wood of the hanger is engraved the following:

Pelze
Wittelsohn
Munchen 15, Tel. 55012
Schwanthalerstr. 30

We always referred to Szaja by his first name. Not Jaja Szaja or Zeida (Yiddish for grandfather) or any other grandfatherly moniker. We never lived in the same country so no grandfatherly relationship was ever forged. Buba Rosa and Szaja did not migrate to Melbourne. Why not? Why would Mum and Buba separate after all they had been through together? They were the only two left from their family and together they had been to hell and back. Somehow, in my mind, I always had the following admirable answer. Szaja only wanted to go to Israel. There was no other option for him. For me, with my life-long Zionist fervour, this made perfect sense. To pursue the Zionist dream, even a family can be split up. Later I learned that this was a concoction of my imagination. The only accurate part is that he didn't want to go to Australia. So they didn't.

In Munich, Szaja had two surviving brothers and a sister, Leon, Aaron and Bella. His other siblings, Shmuel and Chayka, did not survive. For four siblings to be alive after the war was a rarity. These cousins of Dad's, the Wittelsohn clan, all appeared in the last, family prewar photo that Dad unearthed. Leon had been a businessman before the war and had never married. Dad remembers that he imported thermometers from Vienna to Lodz. After the Anschluss (annexation of Austria by Nazi Germany) of March 1938, it was no longer possible to source thermometers in Vienna so he turned to London instead. Before the war, Aaron had married someone from Lithuania and Bella had married a Mr Frankel and had a child. After

Szaja Wittelsohn's fur shop, Munich, late 1940s/early 1950s

the war, these siblings only had each other. No wonder the Wittelsohn siblings didn't want to separate. No wonder Szaja was not prepared to immigrate to Australia with Buba Rosa.

How long did they all remain in Munich? My sleuthing endeavours don't get me far. Two pieces of evidence point to the fact that the Wittelsohn siblings and Buba Rosa were still in Germany in 1954. My first piece of evidence is Buba Rosa's international driver's licence authorised in Munich and dated 11 January 1954. The second is a small section of a German newspaper column that reports Aaron Wittelsohn coming across an injured person on the road and racing them into a medical clinic. According to the news item, he was given the 1063rd Kavalier at the Wheel award by an official body called Transport Parliament. The date of this article is 17 September 1954.

Left: Buba Rosa's international driver's licence, issued in Munich, January 1954

Right: German newspaper article about Aaron Wittelsohn's 'Kavalier at the Wheel' award, September 1954

Then a third piece of evidence surfaces. While talking to my brother, Issy, on the phone, I tell him about my detective work. He says he received a present from Buba Rosa in 1954 when he was three years old. "What was it?" I ask. His answer? "Lederhosen." I am silent. Then we crack up laughing. Lederhosen are shorts, or more accurately breeches, that are quintessentially Bavarian. These days they are best known as a favourite Oktoberfest costume worn by men. Do I need any further proof that Buba Rosa was still in Germany in 1954? I rest my case.

And then we find the photo of Issy wearing his lederhosen. Mum and Buba Rosa are standing next to him. It seems that Buba visited us, before I was born, in 1954. She came bearing lederhosen.

Buba Rosa visiting Australia, with Mum & Issy dressed in lederhosen, Melbourne, 1954

I already know that Buba Rosa and Szaja spent a bit of time in the 1950s living in New York, together with Szaja's three siblings. I had always assumed they moved from Israel to New York and then later returned to Israel. What did 'a bit of time' in New York mean to me? Maybe a year or two? I was wrong. About everything. It turns out they went from Germany directly to America. I'm not sure what their visa status was. I can find no evidence of American citizenship or Green Cards. I only have one relevant document regarding Buba Rosa's sojourn in America, a permit to re-enter the United States. It is not easy to decipher. What exactly did it allow Buba Rosa to do? She was not an American citizen and therefore unable to come and go as she pleased. It seems that she was a 'nonquota immigrant,' whatever that may be. In the section entitled 'Country of which a citizen, subject or national' is typed 'Stateless'. I am taken aback. This document was issued in 1960. The war ended fifteen years earlier and my grandmother was still stateless. She was a citizen of nowhere. It seems that at an earlier stage she had applied for an extension of her American permit from 14 September 1959 to 14 September 1960. This new document extended that right for an additional year, until 14 September 1961. Her life in New York was a year-by-year proposition.

Perhaps even more interestingly, this document was issued in Melbourne. By Joseph P. Leahy, the American vice-consul. His stamp was embossed with the words, "Consular General of the U.S. of America. MELBOURNE, AUSTRALIA." She was visiting us when she applied for this extension. This matches with my brother's memories of going on a holiday with Buba Rosa to Surfers Paradise in Queensland in 1960. The timing makes sense. What doesn't make sense is that neither Dad nor my brother can remember her living in America when she visited us. They now have no idea at all.

Back in New York, I don't know whether Buba Rosa and Szaja lived with Szaja's siblings. The only relevant address I can find is for Aaron Wittelsohn. It is 790 Riverside Drive, way uptown in Washington Heights. Dad says, "I'm sure that they all lived together in the same apartment."

If Buba Rosa and Szaja were in Germany at least until 1954 and then went to New York, how long did they stay? Their Aliyah Certificate booklet notes that they arrived in Israel on 23 April 1964 on the ship *Olympia* from the USA and docked at Haifa port. Could they have lived in New York for ten whole years?

At the forefront of my mind is that at last my grandmother was not stateless. At last, in 1964, after nearly two decades from the end of the war, she had citizenship and a state to call home. I know I am a hopelessly romantic, old-school Zionist.

I do wonder if there was ever a consideration, even a minute one, that Buba Rosa and Szaja might go to Australia from America. Was there ever a 'fork in the road' moment? Or was it a *fait accompli* that Israel would be their next, and presumably final, destination?

I also wonder why my parents didn't go with them to America? Dad says, "There were never any conversations about it; things just sort of happened." This amazes me. How could this be? Dad just shrugs.

As an aside, Buba Rosa's Israeli Dental Association membership card is dated 13 November 1964. Seven months after their arrival. As another aside, their Aliyah Certificate booklet states that Szaja's mother's name was Malka Chana and his father was Henoch. Dad remembers that his father used to call him, "*Fetter* (uncle in Yiddish) Henoch."

In April 1966 our family (minus Issy who stayed in Melbourne because he was in Year 11) visited Israel for the first time. The trip was beyond exciting. Mum, Dad and I undertook the tedious plane trip with a sense of longing and adventure. The longing was to visit Buba Rosa and the adventure was to tour the State of Israel. It was a fulfilling and exhilarating journey. I may have been only eight years old but I was delighted to spend time with my grandmother. Szaja was a side-show, I'm afraid. I can still recall going shopping and visiting cafes in Dizingoff Street, Tel Aviv, the chicest place in 1960s Israel. Having coffee in sidewalk cafes was *de rigeur* in Tel Aviv long before it became a popular Melbourne pastime. I am forever grateful that my parents included me in all their tours. Often, I was the youngest person on the bus which made me feel privileged and lucky. Together, we explored the length and breadth of

Israel. I don't recall feeling bored at all, but rather awed and exhilarated. This was the incarnation of all that I was learning in my Jewish Zionist school education. The fact that I could read the public signage in Hebrew enhanced my sense of belonging and comfort.

It's only now, more than five decades later, that I realise that Buba and Szaja had been living in Israel for a mere two years before our visit. They were not long-time Israeli residents as I had imagined. Far from it.

What about Szaja's siblings? Leon, Bella and Aaron. On our next family trip to Israel in 1972-73, when I was fourteen years old, I met Aaron and Bella. Leon had already passed away. Were Bella and Aaron visiting Buba Rosa and Szaja, like we were? Or had they also moved to Israel? I'm not sure. My gut tells me that they had moved to Israel. I don't think the Wittelsohn siblings were ever going to live apart. In addition, it was winter in Israel. No-one who can help it visits at that time of year. Especially older people. Only us, southern hemisphere residents, do such a thing. Therefore, according to my logic, Bella and Aaron must have immigrated to Israel.

The farewells from these trips must have been emotional and heartrending. However, I do not remember them. I do remember Mum, in Melbourne, waiting for the mail to be delivered. Every single day. She would wait outside for the mailman to deliver those treasured green Israeli aerogrammes. A few years ago, in Dad's garage, I found a box full of those letters dated from 1968 to 1972. Written by Buba Rosa to Mum in Polish. It's a one-way correspondence; I don't have Mum's letters to her mother. I took this cache to my place to sort them into order, following the postal imprints. Sometimes these were blurred or faded. Luckily, Buba had dated every letter, just before she began with her customary, "*Moi kochani*" which translates from Polish to "My beloved." Firstly, I sorted them into piles according to the years in which they were written. Secondly, I sorted each pile chronologically. Then I proposed to Dad that we embark on a project translating the letters together. Dad and his mother-in-law had adored each other. I always knew that. Maybe, they even occasionally colluded against Mum.

Dad and I sat opposite each other at my kitchen table. Dad had the first letter in his hand. I was poised over my laptop, ready to write. However, it wasn't all that easy. Nor that enjoyable. Obstacles included Buba's loopy handwriting and lack of context. Dad's deteriorating eyesight didn't help either. It took him ages to read, re-read, translate and then go back over that translation. All this toing and froing didn't always lead to a coherent narrative. I tried to curb my frustration—which I'm not particularly good at—and even had a bash at translating myself. Desperate means for desperate times. After half an hour of irritation, with little to show for it, I realised we would not be completing this project. I wasn't quite ready to surrender but could see that the pleasant pastime I had envisaged was a futile fantasy. We continued trying in half-hour bursts over the next few weeks and ended up completing six letters. Even though the results were heart-warming for me, the undertaking was just too painstakingly aggravating. I could see that Dad also was not looking forward to these sessions together. So, we dropped the translation project. Of course, I still have the letters. They are filed, in order, in zip lock bags, awaiting others to pick up where we left off.

Less than two years after our second trip to Israel, Szaja passed away. Buba was visiting us at the time. She was not by his side, she was at the other end of the world. We received a phone call in the middle of the night. I now ask Dad who called us. He remembers that it was a distant relative of Szaja's. "He was from the other side of the family. Not our side. Not the Wittelsohn side." This is a reminder that Szaja was related to the Prince side of the family way before he married Buba. Dad remembers the precise words this person said to him in Yiddish: "*Szaja gegangan shloofen.*" Szaja has gone to sleep. Dad and Buba flew immediately to Israel. There were many expensive international telephone conversations between my parents. A decision was made that Dad and Buba would pack up her life in Israel and she would return, with Dad, to Australia. How was this decision made? Whose input was dominant? Is this really what Buba wanted? Perhaps she remained in Israel all those years only because Szaja wanted to be there? Was it inevitable that without him she would live in Australia with us? I now ask Dad about this too. He looks at me in the way he does when I am exasperating him. He says, "You always look for complications. There was no discussion and decision. It was obvious that she would now come to Melbourne. What else was she going to do?"

My gut reaction response is, "Carry on with her life in Israel?" Dad shakes his head at what he perceives to be my total lack of comprehension of the situation. I guess I have superimposed my own sensibilities onto a far different scenario.

He adds, "I remember something she said to me over there. I've never forgotten it." My attention is more than piqued. "*Ja nie mam juz meza,*" he says in Polish. I no longer have a husband. I find these words sad and poignant.

I ask Dad what he did in Israel. Basically, he and Buba packed up her life. He tells me, "I went to the post office every day. Buba made packages of things she wanted to keep and send to Australia. The rest of her belongings she either gave away or threw away." That's it.

My grandmother was preparing to make her next, final, immigration. It was 1974. Buba Rosa was 71, Dad was 49 and Mum was 47. I was sixteen.

Buba lived with us for a short while before moving into a nearby flat on her own. Then her decline began. Perhaps it had started earlier, but this was when it became sorely obvious. We received a phone call from the police in the middle of the night. She had been found wandering down the road. We hoped, perhaps naively, that this would be a one-off occurrence. However, it happened again and again. My parents made the agonising decision to place her in an aged-care home. She absconded from there as well and was moved to a higher-security section. Her demise was tragic. We watched as her mind clouded over. The diminishing of a human being is wretched. Buba Rosa passed away in 1982.

Standing: Aaron Wittelsohn, Josek and Malgosia Drzewiecski (cousins living in Israel), Bella Wittelsohn, Mum & me (aged 14, looking suitably bored)
Seated: Buba Rosa & Szaja Wittelsohn, Tel Aviv, December 1972/January 1973

UNITED STATES OF AMERICA
DEPARTMENT OF JUSTICE
IMMIGRATION AND NATURALIZATION SERVICE

File No. A11 042 961

Permit to Reenter the United States

PURSUANT to provisions of section 223 of the Immigration and Nationality
Act, this permit is issued to bearer,

ROSA WITTELSOHN

an alien previously lawfully admitted to the United States, to reenter the United
States, if otherwise admissible, as a nonquota immigrant ☒
as a treaty merchant ☐

PERSONAL DESCRIPTION OF BEARER

AGE	HEIGHT		WEIGHT	COMPLEXION	HAIR	EYES
10/20/03	5	3	120	FAIR	LT.BROWN	BROWN

VISIBLE DISTINCTIVE MARKS

NONE

SEX	MARITAL STATUS	
☐ M ☒ F	☒ Married ☐ Widowed	☐ Divorced ☐ Single

COUNTRY OF WHICH A CITIZEN, SUBJECT, OR NATIONAL	COUNTRY OF BIRTH	COUNTRY OF DESTINATION
STATELESS	POLAND	AUSTRALIA

UPON THE EXPIRATION OF ITS VALIDITY, THIS PERMIT MUST BE SURRENDERED TO THE IMMIGRATION AND NATURALIZATION SERVICE

Rosa W. Wittelsohn

The validity of this permit expires

MONTH	DAY	YEAR
SEPTEMBER	14	1960

ISSUED AT
NEW YORK, NY

MONTH	DAY	YEAR
SEPTEMBER	14	1959

APPLICATION FOR EXTENSION SHOULD BE
SUBMITTED TO DISTRICT OFFICE AT:
NEW YORK, NY

Approved:

NOTE.—Any erasure or alteration shall render this permit null and void.

EXTENSIONS

Joseph P. Leahy
American Vice Consul

Extended to and
invalid after

September 14, 1961
(Date)

Extended to and
invalid after

_____
(Date)

ADMISSION STAMPS

Arrived by	Arrived by	Arrived by	Arrived by
	DEC 1 1959 N.Y.		

Form I-182
(Rev. 12-1-56)

| Immigration Officer. | Immigration Officer. | Immigration Officer. | Immigration Officer. |

Buba Rosa's Permit to Reenter the United States, extended from September 1960
to September 1961. Issued by the American vice consul, Melbourne

Top: Buba Rosa & Szaja Wittelsohn's *aliyah* certificate, 1964

Wednesday 17 June 2020

We have made a substantial digression from our reading. We get back to Emanuel Tanay. He writes, "My life in Munich revolved around my studies and the activities of the student organisation." Dad pipes up, "Mine too." When Emanuel mentions a close friend named Natek Birman, Dad opens his eyes and says, "That was Adolek's sister's boyfriend. He was a good-looking man. He dropped her and she then left to go to Palestine. But she got stuck and was imprisoned by the British in Cyprus. She returned to Munich for a short while to see what was happening and then returned to Israel." I try to tease out some more details about this little saga. What does 'to see what is happening' mean? Was that something to do with Natek? Was it part of deciding whether she should or shouldn't go to Israel? Had the State of Israel already been declared when she returned there? Dad can't remember these details. We go to our treasure trove of photos, in particular those from the 1998 reunion. In one of the two photos I took of Survivor Students, there is Natek (now Nathan) Birman standing next to Emanuel and Sabina. Their arms are around each other's shoulders. I try to picture what Natek may have looked like 50 years earlier. It's not easy. But I can see an enduring charming smile.

Sabina Zimering, Emanuel Tanay & Natek (Nathan) Birman,
Jewish Students' Union reunion, New York, 1998

We come across another close friend of Emanuel's, Israel Borenstein. Like so many of the others, he sounded exceedingly capable. I Google him and stumble upon a memoir written not by Israel *Borenstein* but Israel *Bornstein*. Also a Survivor Student. It's been translated from German into English relatively recently. That's why it is so easy to come across. I order it immediately. According to Emanuel, his friend, *Borenstein* went on to have a distinguished career with the United Nations armed with a PhD in political science. My *Bornstein* studied dentistry and then medicine in Munich. I prefer my *Bornstein* to *Borenstein*. There is a greater chance, given the courses he studied, that he knew my parents.

Monday 22 June 2020

The Long Night: A True Story by Ernst Israel Bornstein arrives. The glowing accolades on the back cover are all from major community and political leaders in England. Jewish and non-Jewish. There must be an English angle to the book. It transpires that Bornstein wrote his memoir, in German, way back in 1967 and his eldest daughter has recently translated it. This edition was published in 2015. It is a gruelling read. Raw. It does not spare its reader any horror or cruelty. He has somehow found the words to describe the indescribable. And so has his daughter.

Dr (or double Dr, as he graduated both from dentistry and medicine) Ernst Israel Bornstein was one of the few Survivor Students who remained in Germany and made a life there. He established a career as an oral surgeon, married, had three children and became a leader in the Munich Jewish community. I am absolutely convinced that Mum must have known him. Even if they weren't in the same year, I have no doubt that all the Jewish dental students knew each other. I also suspect that Buba Rosa may also have known him in Munich. Especially since my recent revelation that she was still in Munich for a number of years after my parents immigrated to Australia. The Jewish dental world in Munich must have been interconnected.

To say I am saddened by Bornstein's premature death is an understatement. He passed away in 1978 at the age of only 55. His children were twelve, eleven and seven years old at the time. I feel gutted. His memoir recounts terrifying violence and brutality. Laced with drops of mitigating kindness. But it is the 'after' narrative that I look towards as a sort of salve to balm the souls of survivors. And his postwar life did not last long enough for him to reap the joy of adult children and grandchildren.

I decide to deepen my internet search to find out more about Bornstein's family. There is much to find including articles about his translator, his eldest daughter, Noemie Lopian. I read voraciously. I decide to send Noemie an email.

Hello Noemie

My name is Frances Prince. I live in Melbourne, Australia. Both my parents were Polish Holocaust survivors.

I have just completed reading your translation of your father's book. It is both harrowing and moving, as you well know. In my opinion, your undertaking has been a well-accomplished and important one. I am sorry that you lost your father at such a young age (both his and yours).

Both my parents studied in Munich after the war. They met there. They studied at the Ludwig Maximilian University, thanks to the Jewish Students' Union. My father, who is 95, studied pharmacy. His name at that time was David Prinz. Today it is David Prince.

My mother, who passed away over six years ago, studied dentistry. Her name at that time was Rachela Salzberg, then Rachela Prinz, and later Ella Prince. My parents married in Munich in December 1947. Our parents must have known each other. Mum and Dad left Munich for Melbourne in December 1949. Dad had graduated from pharmacy. Mum did not graduate from dentistry. She completed her 'half-diploma'. My father is in good shape, but his memory is not as sharp as it once was. He doesn't remember your father, but feels that he should. His name is familiar to him.

Are you aware of friends of your father's from those days? Those who went to America and those who went to Israel? Only a very small number immigrated to Australia. Would you have any of their names or documentation from that time in the late 1940s?

Looking forward to hearing from you.

Regards

Frances

Tuesday 23 June 2020

I do not wait long for a reply.

> *Dearest Frances*
> *Am full of goose pimples ...*
> *Thank you for writing to me*
> *Am so interested*
> *Will make some enquiries*
>
> *Can we chat?*
> *Let's arrange a time*
>
> *Thank you*
> *Love*
> *Noemie*

I think I have found a new friend. Noemie lives in Manchester. A year after her father died, her mother packed up the three little children and moved them from Munich to the UK. As I learn later, they had already planned the move.

We email back and forth and make a time to speak on WhatsApp the next day.

Friday 26 June 2020

Noemie has passed my emails onto her brother, Alain. He sends me an email. Also, very excitedly. We discover a number of connections. Including the fact that their sister, Muriel, lives in Israel, less than five-minutes walk from my Jerusalem home. And that Noemie's husband is a first cousin of a close friend of ours in Jerusalem. And that their mother, Mrs Bornstein, had been very close friends with the only friend my parents still had in Munich, Dr Ewa Horowicz. Another dentistry-followed-by-medicine graduate. I met Ewa Horowicz in 2009 on my 'pilgrimage' there with Dad. We knew she had passed away but didn't know when. Now we find out that she died in January 2016 and was buried in Israel. I tell Dad. He says, "Yes, I remember now that her husband was buried in Israel." Dr Samuel Horowicz passed away in July 1989. Dad adds, "We became closer with her after he died." I do know that Mum and Dad had stayed at her place on earlier visits to Munich. Noemie tells me that Dr Ewa Horowicz practised as an obstetrician and gynaecologist in Munich. And that she was highly respected in her field. Noemie and I make a time to chat again on the phone the following week. A new friendship is a blessing.

***

Back to Emanuel. Dad and I think we pick up an error in his memoir. Dad is a stickler for the facts. I quite like them too. They firmly ground subsequent musings. We simultaneously identify the mistake. For us, it is an important one. Emanuel tells the reader about an exam that he undertook in physics. He doesn't remember the name of the professor, but "…I believe he received the Nobel Prize."

"Wrong!" shout the two sticklers for detail. We know that the professor who won the Nobel Prize was Heinrich Wieland, and that he won it for his work in chemistry. I ask Dad, "Maybe there was another Nobel Prize winning professor there?" I like to give Emanuel the benefit of the doubt.

Dad stares me straight in the eye and says, "There was one, only one, Nobel Prize winner. My chemistry professor. Professor Heinrich Wieland."

Emanuel tells us about his former girlfriend, Halina, being courted by Edek Langer, a student of dentistry. I don't need Dad to jump in here. I know Edek Langer. Edek and Mum were dental students together. My parents spent time with him and his wife when they visited Israel. But I wonder, who was his wife? Did Edek end up marrying Emanuel's ex-girlfriend, Halina? I rush to Dad's photo album of the 1995 reunion in Israel and read the list of names of the 144 attendees. I quickly find the two Langer bothers and their wives. They lived in Israel. I know this already. My eyes land on Halina Langer. Bingo! Could it be another Halina? I choose to decide that this is the one and same Halina.

Dad adds, "Not only was Edek Mum's good friend, but he was also friendly with Buba. They remained close when both he and Buba lived in Israel. They were both dentists there."

We read about another young medical student, Marion Landau. Emanuel and Marion fell in love and got married and divorced by the time he was 21 years old. I ask Dad, as I do whenever a new name from the Munich student days is introduced, whether he remembers her. He shrugs his shoulders and says, "No." It seems that Marion had quite an unusual heritage amongst the students. Her mother was a non-Jewish German and her father is described as an "assimilated Jew". Dad interrupts—though I don't see it as an interruption as such, but as another gem—"There was this one girl in the year above doing medicine who wasn't really Jewish. Now I remember. She wasn't skinny." I laugh at this last comment. I am thrilled with the recollection. We decide that she must be Marion.

Emanuel's memoir is dotted with names. I seek more information about these people. It's not sufficient for me to read about a friend, I want particulars. Emanuel mentions Felek Korn as another leader in the Jewish Students' Union. We know Felek. He became Felix after immigrating to America. We have a photo of him in Dad's album from the 1995 Israel reunion. Dad and I rejoice with each discovery.

Emanuel is coming to the end of the autobiographical section of his book. He graduated and immigrated to America. Not all that long after his arrival he began his medical career. Life in his new homeland was set to soar.

The next section, entitled 'Reflections', consists of 60 pages of Emanuel's ruminations on all manner of topics. It's a combination of opinions and attitudes that he has developed over the span of his life laced with literature, psychology, philosophy and sociology. It bears the hallmark of a sharply intelligent and widely read person who is engaged with many of life's great questions. And, of course, it is all underpinned by his Holocaust experiences.

I make a unilateral decision. Dad and I don't read 'Reflections' together. We have been engrossed in the life of Emanuel Tanay for weeks now. It feels like we must now take leave of him, so that he can live out the remainder of his accomplished and complex life.

Dad (seated, second from the right) with Emanuel Tanay (seated, right) and other students, including Lusia Frydman (standing, left) who also immigrated to Melbourne, late 1940s

Sunday 28 June 2020

Dad asks me to choose the next book but I really want him to decide. He decides on:

A Lucky Human Being: An Incredible Story of Survival,
Hania Harcsztark-Goldfeder Mayer

Published by Makor Jewish Community Library, 2009

'To dear Frances! A child I know since she was born! My love, Hania'

Hania is one of the most elegant of our family friends. She is always stylishly dressed with immaculate hair and nails; her make-up is always perfect. And she is warm and wise.

Hania was born in Lodz, three years earlier than Dad. The opening scene of her memoir is set in a close-knit, religious family with serious 'yiches'. This Yiddish word probably requires a whole paragraph to explain. In short, it refers to a family lineage and heritage to be proud of. Hania's forebearers are religious scholars with solid reputations for outstanding learnedness and erudition in the traditional Jewish texts. This scholarship together with wisdom and compassion add up to major *yiches*. Hania's family had it in spades.

We read about her maternal grandfather, Rabbi Biderman of Ruda Pabianicka, a town near Lodz. Dad stops me. "Ruda Pabianicka? My father took me to the rabbi of Pabianicka after I broke my arm." The broken arm story I know. The rabbi of Pabianicka story I do not know. When the family was away on holidays in 1938, Dad fell, landing heavily on his elbow and broke his arm. A doctor at the children's hospital in Lodz gave him an anaesthetic and manipulated his arm. Later, when Dad started physiotherapy, he realised that he couldn't fully stretch his arm out. The family narrative is that the doctor was an antisemite who purposefully botched it. So be it. I can't make any comment on the matter. Dad was taken all the way to Warsaw to see another doctor. This doctor said that the arm could be left as it was with a permanent bend or he could operate to break and re-set the arm.

So, what's with the rabbi of Pabianicka? It is not clear to me the exact purpose of this visit to the esteemed rabbi. Dad thinks it could be that his father was seeking advice in a tricky situation.

I ask Dad, "Do you think it was about whether you should have that operation? Or maybe he wanted you to be blessed by the rabbi?"

Dad responds, "I'm not sure. Probably something like that." We are left wondering whether the venerated rabbi of Pabianicka that my Dad and grandfather visited was Hania's grandfather, Rabbi Biderman.

Dad remembers his mother saying to him, "David darling, do you want this operation? One day, when you grow up, I don't want you to blame us for your arm. So, we are going to leave the decision to you." He decided against breaking and resetting his arm. I ask Dad now whether he thinks he made the right decision. Without hesitation, he answers, "Yes I do. I think that the surgery could have made it even worse. I would end up with an arm with a worse bend."

Dad has always said that he was lucky his crooked arm was not noticed in Auschwitz-Birkenau. The repercussions could have been fatal. The other, significantly less serious, but ongoing, legacy of that injury is that Dad can tell, by the feeling in his arm, if it will rain the next day. He is his own weather gauge.

Hania's parents packed up their belongings and went on *aliyah* to Eretz Yisrael, then Palestine, in the mid-1920s. Hania was very young at the time. Dad chimes in, "None of my family went to Palestine." It's like an apology for his lack of Zionist credentials. On the other hand, Mum's maternal grandfather, David Ber Gringlas, did immigrate to Palestine in 1932. As a child I was proud of that link. However, as the story goes, the matter was a little more complicated. Zaida David's wife, Brindla, passed away. He then married his very young niece. (Her name has been lost.) I don't know if they were advised by family members that it might be better for all concerned if they left town or whether they decided this for themselves. Either way, I imagine a delicious scandal. Tragically, they decided to visit relatives back in Warsaw in August

1939—an inauspicious time for a Jewish family reunion. They, together with virtually all family members, were indeed reunited. In Treblinka.

Back to Hania. After two years in Palestine, due to her father's ill health, the family returned to Lodz. Their fate was similar to that of Zaida David Ber Gringlas and his very young niece-wife.

Monday 29 June 2020

Hania tells us about her schooling in Lodz. Her secondary school was called Wiedza. Dad stops me, "I know exactly where that is. That is where I went to school at the start of the war, until education was totally stopped. It wasn't called Wiedza then. It wasn't called anything. I think it was on Poludniowa Street." Dad's internal Lodz atlas is never far away.

Hania was fifteen years old when her mother died. She was devastated. However, she was still surrounded by the love of her father and three much-older brothers. The only brother still alive after the war had moved to Palestine before the Germans invaded Poland.

Like all of Lodz's Jews, after the German invasion, Hania and her family were ordered into the ghetto. During her time there, she lived at three different addresses: Mlynarska Street, Marynarska Street and then Dworska Street. As we read about each of Hania's moves, Dad's hand is again following the twists and turns of his internal map of Lodz.

Hania describes how she, her father and one brother decided which of their possessions to take with them into the ghetto. Dad tells me about his relocating experience. He thinks his parents did all the packing while he and his brother did the *schlepping*. They tied their chosen belongings on a type of sleigh and made multiple trips to Ciocia Mala and Wujek Salek's place at 30 Brzezinska Street in Baluty, a fifteen-minute walk away.

We read about Hania's search for work and some of the personalities she met and situations that arose. She mentions a Mr Radzyner who was in charge of a factory making metal goods. Dad stops me. "One of his sons, much older than me, was in the Friedland labour camp with me." Another snippet.

Jews from other parts of Poland, and indeed other parts of Europe, were sent to the Lodz Ghetto to be incarcerated. Hania's description of the arrival and rapid demise of Czechoslovakian Jews is devastating to read. Dad and I discuss their precipitous deaths. He surmises, "They didn't gradually get used to deprivation like we did. For us, things happened in stages, over time. They arrived and they didn't know what hit them. Squalor, starvation. They didn't have time to get used to it. They just couldn't take it."

Hania briefly mentions the Gypsy camp within the Lodz Ghetto. Dad pipes in. "Yes, I remember them. They did have their own section. We weren't neighbours." As usual, whenever the geography or topography of Lodz is relevant, Dad's hands get moving, as if to direct me to the part of the city he is describing. He continues, "They weren't there for long. They were deported altogether. It's like they were there and then they weren't."

Tuesday 30 June 2020

Marriage in the ghetto. Who would've thought? Hania met Janek, fell in love, and they married. On the very same day, another 39 other couples married. Surely you need to believe in a future if you are going to get married in these circumstances. Were they all that naïve? Were they so besotted with each other that they just went with it? Whatever the future holds, at least they'll be together? Admittedly, I find it romantic as well as heartbreaking.

Three weeks after their wedding, Hania and Janek were sent to Auschwitz-Birkenau.

We are about to read Hania's description of their arrival at the death camp. Dad and I brace ourselves for the onslaught of images that we are about to expose ourselves to. Yet again.

Each arrival testimony we read is the exception to the rule. Each written by one of the very few who survived. The vast majority of Jews who arrived in Auschwitz-Birkenau were murdered. They wrote no memoirs.

Separation of men and women, the selection, the violence, the confusion. Hania endured it all. At least she was with two cousins. Being with loved ones couldn't save you from the randomness of murder. But perhaps it could contribute to perseverance and fortitude. It also meant that someone was looking out for you. This mightn't save you, but I believe it could be an important factor in finding the tenacity to cling on, somehow. I believe this to be true for Dad, with his father and brother. I believe this to be true for Mum, with her mother.

Hania tells us about the paltry diet, the constant *appel* (line-ups), the straw bunks and the back-breaking work. There were clandestine rendezvous with one of her brothers. In Auschwitz-Birkenau. "Unbelievable," comments Dad. These surreptitious and dangerous encounters create a surreal picture in my mind's eye. Most people dream of exiting from Birkenau. Hania wanted to stay. Why? So she could continue meeting her brother. However, in October 1944 she was transported out. Her brother did not survive.

Hania was sent to a camp called Pirszkau Szlesensee. Yet another place neither Dad nor I have heard of. Again, the women were assigned to carry out wretched labour in appalling conditions. As the Russians approached from the east, the Germans mustered the women and forced them to walk in the opposite direction in the freezing cold. A death march. Any woman who could not continue was shot. Hania's strength was slowly ebbing. As implausible as it sounds, she made a desperate escape before she was found and returned to her imprisoned group. For some unknown reason, she was not shot. The women were forced to stagger on to the concentration camp of Bergen-Belsen. The conditions there were indescribable.

British forces entered Bergen-Belsen on 15 April 1945 and Hania was liberated. Dad drops his inevitable lament, "I was still in camp for another three weeks after that." Hania's ill-health upon liberation reminds me of Willy Lermer's. She had literally been left for dead. After three months recuperating in hospital, Hania and her cousins sailed to Sweden. Most of the survivors we have been reading about spent the postwar years in Germany, but not all.

Thousands of Jews spent the postwar years in Sweden. A program called the White Buses[33] instigated by the Swedish Red Cross, brought concentration camp survivors to the Scandinavian country to heal and to recuperate. Reading between the lines, I think Hania and her cousins were part of this program. I have a close friend whose mother and two aunts were also brought to Sweden at this time.

Wednesday 1 July 2020

Hania spent five tumultuous and eventful years in Sweden. Early in her Swedish sojourn, Hania and other survivors performed in a concert, singing a Polish song from their childhoods about "mountain people who sing about their lives". I ask Dad if he has any idea what song this is. "Nope, no idea," he shrugs. About two pages later he starts to sing. Just a few words. He stops and says, "I've forgotten the rest." I ask him to sing those few words again, hoping the repetition might lead to a continuation of the song. It doesn't. I ask him to spell out the words to me. "*Goralu czy ci nie zal*?" Dad translates this as, "Mountain man, aren't you sorry?" Google Translate interprets the words as, "Highlander, don't you regret?" Same thing.

Dad and I read about Hania's trials and tribulations and her happy reunion with her husband, Janek Goldfeder. Hania experienced great kindness from many people. Not perfunctory kindness, but purposeful and compassionate open-heartedness. No wonder Sweden is considered a convalescence haven. We read with not much commentary and overlay. It was a very different postwar experience from Dad's.

In time, Hania tells us about their voyage to Australia. Now, we are back on familiar ground. She complains about the smell of tomatoes which were an essential ingredient for meals on an Italian ship. My parents

---

33. The White Buses was a program initiated by Count Folke Bernadotte, vice-president of the Swedish Red Cross, to rescue prisoners in Nazi Germany, towards the end of the war. More than 15,000 concentration camp prisoners were rescued and transported to Sweden in buses painted white so they were not mistaken for military vehicles.

came to Australia on a Dutch ship, *MS Volendam*. Dad says, "We were fed meat from sheep—mutton—every single day. For breakfast, lunch and dinner." He adds, "There were many Dutch people on our ship who had lived all their lives in Indonesia, a Dutch colony. When Indonesia gained independence in 1945, they had returned to the Netherlands. But they weren't comfortable back home, they didn't feel that they quite belonged and were now immigrating to Australia." Are these riveting facts for me? Not really. But they are more of the little snippets that I enjoy.

Thursday 2 July 2020

Hania and Janek were greeted by distant relations at Station Pier in Port Melbourne. This is where all the ships docked, including *MS Volendam*, with my parents on board.

This prompts me to ask Dad, "Who greeted you at Station Pier?" I've never asked him this before. I've never even thought about it.

"Isaac Sussman was there. So was Adolek Kohn." Isaac Sussman was my grandfather's first cousin. He had immigrated to Australia in the 1920s. I ask Dad why he came to Australia. Dad enlightens me, "Isaac was visiting a brother who lived in England when his visa expired. He wanted to stay there but was refused residency. However, he was given permission to migrate to Australia." I wonder what Isaac thought of his consolation residency.

Adolek Kohn was Dad's friend. They always boasted about how they met. In a concentration camp, Friedland. They had arrived there from Auschwitz-Birkenau on the same transport of 300 supposed metal workers. In the rush to secure a bed upon arrival, Dad's father and brother pushed together towards a bunk and got separated from Dad. In the confusion, he looked around and grabbed the nearest spare top bunk. There was someone already in the bunk next door. Dad recounts, "He turned around and introduced himself. We slept in adjoining bunks from 8 September 1944 until 8 May 1945." This was the beginning of a lifelong friendship. No wonder Adolek was at Station Pier on the day Mum and Dad sailed into Melbourne.

Isaac, Cela & Geoffrey Sussman, Melbourne, 1940s

After their arrival, Isaac took my parents to the home he shared with his wife, Cela. Dad says, "They lived at 46 Kean Street, South Caulfield." How does he remember? After all, it was 70 years ago. They had one suitcase each.

Later, the Sussmans took them to what would be their first home in Melbourne, a flat above a shop at 315 Drummond Street, Carlton. Very fashionable these last few decades. Not so much when they lived there. Mum used to tell me about the rats that shared their flat.

Acclimatising to life in Melbourne, Hania tells us about her growing number of friends, including Halinka Zauder. Halinka and her husband, Steve, were also friends of my parents. I remember them as delightfully engaging people. Hania also mentions Halinka's father, Dr Rozaner, who was a well-known dermatologist in Lodz before the war. Dad nods vigorously, acknowledging this fact. He tells me, "We got to know him quite well here, in Melbourne. He lived with Halinka and Steve. We were over at their place a lot and therefore saw him often too." My parents only met them in Melbourne. Dad didn't know Halinka from Lodz but had heard of Dr Rozaner. "Everybody knew Dr Rozaner. He was famous in Lodz." Dad bursts out laughing.

"What's so funny?" I ask. He can hardly control himself.

"As kids, we used to go to his practice where his shingle was prominently displayed. We would read it, 'Dr Rozaner: Specialist in Skin Treatments and Venereal Diseases' and then run away laughing ourselves silly." My 95-year-old father sounds like a twelve-year-old child.

As a postscript, Dad tells me that during the war, Dr Rozaner was imprisoned with Polish officers at a German POW camp. He was the camp doctor. Evidently, both the Poles and the Germans knew he was a Jew.

In Melbourne, the medical qualifications of Lodz's famous Dr Rozaner were not recognised. Such are the insurmountable obstacles for an older immigrant.

Friday 3 July 2020

Hania's managerial skills and elegance landed her a job running a chic boutique located at the end-of-the line tram stop at Acland and Barkly Streets. Dad pipes up, "I took that tram, the number 15, every day to the Pharmacy College." This was the mid-1950s. My parents had been in Melbourne for over five years already. At last, Dad was beginning to fulfil his dream of re-studying, to becoming recognised as a qualified pharmacist in his new country. My parents were living in Flat 5, 26 Blessington Street, St Kilda.

We read about the birth of Hania and Janek's daughter, Marcia. The joy is palpable. The drive to earn a respectable living and provide for their daughter led to a path of sheer hard work. "We all worked so hard to get on our feet," comments Dad. Hania and Janek explored different parts of the city. They sound curious and mostly optimistic to me. They met helpful and kind people and Hania's burgeoning career at Myer was seriously impressive. I feel so proud of her. I sense a *joie de vivre* in Hania that I can't imagine in my parents during their first years in Melbourne.

Perhaps I am being overly judgmental and harsh. When talking about their early years in Melbourne, my parents focused on the dullness. Especially Mum. Doing 'piece work' while isolated at home in North Balwyn with a crying baby (my brother) sounds pretty grim to me. 'Piece work' refers to the nearly finished garments that clothing factories would outsource to be completed in the homes of (mostly) women. Stitching hems and the like. Workers were paid per completed garment, or piece. Dad recalls, "After I came home at night from a full day's work, I helped Mum with this. We sat at our little table together, listening to the radio, to Bob Dyer, just sewing." What a contrast (come down?) from their life as students at the Ludwig Maximilian University a couple of short years earlier.

In my understanding, Mum poured all her efforts and energies into supporting Dad. And looking after my brother and me. She identified and was united with Dad in his endeavours. Whatever it took to save up for Dad to go to Pharmacy College and qualify in Australia. Once Dad eventually began re-studying, Mum took care of the home and ensured their living conditions were suitable for studying. Everything was geared towards their shared goal and dream. My brother Issy remembers those days, before I was born. I arrived the year Dad graduated. This explains our seven-year age gap. He was born the year after my parents immigrated to Melbourne. Then we had what could be termed 'the seven lean years'. The years of factory jobs, sewing piece work, and study. I was my parents' graduation present.

Throughout this time, Mum and Dad planned the purchase of their pharmacy in Richmond. They shared the inevitable problems and burdens. As they slowly became successful, they bought our home in Caulfield, the first home that I remember. In my mind's eye, it was huge. Objectively, I think it actually was rather large. Then, a number of years later, my parents bought a block of land with a dilapidated house on it and began to plan their dream home. Also in Caulfield. That demolition happened quickly. Mum was immersed in every step of the building of our next, and final, family home. She pored over architectural drawings, tested different designs, and consulted many experts. I'm not sure whether she enjoyed the process or was just focused on the end result. The house, and its furnishings and decorations, gave Mum and Dad a great deal of joy.

Sunday 5 July 2020

Hania felt a constant draw to Israel. She was strongly influenced by the Zionist values of her parents. And her one and only surviving brother lived there. I identify strongly with this lifelong powerful pull. Mine emanates more indirectly from my upbringing. My school education (including unbroken Hebrew language classes), trips to Israel at formative stages, reading tomes of Zionist literature, conclusions reached through my own intense Holocaust education, combined with a sense of adventure and challenge, have contributed to my own Zionist attraction. Interestingly, my grandmother, Buba Rosa, lived in Israel from 1964 until 1974 and while Mum missed her terribly, this did not draw her to the country. Perhaps more than familial love is required to emigrate from a country like Australia. Much more, it seems.

Hania, Janek and young Marcia went to Israel for three months. Hania wanted to stay but it became apparent that it was not practicable to do so and they returned to Melbourne. Tragedy struck. Janek died suddenly and Hania's life was upended. Even though I am aware of what happened to Janek, reading Hania's reaction, in her own words, is gut-wrenching. After soul-searching, and with her brother's encouragement, Hania and Marcia packed up and moved to Israel. It was a lifelong dream. But not under these circumstances. After two years, they returned to Melbourne.

Once again, Hania picked herself up and started again. Home, job, school for Marcia. Her resilience floors me. She remarried, Marcia completed her education, then married and had children. Hania's life in Australia and the arrival of her grandchildren clearly brought her much joy.

As we conclude our reading of *A Lucky Human Being*, I have an epiphany. I know that Hania is alive and that she is 98 years old. I text Marcia to ask after her welfare. It sounds like she is doing well while living in a high-quality aged-care residence. Marcia sends me a recent photo of Hania looking as elegant as ever. Her grey hair is coiffed stylishly and her scarf is draped smartly around her shoulders. The electric blue colour of her scarf is stunning. The yellow design that dots the scarf matches the sweater that Hania is wearing. In addition, she is wearing a necklace and has donned a large pair of sunglasses. She has applied red lipstick. Her hands rest on the blanket on her lap. Immaculately red-painted fingernails protrude from her hands. She truly is a picture of studied chic.

I ask Marcia whether I can visit her mother. Given that most of our memoirists are no longer alive, it would be a wonderful chance to actually speak with her and not just read her words. I wonder how she now reflects on her life, given her fabulous great age. Marcia is happy to facilitate such a visit (not so easy to organise these days). A date is set. I find that I am very much looking forward to seeing Hania.

Tuesday 7 July 2020

The day of my visit with Hania approaches. However, the number of coronavirus cases is rising. It seems that Melbourne is heading towards a second wave. Another lockdown is announced, set to begin at midnight on Wednesday. My scheduled visit is for Thursday. I expect it will be cancelled. Aged-care facilities are understandably very vigilant. I text Marcia. She informs me that it's still happening. Wonderful.

Thursday 9 July 2020

I meet Marcia outside the facility and we enter together. We sign in and have our temperature checks. Then we are escorted to the bathroom where we must wash our hands under strict supervision. Evidently, this is a brand-new protocol. So be it.

Hania has been wheeled into a separate glass-enclosed room designated for visitors or meetings. She seems overjoyed to see me. The feelings are indeed mutual. We sit opposite each other across a small table. Marcia sits on the side. Hania looks as elegant as always.

I tell her that I have been reading her book, out loud, to Dad. She seems flattered and appreciative. We chat about her family. Her original, nuclear family. We talk about her love of Israel and her bond to the Jewish homeland. Do I tell Hania and Marcia that I have written about Hania, and tied her story to my dad's life? Will they think me mercenary and opportunistic? I certainly hope not. My fears are unfounded. We have history together. They both know me and hopefully trust that my intentions are honourable. Marcia finds my writing project an interesting proposition. Do I dare take a further step? Do I suggest reading to Hania an extract from my writing? Of course, I ask Marcia first. She is enthusiastic. And so, I begin. I read, out loud and slowly, the first five paragraphs of my writing about Hania's memoir. I'm probably reading too slowly, and too animatedly, for a younger person. But at 98 years old, I figure that for Hania, I should slow down, exaggerate my gesticulations and overmodulate my voice. She is attentive, actively listening and nodding in various places. I'm not sure about her total grasp, but she certainly seems to be following me attentively.

I do not want to overstay my welcome. Less is more. A short enjoyable visit is to be cherished by all concerned. I am gratified to have seen Hania and shared some of her own reminiscences and my literary (?) appreciation of her remarkable life.

Visiting Hania Mayer, July 2020

Friday 10 July 2020

I decide that it is finally time to tell Dad about this writing project. It might seem surprising that I haven't already done so. However, I have been reluctant, fearful that Dad would be self-conscious about having his thoughts and reflections recorded. I didn't want his spontaneity or gut reactions to be stymied. I wanted us to talk naturally without even a thought about what others might think. Perhaps, reading a small extract to Hania Mayer made me think that Dad is, at least, entitled to know that I am using our time together to write a book. In addition, a significant number of people have been told about it, by me. Quite a number have been read snippets, by me. A few people have been read rather large snippets (an oxymoron, I know) by me. Meanwhile, Dad has been oblivious that I am mining him and his life for writing material. I am beginning to feel a little uncomfortable. So, I tell him. He is not sure exactly what I am telling him. I try to explain my aims and methodology. He is confused. Believe me, he isn't the only one. I guess the concept is best understood by an actual reading. That is why I have read excerpts to a few friends. No-one quite 'gets' what I'm doing until they hear a sample.

Which section should I read to him? I decide to start at the very beginning of my first draft. This will certainly give him a strong sense of the framework of my writing project. We get into our usual comfortable reading positions on the couch. With our blankets.

We step inside our own story.

Epilogue

My writing may have ended but our reading project continues. After all, this began as a way of spending time with Dad, keeping him company and engaged in the best way that I can. As 2020 draws to a close, Dad continues to arrive at my place every day at 3pm so that we can read together.

The spread of the coronavirus in Melbourne seems to have been curtailed, if not eliminated. Lockdown is over. Few restrictions remain. Melbournians feel liberated and many people have resumed their usual lives. The weather is warming up and the days are longer. However, for Dad, little has changed in his daily life. Except that he has become frailer, more forgetful, less confident. And he knows it. When I go away for an occasional weekend, Dad misses our cherished time together. So do I. The hours we spend together have become sacrosanct. I have bestowed an almost Sabbath-like sanctification of time onto our daily reading schedule.

We maintained the same genre—Holocaust memoirs—throughout. Occasionally we attempted to change categories, to perhaps lighten things up. However, neither of us are drawn so intensely to other stories; we lose interest embarrassingly quickly. Other stories just don't suit us.

Dad continues to bring documents to my place. In dribs and drabs. The most enlightening of these is a bundle of newsletters that Survivor Students published in the late 1990s. I knew of the existence of these newsletters and had read or skimmed through some of them years ago. I remembered that Emanuel Tanay was the industrious editor. However, I assumed that Dad no longer had these newsletters. Until the day he brought over another one of his green folders packed tight, nearly overbrimming. I asked Dad, "Why didn't you bring these newsletters over when we were reading Emanuel's book?" He shrugged his shoulders and said, "I am bringing them now."

The newsletter is called *Reunion*, a most appropriate title as the mission of the publication is to reunite friends who shared an amazing connection forged half a century earlier. The newsletters were published and the reunions were organised over the same time period. This included the reunion in New York that I attended with Dad in June 1998. At that time, the Survivor Students were nearing the end of their professional lives, some were retired or semi-retired, and had time and energy to devote to other matters. Perhaps it is a time to pause and reflect, when a person is still (hopefully) full of energy and creativity, as well as sentimentality and nostalgia. A time before the vicissitudes of old age creep in.

I was thrilled to come across an article Dad wrote in Volume I, Issue 1 in June 1997. The very first edition! My dad was in on day one. I was thrilled but not surprised. This was Dad as a younger man—involved, motivated and sociable.

Many of the articles and letters in the various *Reunion* issues were written by those Survivor Students Jeremy Varon interviewed. I certainly don't see this as a coincidence. These people were already connected to each other and committed to preserving their stories and memories.

And then I hit the jackpot!

In Volume IV, Issue 1 (published in late 1998) I come across the following article written by Sabina Zimering:

Dear Friends,

On the last day of our Concord Reunion in June 1998, after the meeting was over and everyone was ready to leave, Frances, David Prince's daughter from Melbourne, Australia approached us with an unusual request.

She said that watching her father enjoy his colleagues and friends from five decades ago was a moving experience for her. Frances was one of the eloquent speakers of our Second Generation guests. She felt that we, the students of Munich and other universities, most likely don't realize how unique our situation was in postwar Germany. She considered our experiences historically significant and worthy of documentation.

She suggested we find a professional historian, not an amateur writer, who would be able to do the research, the writing, and most likely the publishing.

Since I had become a member of the new committee, she asked me to present her idea to the other members during a teleconference. I presented Frances' suggestion. Everyone liked the idea.

I also had names of two historians who expressed interest in our project: Dr Stephen Feinstein, Acting Director of the Center for Holocaust and Genocide Studies at the University of Minnesota, and his assistant of 1997, Dr Jeremy Varon, presently of Santa Barbara, California.

If anyone would like some information about the two historians, please contact me.

Unbeknownst to me (or at least, unremembered by me) I was, in actual fact, an instigator of the monumental historical study that resulted in Jeremy Varon's *The New Life: Jewish Students of Postwar Germany*. I seem to have been the one who sewed the seeds for this undertaking. I remember vaguely a discussion of some sort. I certainly had no idea that I had been taken so seriously. A full circle has come to pass.

***

While Australia is patting itself on the back for its stellar handling of the coronavirus pandemic, countries in the northern hemisphere (and other places) are descending into a quagmire of increasing numbers of afflicted people and deaths. All of this while the harsh winter weather and darkness descend on that part of the world. The part of the world where my children and grandchildren live.

The Australian government has forbidden its citizens to leave the country. With few exceptions. Though I understand the motivation for this ban, I acutely feel the resultant emotional and familial fallout of this ruling. Of course, I am not the only one.

During 2020 many people were impacted in devastating ways. Illness, death, unemployment, domestic violence. Repercussions will be ongoing for many years to come. While cognisant of my many blessings, my anxiety has been centred around taking care of my elderly father and concern for my children and grandchildren overseas. I imagined myself as a jaffle sandwich. Dad is one piece of bread. Children and grandchildren are the other piece of bread. And I am the scorching and blistering cheese and tomato in the middle.

Spending time with Dad and writing this book has brought profound meaning and connection to a year in which the entire world faced one of the most significant challenges of my lifetime. In some ways I have 'lost' this year. In other ways, it has been grand.

Dad watching the *brit milah* (circumcision ceremony) of his newest
great-grandchild in Jerusalem via zoom, 5 April 2021

Afterword

THE GIFT OF *GIFT OF TIME*
Jeremy Varon

In a pivotal scene in *Gift of Time*, Frances recalls gently trying to wrest from her reluctant father, David, the precious artifacts of his past—university certifications, photos, and ephemera from his time in postwar Munich and then Australia. "This conversation," she shrewdly observes, "is really about mortality." Keen to the subtext, David turned them over.

This encounter brought to mind a similar, if inverted, episode during the late stages of my research on the Survivor Students in postwar Germany. Roman Ohrenstein, a leader among them and an interview subject of mine, reached out to me with a special urgency. He had been to the doctor and the news was not good. If I wanted to use items in his possession for the book, I best get them now from his home in Queens, New York. Within days, I did.

Both episodes signal the awesome responsibility I felt when writing *The New Life: Jewish Students of Postwar Germany*, about the remarkable student cohort that included David Prince. Sharing their recollections and documents, the alumni entrusted me with nothing less than their collective legacy as Holocaust survivors and as Jews. My words were both their history and memorial.

Central to the entire effort was Bella Brodzki, born in Munich in 1950 to displaced Jews. A professor of comparative literature in the United States, Bella propelled the research in its key phases, alert to both its historical and existential significance.

The gift of my time with the Survivor Students proved finite, adjusting my hopes for the book. By its publication in 2014, most all of the alumni (including Dr Ohrenstein) had passed on. Those still living were generally too infirm to absorb the book's content. Its ideal audience—indeed those for whom it was fundamentally written—were gone. Their knowledge that the book was on the way would have to be satisfaction enough, for them and for me.

Imagine then, my elation to learn in the spring of 2020 that half a world away a devoted daughter was methodically reading my book aloud to her 94-year-old father, alert to its every word. Their daily readings prompted David to unearth his own trove of documents. With these, he elaborated to Frances the details of his life in a postwar world made newly visible by my years-long labours.

By this process, her knowledge as the primary bearer of his personal legacy grew exponentially. Among her epiphanies was the discovery of an article he had penned for the Jewish Students' Union newspaper in 1947 about his time in a Nazi labour camp. David was, his essay makes clear, an astute observer and gifted writer, complicating his self-image as something shy of an intellectual. Frances, who rightly rushed the text to Holocaust researchers, appreciated her father anew. Done with my book, they extended their reading to the memoirs of fellow Munich alumni and survivors mainly in Australia known to their family.

The New Life had set all of this in motion. No author could ever ask for more.

***

My gratitude for this special father-daughter undertaking is greater still. Here my appreciation is for *Gift of Time* itself, a masterpiece all its own.

The book is surely different than most all of the thousands of memoirs of Holocaust survivors or biographical profiles of them. Fundamentally, it captures a dialogue—both between a child and parent, and between them and a devastating, but also exhilarating, past.

Doing so, it calls to mind the template established decades ago by Art Spiegelman's iconic *Maus*. More than recounting his father's harrowing survival, Spiegelman chronicles the painful extraction of his father's story by means of his own anguished curiosity. Like Spiegelman, Frances leads her father in the journey of remembrance. She has her own 'tell me more' urgency, approaching an obsession. And she too plays ethnographer to the entire voyage, recording its moments of tenderness, terror, triumph, exhaustion, frustration, humor, and grace.

Yet much also separates *Gift of Time* from *Maus*. Frances' knowledge of her father's Holocaust experience was already prodigious prior to this new sharing. For her, the principal revelations concerned her father's revival in postwar Munich. Like my own book, *Gift of Time* is substantially about that other, less appreciated side of survival: the drama of rebirth, the winning again of a sense of purpose and power and a positive vision of one's future, in spite of devastating loss.

Indeed, so much of what may seem counter-intuitive or even implausible about David's postwar life made perfect sense to me, given my extensive research. With just a year of high school in his native Poland, David studied mightily to pass a rigorous entrance exam and then succeeded in a pharmacy program in one of Germany's leading universities. Like his Jewish peers, he was driven to make a future for himself, requiring a nearly uncanny single-mindedness of purpose.

David was able to function at such a high level, in large part, by repressing the terrible trauma of his recent past. His fellow Jewish students similarly brooked little talk of their wartime experiences. This silence was a de facto condition for their energy, basic sanity, and resolve in the present.

David and his future wife, Frances' mother, Ella, whose persecution was extreme even by Holocaust standards, were "deliciously happy" in postwar Munich. Their existence, writes Frances, was "imbued with the optimism and vigour of fledgling independent young adults." Others of the alumni confessed a similar thrill at the rediscovery of life, the joy of outings in nature and to the opera, and the bond they formed with one another.

The Holocaust was unfathomably brutal, as *Gift of Time* amply affirms. Much of the reading Frances and her father did together, narrated in detail its death and destruction. Among the most chilling refrains in the narrative are moments of reading so painfully resonant that Frances and David have to stop and sit in silence. I myself periodically sat in silence when reading *Gift of Time*. Such moments are the faint way we pay honor, to both loss and its overwhelm.

Life destroyed was an ineliminable part even of a restored life, like that of David Prince. But we distort and diminish the idea of survival if we present it simply as the narrow escape of death and a perpetual haunting thereafter. Revival, however qualified, was an achievement—the assertion of Jewish agency, both individual and collective, that the Nazis had tried to permanently annihilate. David Prince's life, illuminated by his daughter's book, is testament to that achievement.

***

Gift of Time is a tribute to the power of books. In truth, the Prince dialogue is with more than each other and with the past. It is also a multidirectional conversation with works of history and memoir. Each title shaped their dialogue and suggested the next reading. The most luminous star in this constellation of books turns out to be Frances' own. With it, she all but invents a new genre: reading books, under cozy blankets, to an elder! With the flourish of a seasoned dramatist, she has the book's tail catch its head: the last text she reads to her father is the one she has just written herself.

Gift of Time, finally, is about time itself. In this aspect it is for me inseparable from the moment of its inception in March 2020. Covid had much of the world in lockdown, elongating time and enforcing what could feel a dull and uncomfortable isolation. Frances turned that burden into an opportunity to bond with her father, largely by travelling via memory through time.

Most personally, Frances' readings with her father were perfectly coincident with the final demise of my own father. In late February he—Bension Varon, a Sephardic Jew from Istanbul and émigré to America—had a fall at age 87. He was never again quite himself. Due to Covid restrictions in his facility, I was able to see him just once in his last months. It was a 20-minute 'end-of-life' visit. On June 23, just hours after my goodbyes, he died.

More than his Jewishness connects my father to Frances' book. He himself was a man of great learning. Late in life, he became the author of many fine books—mostly self-published because he feared he would not survive the production schedule of conventional presses. Among their topics were books themselves. One such volume was about a single, rare book from the Spanish 17th-century. ("A book about a book" was our family's affectionate description of it.) Another was his musings on bibliophilia, which he titled simply *Book Love*. His pride at the authorship of me and my sister, an eminent historian of America's Civil War, was immense. I had dedicated my book about the survivor students to him.

Little cheered my father in his final months. Knowledge that someone was writing a book about reading my book to an old, Jewish father like himself surely would have. I likely made too little of the time I had with him. Perhaps most of us feel that way about our aged parents.

Frances reminds us how precious, and finite, the gift of time is, no matter who our beloved elders are. Should her book inspire us to be better guardians of time and love, its gift will grow greater still.

***

Acknowledgements

Where do I even begin?

With much sensitive trepidation and deep compassion for all the suffering and loss in the world, I need, bizarrely, to 'thank' the coronavirus for this book. The truth is that it would not have been written without the circumstances that arose due to this pandemic.

On a more comfortable note, my gratitude first and foremost goes to Dad, David Prince. He is the star of the story. As is abundantly clear throughout the book, it is Dad who has shared and opened up to me. He has honoured me with his time, company and reminiscences. He would see it differently and would thank me for my time, company and interest. In truth, we enjoyed a mutually enriching experience.

Even though this is predominantly Dad's story, each page is infused with the presence of Mum, Ella Prince. May her memory continue to be for a blessing. In this book I have shared some of my intimate thoughts about Mum. I hope that I have not diminished nor dishonoured her, but have given the reader a sense of the complexity of her character. (Both Dad and my brother, Issy, approved of my portrayal). Even though she sometimes became exasperated (and rightfully so) by my wilfulness, she would have been the proudest person in the universe upon the publication of this book. When the launch takes place, I will be able to conjure up the image of Mum sitting in the front row.

I am greatly indebted to Jeremy Varon, author of *The New Life: Jewish Students of Postwar Germany*. It was his many years of research, travels far and wide for interviews, and scholarly, yet accessible writing, that gave Dad and me our original reading subject matter. However, Jeremy gave us so much more. He gave Dad back his younger self. He managed to peel back over 70 years of Dad's life and thus enabled him to reveal and relive who he was as a man in his early twenties. I was privileged to witness this astonishing daily transformation. In addition, Jeremy provided Dad with many missing or forgotten details of his time as a university student in Germany. Dad was reminded of key people and learnt the backstory of long-ago events. He had countless 'aha' moments that gave both of us equal delight.

In addition, Jeremy's unreserved pleasure when learning about my own book, will forever warm my heart. His enthusiasm and sheer joy that my book was an outgrowth of his work was beyond my wildest expectations. His generosity in reading my penultimate draft in its entirety and writing such a meaningful afterword, is profoundly appreciated and deeply valued.

I would like to thank Danielle Charak for her superlative translation of Dad's Yiddish article in the January/February 1947 edition of the Jewish Student Union newspaper, *The New Life*. I am grateful to Jayne Josem, director of the Jewish Holocaust Centre (JHC) in Melbourne, for recognising the worth of Danielle's translation of Dad's article, and to Ruth Mushin, editor of JHC's *Centre News*, for publishing it in the September 2020 issue.

My appreciation of the authors of the books comprising Part Two is boundless. They provided Dad and me with hours and hours of fascinating and moving material to discuss and to prompt Dad's memories. Thank you to: Sabina S. Zimering, Simon Schochet, Diane Wyshogrod, Willy Lermer OAM, Guta Goldstein, Martin Lane, Lidia Eichenholz, Tova Tauber, Emanuel Tanay and Hania Harcsztark-Goldfeder Mayer.

Most of the survivor-authors are no longer alive and will never personally receive my special gratitude. May their memories be for a blessing. However, I would like to thank and acknowledge the following survivor-authors and/or their children.

Thank you to Diane (Dina) Wyshogrod for writing about her late mother's life, and more. Helen Lutka Rosenberg Wyshogrod's story is told by Dina with reverence, reflection and love. It is her priceless legacy to her family, and beyond. Dina is the only author of the next generation, my generation. Given that Dina lives in Jerusalem, I emailed her the final relevant section. She asked me point-blank what I would like her to comment on during her reading. Knowing Dina's razor-sharp intelligence, I was quick to request no critique but merely her thoughts and reflections. (Enough drafts already.) To my absolute delight, I received her insightful comments and additional remarks interspersed, in red print, with my own writing. Another layer had been added to my project! But this will remain a private layer between Dina and myself.

Thank you to Guta Goldstein, whose beautiful prose about her Lodz childhood evoked so many joyful memories for Dad. As we sat in her kitchen and I read aloud to her, Guta was attentive to every word and finetuned a couple of points. I immediately tweaked what I had thought was my final draft. Guta remains one of the few Melbourne survivors who continues to robustly speak about her experiences to different audiences. May she remain strong and healthy in body and mind until 120.

Thank you to Judy (Tauber) Ifergan, daughter of the late Tova Tauber, who was moved to tears when I rang her out of the blue to tell her about this reading project. I went to her home and read her the section based on her mother's book. Neither of us were able to hold back the tears.

Thank you to Marcia (Goldfeder) Janovic for allowing me to accompany her on a visit to see her mother, Hania Harcsztark-Goldfeder Mayer, in her aged-care facility. Hania and Marcia listened attentively as I read aloud part of an early draft based on Hania's childhood. When I originally organised this visit, I was unsure whether I would actually share my writing with them. I am so glad that I did. Hania was genuinely pleased to hear long-ago recollections of her parents and brothers. And Marcia was equally delighted. Upon near-completion, I invited Marcia to my home to listen to a final draft based on her mother's memoir. I hope I have honoured Hania appropriately.

I want to pay tribute to all the survivor friends of my parents. The vast majority are no longer alive, but they inhabit, between the lines, all the stories in this book.

My gratitude to my editors and publishers, Romy Moshinsky and Georgie Raik-Allen of Real Film and Publishing, is boundless. The relationship that has developed between us is one of the most unusual, yet rewarding, relationships that I have ever experienced. Romy and Georgie knew the inside of my head and heart before we even met. By the time we were able to get together for our first face-to-face meeting, after a long coronavirus-induced lockdown, the editorial process (via modern technology) was well underway. My writing had already revealed to them my innermost self, which they treated with the utmost respect and sensitivity.

Romy and Georgie are an amazing team dedicated to excellence in their profession. They have found the perfect combination of meticulous editorial acumen laced with kind advice and generosity. Their insightful guidance and support made the editorial process a fascinating and enjoyable one. At least for me. I looked forward with enthusiasm to every single draft that Georgie sent back to me, complete with her astute comments and suggestions. Discussing words, phrases and the craft of writing was joyous. Their profound commitment to me and to this book was unwavering. I am indebted to both of them for their skills, wisdom and friendship.

What a pleasure it has been to work with Marianna Berek-Lewis, a book designer extraordinaire. Her cover design, layout, typesetting, choice of colours and shades, and placement of photos and documents, are all evidence of her artistic talents and keen eye. This book would be a much poorer one without Marianna's indispensable contribution.

Thank you to the wonderful photographer, Steven Gringlas, creative director of Picos, who captured more than the outer layer of Dad and me. The exquisite front cover photo of this book is a testament to his talent. Unbeknownst to him (until our photo shoot) was the fact that we are family. Those who are good at remembering names will recall that Gringlas is my maternal grandmother's maiden name. So yes, we are cousins from Warsaw.

I am grateful to those few people who listened to snippets of drafts along the way. I am equally grateful to those friends and family members who, without reading a word, encouraged me and cheered me on. Female friends (and male ones too; I just have fewer of those) are a treasure and I feel blessed to have them.

And now back to family.

Thank you to my amazing mother-in-law, Judy Kolt, for her consistent support and unstinted enthusiasm, not just for this writing project but for all that I undertake. She has always been a model of a non-judgemental and open-minded person. I have learnt much from her.

It is with deep emotion that I pay tribute to my brother, Issy Prince. A more caring and generous sibling could not be imagined. I cherish our unflagging solidarity. Our vital teamwork in the venture of caring for our aging parents would be difficult to surpass. However, believe me, he has always done the heavy lifting. Adherence to the Fifth Commandment, to honour one's father and mother, has never been practised so fully as Issy has done and continues to do.

I sincerely thank Wendy Prince, Issy's wife, my sister-in-law, for understanding and accepting Issy's essential need to care so intensely for Dad, which is bound up in his very essence.

I thank our sons, Gali Kolt and Noey Kolt, for their eager support of this project. They realised immediately that my writing would be their legacy. Both devoured parts of early drafts and urged me to send more and more sections. I hope that they will savour the final result. It is an underestimated but delightful paradox to have adult children taking on the role of encouraging their parents. I have thoroughly enjoyed being on the receiving end of their enthusiasm. I also unreservedly thank their wonderful partners, Rebecca and Bat Sheva, who support them.

And finally, to my husband, Steven Kolt, who was, and is, with me every step of the way—not only with this writing project but with the much more significant project of life. This does not imply that he was a consistent reader. I didn't need him to be. However he was, as always, my champion. He respects and guards my time and efforts and mitigates my self-doubt. He was the one who realised that I was writing a real book way before I did. Over the decades, Steven has enabled me to grow into a much better version of myself. He has empowered me to be more adventurous, bold and confident. His steadfast support for all that I do has been unwavering. My life would be a smaller one without him.

Frances Prince

Appendices

An epizod fun trojerikn owar *Prinz Dawid*

A uzejger nochmitog. Der gong hastik un nerwejisz: ojfsztejn, ojfsztejn...

In szlof her ich zajn ruf, er treft wi a diner fun heln, szejnem hint. A grojzame mojre gejt adurch majne bejner... Erszt gelejgt ich szlofn un wider cu der arbet? Wider cu der arbet? Nejn! Ich 'ken nyt, ich wil nyt!

Ich ci sznel majn kop cwiszn di akslen un farsztek mich unter di szmeide-dek. Un efszer hob ich a toes? Ober a minut arum her ich di sztim fun majn sztubn-eltstn: „Piotruś auf!" (men hot mich Piotruś gerufn). Ich ze, az es iz kejn cholem. In kop rojszt, di bejner tuen wej, ich bin mid un hungerik. Dan her ich wi majne chawejrim cijen arojf in der sznel zejere malbuszim. Jeder fun zej wil lojfn wiamsznelstn in di kich brengen dem kesl esn. Er hoft cu bakumen noch a lefl hejs waser.

Langzam zec ich zich ojf un kuk tempf ojf di blumelech, wos badekn di fenster fun undzer barak... A trop ajz-kaltn waser fun ojbn falt grod ojf majn opgegoltn kop. Ich geb a citer... Glajcheejtik loz ich arop di fus fun majn ojberszter prycz, glajch ojs majn pekl bejner, wikl arum di fajchte fuś-lapn un lojf arajn in waszrojm. Ich wasz mich mit sznej, wajl di waserlejtung iz gefrojern, un wisz op in a smate, welche dint mir ojch als haldz-tuch, majne hent un majn ponim.

Mir bakumen noch ojf der sznel undzer ojsgetrojmte zup, kimat an tropn cu fun der szisl. Nyt jeder hot a lefl un nyt jedem lojnt zajn lefl ajneurachtn. Ingichn mach ich majn prycz, wasz ojs di szisl un mach fartik majn garderobe. Zi basztejt fun a sowjetiszn zumer-mantl mit grojse buchsztabn S. U. un cejfems ojfn ruku un erml. Ich wikl mich arum, cieu mit drot — es zol zajn waremer. Ch'ei arop dos heftlings-hitl iber di ojern un wer fartik noch grod cum gongszlag, welcher ruft cum apel un cum opmarsz.

Mir gejen arojs fun barak. Di frost bajst, di kalte winter-nacht falt-cu. Noch hern mir di komando: „Stillstand! Mützen ab! Marsch!" Un szojn gejen mir ariber dos lager-tojer. „Links, links, eins, zwei, drei, vier!" Mir marszirn in glajchszrit. Di erszte por meter bamit zich jeder noch cu haltn dem szrit, ober szpeter gejt es ojch bajm bestn wiln nyt. Der frisz-aropgefalener sznej klebt zich cu cu undzere hole-szich. Mir hobn szojn kejn kojach nyt, undzere hercer klaph hastik, mir gejen un faln. Ojf dem wartn undzere S. S.-lajt mit an ejgnartiker frejd. Zej szlogn mit di kolbes fun zejere biksn, szrejen un szeltn, ojslodndik di gemejnste kloles fun dem dajczn leksikon. Doch derlebn mir arajncukumen in di fabryk.

Mir rejdn gornyt, mir farszlejen zich ale: Ici zoln mir ojshaltn in a kaltn zal 12 szo? Es iz szwer cu glojbn, ober mir wejsn es fun der praktik, dos es iz nyt undzer erszte nacht-arbet, un lejder, ojch nyt di lecte. Mir hofn zi ojch beszolem adurchcuhaltn. „Jeder zu der Arbeit!" — ruft der szicht-firer. Mir cegejn zich in gewaltik nyt bahejtn zal fun di V. D. M.-Werke. A minut batracht ich noch majn 5-meter lange drejbank, kontrolir dem Norton-kastn un loz kraft in majn maszin.

Ich fil zich hajnt on ojsnam szwach. Es szojdert mich fun kelt un fun fiber. Der gerojsz fun di zejgn un szlajf-maszinen geinjt zajn opklang in majn brenendikn kop. Ich arbel szojn azoj a por szo. Was amol ober langzamer, langzamer... Di ojgn faln cu, di fis trogn nyt.

Pluclung bamerk ich, az ich wer obserwirt. Jo, majn huntiszer majster (Kurt Herdeker fun Hamburg), est rujik zajn' szynkn-brojt un lozt nyt arop fun mir zajne ojgn. Ich pruw mich dermonen wi lang er sztejt szojn lebn mir. Ich ztreng on majne lecte kojches, kdej cu arbetn gor sznel un zicher. Derwajt dernentert er zich cu mir. Zajne szpicike ojgn bojern mich adurch. Ici farlir ich szojn genclech majn glajchgewicht. Di hant get mir a citer un der mikrometer iz arajngefaln in waser arajn. Ici iz szojn di skala krin skala nyt, der eapfn iz arojs cu din. „Ha! Hund einer! Du hast heute keine Lust zu der Arbeit, Verfluchter!"

Ich wil rejdn, ich wil im zogn, az... Ober ejder ich ken noch efenen majn mojl derfil ich szojn fun zajn brejter lape di „Backpfeife" wi er hot gerufn zajne klep. Ich bin szier nyt umgefaln. Dos blut hot mir geszlogn in kop arajn. Er ruft cu dem posłn un hejst ajnszrajbn majn numer 56497 cu „Verpflegungs-Sperre". Ich bin szojn nyt bekojach mer cu klern. Wer han noch klern wegn dem, wos wet nochkumen — wen ich fil, az hajnt muz noch epes geszeen, epes ojsergewenleches un halwaj gutes. Zol zajn wos es wil, zol es kumen! Ejnmol far alemoll.

Ich hob gajstik un fizisz gaue cebrochn. Ich szpir. — es dernetert zich di lecte minut fun majn bawustzajn. Ich szpan ojs dem fartikn proneller, probir im awekcusztein, un fal um. Der 80-funtiker Propeller falt mir arojf ojfn fus.

Der klang fun fahndikn metal, hot cugecojgn dem majster un dem S.S.-man. Er lojft cu cum Propeller un hojbt im sznel ojf. „Hund einer du hast alles beschädigt! Ich werde dir zeigen!" — un nor noch di ojern majne zogn mir wegn di klen mit welche es balejgt mich majn majster. Majn kerper hot szojn ojfgehert cu film. Ich rangl mich in wejen, biz majn capo nemt mich ojf di plejces un firt ahin cum dajezn sanitets-punkt.

A libe warem nemt mich arum. Der fus iz szojn geszwoln. Di kranken-szwester glojbt, az er iz gebrochn. Noch a prowizoriszn farband nemt men mich arajn in es-rojm, wu mir flegn zien ojf di pauze. Der majster wil, az ich zol curikgejn cu der arbet. Ich zog im, dos es iz ummeglech. Er drot, az er wet mich curikszikn kejn Grossrosen oder... szisn. Mach wos du wilst, zog ich im. Er lozt mich zien. Ich blajb alejn.

Efszer iz es gor cum gutn? — kler ich mir. Ich wel mich in der kranken-sztub ojsruen un... ojssztofn. Ojssztofn, nor richtik ojssztofn. Ich sztel mir szojn for wi ich szlof, 3 teg un 3 necht. Dos brojt fun di 3 teg wel ich szpeter mit ejnmol ejffesn... Ich celejg mich bakwem ojf der bank un troe majne szmeren szlof ich zofort ajn.

„Sztej ojf, mir gejen ahejm", — hobn mich ojfgewekt majne chawejrim. „Szojn?" — freg ich, es ducht zich mir, wi s'wolt gewen erszt 5 minutn zajt ich hob mich geleigt. Zej hobn mir ihergerisn azn zisn cholem... Tate... Mame... Wareme szlub... A gedekter tisz... A wajs het ... Wel ich dos amol noch derlebn?

PRINCES PHARMACY

DAVID PRINCE, Ph.C., M.P.S., M.C.P.P.
JAMES PRINCE, J.P., Ph.C., M.P.S., M.C.P.P., M.A.I.P.M.
Member Society Hospital Pharmacists of Australia

350 BRIDGE ROAD, RICHMOND, VIC. 3121
TELEPHONE   9428 1953
FAX   9427 0160

Reminiscences

Fifty years ago ... where were we all ?

In Munich - 'die Stadt der Bewegung' in Bavaria-Germany.

For us it was irrelevant - city on the move or not.
We did not care. Boys, girls a loose bunch, which became a very
close- knit bunch in no time.

Jews and half Jews (I remember at least one). Jews from
Germany, Poland, Hungary, Czechoslovakia, Rumania, Latvia,
Lithuania and Russia. Among them survivors of concentration
and labour camps. Survivors driven out from bunkers, from across
borders, the vast steppes of Asia, freezing cold Siberia and
many other remote regions. Kids - hunted like wild dogs over
a period of years. They escaped death and somehow found their
way to Munich, in some instances to Erlangen, Frankurt, Stuttgart
and Heidelberg.

Engineer Alexander Piekarczyk, was probably instrumental
in the logistics pertaining to the entry of tertiary
institutions. I and many others who have a snapshot of him,
(or were phtographed together) aprreciate his more recent photo
featured in Theo Richmond's book Konin - A Quest (Jonathan Cape,
London). Piekarczyk represents one of the most practical
sources of encouragements to study - to those eligible, as
well the ones who missed out on formal education through the
war and depended on individual adaptation.

PRINCES PHARMACY

DAVID PRINCE, Ph.C., M.P.S., M.C.P.P.

JAMES PRINCE, J.P., Ph.C., M.P.S., M.C.P.P., M.A.I.P.M.

Member Society Hospital Pharmacists of Australia

350 BRIDGE ROAD, RICHMOND, VIC. 3121

TELEPHONE   9428 1953

FAX   9427 0160

We rolled up our sleeves and prepared ourselves for the Verification Commission to gain admission to the Ludwig Maximillian 'Universitat or Technische Hochschule.'

Our attempts to succeed at all cost were sustained by willpower and determination which offered the basis for the goal Jewish post-war students strove for. Föhrenwald, Feldafing, Landsberg and few other camps were of great help.

With few exceptions we lived in rooms rented from German families. Life was not easy, but with youth on our side, we had the capacity to cope.

We also had fun. Dances, excursions, flirtations, romantic encounters even marriages. As for me, I met Ella at the Isator Pl. Jewish students cafeteria. We were married on 23 December 1947 and hope to celebrate our 50th. Wedding Anniversary this year. We have two children and four grandchilren.

Most of us left Germany (apart from a handful). However only Israel recognized our qualifications in medicine, dentistry and pharmacy. Consequently all those who settled in other countries had great difficulties to say the least, to have the hard earned degrees recognized. Once again it was a matter of perseverance with the logistic formalization of the kind we strove for in Germany.

PRINCES PHARMACY
DAVID PRINCE, Ph.C., M.P.S., M.C.P.P.
JAMES PRINCE, J.P., Ph.C., M.P.S., M.C.P.P., M.A.I.P.M.
Member Society Hospital Pharmacists of Australia

350 BRIDGE ROAD, RICHMOND, VIC. 3121
TELEPHONE   9428 1953
FAX   9427 0160

Some of us attained high academic status, others prominence
in their respective profession or material wealth. Even the
less ambitious lead a comfortable life. Roughly stated, the
post-war years spent at a German university prepared most of us
for independent adult life in a realistic and at times harsh
rather, than a perfect world.

Reflections on the reunion in Israel, which renewed and
strenghtened old friendships, can be summed up by that most
relevant definition - it was wonderful !

In Australia, the USA and other Western countries outside
Israel, it is a matter of choice for a Jewish person to maintain
his or her identity and give coherence to Jewish values; to
observe the Jewish religion and/or participate in Jewish cultural,
intellectual, social and political life.

Born a Jew I identify with my heritage. I am a participant
and active supporter of most branches which spring from the
immense terrain of Jewishness.

David Prince
(David Prinz)
Melbourne-Australia

. ranslation from   GERMAN   into   ENGLISH

No 11/54

VERIFICATIONS COMMISSION

FOR JEWISH UNIVERSITY CANDIDATES

MUNICH

(PHOTO)

MR. PRINZ DAWID, BORN AT LODZ ON JULY 21, 1925
WHO NO LONGER POSSESSES THE MATURITY CERTIFICATE
THAT WAS AWARDED TO HIM BY THE JEWISH HUMANISTIC
GYMNASIUM IN 1943, AFTER PASSING THE VERIFICATION EXAMINATION
IN JUNE 1946, PURSUANT TO THE MINISTERIAL DEGREE OF THE BAVARIAN
STATE MINISTRY OF EDUCATION AND CULTURE, DATED 9/9/1947 No.VI
39428,

WITH THE AVERAGE RATING OF

"SUCCESSFULLY PASSED"

HAD MET THE SCIENTIFIC REQUIREMENTS FOR TAKING UP STUDIES
AT A UNIVERSITY.

THE RESULTS OF THE VERIFICATION EXAMINATION ARE SHOWN IN
DETAIL IN THE FOLLOWING TRANSCRIPT FROM THE EXAMINATION RE-
CORDS.

MUNICH, JULY 7, 1948

THE CHAIRMAN OF THE VERIFICATION
BOARD OF EXAMINERS
(SGN) ALEX (2ND NAME ILLEG.)
GRADUATED ENGINEER (1 WORD
(L.S.)   ILLEG.)

.../...

TRANSLATED BY

Fifth Avenue Translation Bureau

505 FIFTH AVENUE (BETWEEN 42ND AND 43RD STS.)
NEW YORK 17, N. Y.

ALL LANGUAGES
ALL SUBJECTS

PHONE MURRAY HILL 7-5774

Translation from GERMAN into ENGLISH

TRANSCRIPT

FROM THE EXAMINATION RECORD RELATIVE TO THE
VERIFICATION EXAMINATION

1) WRITTEN EXAMINATION
LITERATURE............GOOD
HISTORY.................-
MATHEMATICS...........SUFFICIENT
PHYSICS...............SUFFICIENT

II ORAL EXAMINATION
LITERATURE............GOOD
HISTORY...............GOOD
LATIN.................SATISFACTORY
MATHEMATICS...........GOOD
PHYSICS...............SUFFICIENT
CHEMISTRY.............VERY GOOD
BIOLOGY...............GOOD
GEOGRAPHY.............SUFFICIENT

THE EXAMINEE HAS PASSED THE EXAMINATION WITH GOOD RESULTS.
IN WITNESS WHEREOF: THE SECRETARY OF THE VERIFICATION COMMISSION,
(S) R. VENNER
THIS CERTIFICATE ENTITLES TO TAKE UP STUDIES AT ANY BAVARIAN
UNIVERSITY.

(SGN) ILLEGIBLE,
DECEMBER 2, 1949   GOVERNMENT DIRECTOR

THE AUTHENTICITY OF THE FOREGOING SIGNATURE
OF THE GOVERNMENT DIRECTOR BUCK IS HEREWITH CERTIFIED.
MUNICH, DECEMBER 2ND, 1949
BAVARIAN STATE MINISTRY OF EDUCATION AND CULTURE
BY ORDER, (S)DR. TREVVESCH,
(L.S.)   CIEF GOVERNMENT COUNCILLOR
SCALE OF MARKS:
FOR INDIVIDUAL RESULTS: VERY GOOD, GOOD, SUFFICIENT, DEFICIENT,
INSUFFICIENT.
OVERALL RATING: PASSED WITH DISTINCTION, PASSED WITH VERY GOOD
RESULTS, PASSED WITH GOOD RESULTS, PASSED.

STATE OF NEW YORK } SS.
COUNTY OF NEW YORK

THE FOREGOING IS A TRUE AND CORRECT TRANSLATION OF THE ORIGINAL
DOCUMENT TO THE BEST OF MY KNOWLEDGE AND BELIEF.
GERMAN ENTIRE DOCUMENT HAS BEEN TRANSLATED AND NOTHING OMITTED,
THE TRANSLATION HAS BEEN READ BY ME.

SWORN AND SUBSCRIBED TO BEFORE ME
THIS 24TH DAY OF AUGUST 195 3

TRANSLATED BY   (ALBERT LA MOTHE JR.)

Fifth Avenue Translation Bureau

505 FIFTH AVENUE (BETWEEN 42ND AND 43RD STS.)
NEW YORK 17, N. Y.

ALL LANGUAGES
ALL SUBJECTS   PHONE MURRAY HILL 7-5774

ALL LETTERS TO BE ADDRESSED
TO THE SECRETARY.

TELEPHONES FJ 5161
FJ 5162

TELEGRAPHIC AND CABLE ADDRESS
"PHARMACON." MELBOURNE

Pharmaceutical Society of Victoria
ESTABLISHED 1857.

COLLEGE OF PHARMACY
360 SWANSTON STREET.

Melbourne, C.1  2 March 19 51

K.Y
S51.501

Mr. David Prinz,
315 Drummond Street,
Carlton, N3

Dear Sir,

With reference to your application for recognition
of your degree from the Munich University, I am directed to
advise that you make further application at the end of the
current year; and that, in the meantime, you undertake study
with the object of presenting yourself for the preliminary
examination of the Board in the subjects of English, British
History and Physical Science - the first two subjects to
assist you in your progress with the English language - and
the third to help as an introduction to our technical terms.

I would suggest that you endeavour to get as
good a pass as possible at the examination, which is held in
May and November each year.   Details of the examination will
be found in the attached leaflet.

If there is further advice or information you
require, please let me know.

Yours faithfully,

Enc:

Secretary.

Dated: 11 August 1954

Pharmacy Board of Victoria

SECRETARY AND REGISTRAR:
F. C. KENT.

TELEPHONES: FJ 5161
FJ 5162

K/M REF B.54/1756

360 SWANSTON STREET,
MELBOURNE, C.1.

August 11, 1954

Mr. David Prinz,
97 Fortuna Avenue,
NORTH BALWYN.

Dear Sir,

Your letter dated 19.7.54 was submitted to the
Board at a meeting held today.

In reply I am instructed to state that in order
to qualify for registration in Victoria, the Board requires
you, (a) to serve an apprenticeship of three years with a
registered pharmaceutical chemist, in accordance with the
Pharmacy Regulations, and (b) to attend a course of lectures
extending over three years, at the Victorian College of
Pharmacy, such lectures to consist of a combined 1st/2nd
year, 3rd Year and 4th Year, and (c) to pass examinations
set out in the Apprenticeship course of studies, namely;
the College Examination at the conclusion of the 1/2 year
course, the Intermediate Examination conducted by the Board
after completion of the 3rd Year studies and the Final
Qualifying Examination conducted by the Board on completion
of the 4th Year course.

Your copy of the Diploma from the University of
Munich, your Studies Book from the same University and
other documents are retained at this office and may be
obtained by you at any time.

Yours faithfully,

Registrar.

APPENDIX E: LIST OF ATTENDEES AT THE JEWISH STUDENTS' UNION REUNION, ISRAEL, 1995

Abisch-Frenkel Eva (Switzerland/Israel)
Balaban Anna (USA)
Balaban Philip (Fila) (USA)
Ben-Nun Hava (Israel)
Birman Luba (USA)
Birman Nathan (USA)
Blum Emil (Israel)
Blumenau Beno (Israel)
Blumenau Haya (Israel)
Boldo Bella (Israel)
Boldo Pinchas (Israel)
Braude Lea (Israel)
Braude Louis (Israel)
Budanski Shmuel (Israel)
Budanski Ziona (Israel)
Comber Hava (Israel)
Comber Max (Israel)
Cydulka Ethel (USA)
Cydulka Samuel (USA)
Dresner Helena (Israel)
Dresner Jonathan (Israel)
Dresner Mrs. R. (Israel)
Dresner Zalman (Israel)
Dunsky Stefan (Israel)
Dunsky/Amster Halina (Israel)
Edelberg Irka (USA)
Edelberg Lazar (USA)
Eisenberg I. (Israel)
Eisenberg Mrs (Israel)
Elsner Marcus (Mundek) (Israel)
Fiedel George (USA)
Fiedel/Black Renate (USA)
Fink Lucy (USA)
Fink Paul (USA)
Finkelstein Fania (Israel)
Fintel Mark (Burna) (USA)
Fintel Nathan (USA)
Fintel Slava (USA)
Gertel Cecile (USA)
Gertel Leon (USA)
Getzler Israel (Israel)
Goldwasser Marcel (Israel)
Golombek Jo (Norway)
Grynhaus Marian (Israel)
Gurfinkel Gary (USA)
Gurfinkel Irene (USA)

Hauser Edith (Dita) (Israel)
Hauser Heinrich (Israel)
Hertz Nathan (Israel)
Hertz Zahava (Israel)
Hoch Lea (Israel)
Hoch Moshe (Israel)
Horowicz Eva (Germany)
Kastner Pnina (Israel)
Klein Haim (Israel)
Klein Henny (Israel)
Knobler Rina (Israel)
Knobler Yehuda (Israel)
Korn Felix (USA)
Korn Nina (USA)
Kornhauser Hermina (Israel)
Kornhauser Leon (Israel)
Kurz Erich (Israel)
Kurz Mrs (Israel)
Landsberg Ida (Israel)
Landsberg Itzchak (Israel)
Langer Anselm (Israel)
Langer Halina (Israel)
Langer Lea (Israel)
Langer Mark (Manek) (Israel)
Lieder-Mrazek Michael (Marian) (Australia)
Lieder-Mrazek Sara (Suzy) (Australia)
Loew Andrew (USA)
Loew Rita (USA)
Lubash Marcel (Israel)
Luft Maximilian (Israel)
Majewski Georg (Israel)
Majewski Shulamit (Israel)
Marcus Dunia (Israel)
Marcus Zwi (Israel)
Maurer Jadwiga (USA)
Metzger Imek (USA)
Metzger Pola (USA)
Mincberg Helen (USA)
Mincberg Isaac (USA)
Oberman Ziona (Cesia) (Israel)
Prince David (Australia)
Prince Ella (Australia)
Prywes Daniel (Israel)
Prywes Hanka (Israel)
Reiter Frederick (USA)

Reiter Sylvia (USA)
Schindel Helen (Israel)
Schmorak Dov (Israel)
Schochet Paulina (Israel)
Schochet Roman (Israel)
Seibald Sylvia (Israel)
Shani Ziona (Cesia) (Israel)
Shapiro Esther (Fira) (Israel)
Shapiro Pinchas (Pinek) (Israel)
Smulevicz Renate (USA)
Snopkowski Ruth (Germany)
Snopkowski Simon (Germany)
Steinfeld Dov (Israel)
Steinfeld Tova (Israel)
Stern Adolf (Dodek) (Sweden)
Sternheim Lazar (Israel)
Strich Arthur (Israel)
Strich Eva (Israel)
Tiberg Zvi (Heniek) (Israel)
Trachtenberg Dina (USA)
Trachtenberg Leon (USA)
VonSimson Paula (USA)
Weiner David (Dodzik) (Sweden)
Weiner Ruth (Sweden)
Weisfelner Henry (USA)
Weisfelner Irene (USA)
Weissberg Ernst (USA)
White Alexander (USA)
White Inez (USA)
White Jr (USA)
White Jr (USA)
Zahavi Alek (Israel)
Zahavi Frances (Israel)
Zelinger Bernard (USA)
Zelinger Helen (USA)
Zelon Cesia (USA)
Zelon Michael (USA)
Zilberman Elek (Israel)
Zilberman Mrs (Israel)
Zimmering Ruben (USA)
Zimmering Sabine (USA)
Zisbrod Marge (Israel)
Zucker Barbara (USA)
Zucker Henry (USA)
Zucker Jeanne (daughter) (USA)

ADDENDUM

Borenstein Israel (USA)
Kaufer Barbara (USA)
Liebhaber Mark (USA)
Liebhaber Henia (USA)
Stone Bernard (USA)
Stone Beatrice (USA)
Zaphir (Piekarski) Joel (Israel)
Zaphir-Pratt Mrs (Israel)

Frances Prince is an educator with lifelong expertise in Jewish studies and leadership in Victoria's interfaith community.

After graduating from university, she began her teaching career in 1981. Three years later, Frances and her husband Steven moved to the USA where she completed an MA in Hebrew culture and education at NYU. After returning to Melbourne, she worked at Mount Scopus Memorial College for nearly three decades, teaching Jewish studies, writing curriculum and developing interfaith programs. In 2011 she received the National Council of Jewish Women's Sylvia Gelman Award for 'Outstanding Woman Educator in the Area of Jewish Studies'.

Frances' passion for Jewish education has led to significant voluntary endeavours including co-founding March of the Living, Australia, an annual educational program that brings students to Poland to learn about the Holocaust.

Since 2014, she has been an executive member of the Jewish Community Council of Victoria (JCCV) where she holds the multicultural and interfaith portfolio. In this capacity, she represents the Jewish community on the Jewish Christian Muslim Association (JCMA) board and serves as co-vice president of the Faith Communities Council of Victoria (FCCV) board.

Frances is also vice president of the Australian Jewish Historical Society (AJHS) Victoria and serves on the committee of the annual Lodz ghetto commemoration.

Printed in Australia
AUHW011044160821
350398AU00003B/3

9 780645 213119